Canada: The State of the Federation 1986

Edited by
Peter M. Leslie

Institute of
Intergovernmental
Relations

Queen's University
Kingston, Ontario
Canada

Canadian Cataloguing in Publication Data

Main entry under title:
Canada, the state of the federation, 1985

Includes bibliographical references. ISBN 0-88911-425-0

1.Federal-provincial relations - Canada - Addresses, essays, lectures.*
2.Regional planning - Canada - Addresses, essays, lectures. 3.Minorities
- Canada - Addresses, essays, lectures. I.Leslie. Peter M. II.Queen's
University (Kingston, Ont.). Institute of Intergovernmental Relations.

JL27.C36 1986   321.02'3'0971   C85-099586-8

The Institute of Intergovernmental Relations

The Institute, part of Queen's University, is the only organization in
Canada whose mandate is solely to promote research and communication
on the challenges facing the federal system.

Current research interests focus on the respective roles of federal and
provincial governments in the economy, the place of Quebec in
confederation, aboriginal self-government, and a wide range of policy
issues affected by the structure and working of federalism.

The Institute pursues these objectives through research conducted by
its own staff, and other scholars, at Queen's and elsewhere; through an
active and growing publications program; and through seminars and
conferences.

The Institute links academics and practitioners of federalism in
federal and provincial governments and the private sector.

CONTENTS

v Preface

vii Contributors

I Introduction

3 Chapter 1 Rethinking Basic Relationships
Peter M. Leslie

II Focus on the Provinces

21 Chapter 2 B.C. in Confederation
Donald E. Blake and David J. Elkins

45 Chapter 3 Nova Scotia: Optimism in Spite of it All
Agar Adamson

65 Chapter 4 Quebec and the Constitutional Issue
Peter M. Leslie

97 Appendix: Speech by Gil Rémillard to the
Mont Gabriel Conference

III Issues

109 Chapter 5 Tax Reform and the Federation
Ian Stewart

129 Chapter 6 All Talk No Action:
The Telecommunications Dossier
Richard J. Schultz

151   Chapter 7 The Evolution of Canada's New Energy Policy
David C. Hawkes and Bruce G. Pollard

167   Chapter 8 Financing Post-Secondary Education and Research
Ronald L. Watts

189   Chapter 9 Federalism and Free Trade
Richard Simeon

IV Chronology

215   Chronology of Events 1985
Compiled by Stephanie Thorson and Avigail Eisenberg

PREFACE

This is the second edition of the series *Canada: The State of the Federation*. Its purposes are to survey recent events of importance to Canadian federalism and, in light of these events, to comment on present-day and emerging issues affecting the federation. This year's edition follows the format established in 1985, having three chapters focussing on individual provinces, and a series of additional chapters dealing with prominent items on the federal-provincial agenda. A new feature is the inclusion of a chronology of events in the previous year, 1985, affecting the federal system.

The Institute of Intergovernmental Relations is committed to publishing *Canada: The State of the Federation* each year. The first volume in the series appeared late in 1985; the present edition has been regrettably delayed due to an overburdened schedule of work at the Institute. The bottleneck was I. Contributors who laboured to complete their manuscripts in time for publication in the fall of 1985 have, I expect, been chafing at the delayed appearance of the volume. They have graciously refrained from complaining about this, but I apologize to them. It is our plan to publish the next edition, exceptionally, as a double issue (1987-88) during the summer of 1988, in order to get back to our originally-intended schedule of publication in late summer.

I would like to express my heartfelt thanks to the contributors to this volume, and also to various members of the staff of the Institute of Intergovernmental Relations who have performed the less visible but still vital tasks of readying the manuscript for publication. David Hawkes was a great help on the editorial side, as well as contributing his own chapter, with Bruce Pollard, to the book. The main production work was by Valerie Jarus, whose patience and meticulous attention to detail in mastering the mysteries of laser printing is well known at the Institute and is greatly appreciated by all of us. I would like also to acknowledge the help of Andrea Purvis in matters of style, of Patricia Candido in secretarial and general organizational tasks, and of Pauline Hawkes in handling publication arrangements. The production of this book, and other Institute publications, is very much a team effort, and I am glad to have this opportunity to thank all the members of the team.

Peter M. Leslie
February 1987

CONTRIBUTORS

Agar Adamson is professor of political science at Acadia University.

Donald E. Blake is professor of political science at the University of British Columbia.

David J. Elkins is professor of political science at the University of British Columbia.

David C. Hawkes is associate director of the Institute of Intergovernmental Relations at Queen's University.

Peter M. Leslie is director of the Institute of Intergovernmental Relations and teaches political studies at Queen's University.

Bruce G. Pollard is a former research associate at the Institute of Intergovernmental Relations at Queen's University.

Richard J. Schultz is director of the Centre for the Study of Regulated Industries and teaches political science at McGill University.

Richard Simeon is director of the School of Public Administration at Queen's University.

Ian Stewart, formerly federal deputy minister of finance, is Skelton-Clark Fellow at Queen's University.

Ronald L. Watts is professor of political studies at Queen's University.

I

INTRODUCTION

1 RETHINKING BASIC RELATIONSHIPS

Peter M. Leslie

Events in 1986 highlighted four distinct but interlocking sets of relationships that go a long way to defining the character of Canadians as a people, and Canada as a political community. The relationships in question are those (1) between the relatively rich and the relatively poor, (2) between Quebec and its Confederation partners, (3) among economic regions, and (4) between Canada and the United States. We must now, it appears, re-think these basic relationships. A number of current and emerging political issues, each crystallizing one set of relationships, may induce us to face old dilemmas in a new way. The issues, each of which will be commented upon below, are: tax reform and social security, Quebec and constitutional reform, coping with the collapse of prices for resource products, and the bilateral trade agenda.

Tax Reform and Social Security

Federal Finance Minister Michael Wilson, delivering his budget speech 26 February 1986, announced implementation of "the first phase" of a restructuring of the corporate tax system. Its reform was already foreshadowed in a discussion paper[1] released in May 1985. As Ian Stewart notes in chapter 5 of this volume, two white papers were expected in midsummer 1986: one on further changes to the corporate income tax, and one on the reform of the manufacturers' sales tax. However, on 18 July Wilson announced that the two papers would be delayed in order to allow the Department of Finance enough time to draw up proposals for a more comprehensive overhaul of the tax system. The introduction of a business transfer tax – a tax on value added at each stage in the production process[2] – is widely rumoured. In addition, Finance Department officials are working on proposals for reform of the social welfare system (or "transfer payments" system: unemployment

3

insurance, family allowances, old age security, Canada Assistance Plan, and other income maintenance programs.) For reasons discussed by Stewart, a major reform encompassing both taxation and income transfers is urgently called for; it will be important, he suggests, to introduce complementary changes in both aspects of what should properly be viewed as an integrated tax-and-transfer system. Deductions, exemptions, tax credits, and cash payments all have income-redistributive effects.

It is well understood that in Canada income redistribution occurs both through the federal and the provincial governments. 1) The federal and provincial personal income taxes are largely integrated with each other, Quebec alone collecting its own tax according to its own definition of "income"; on the other hand, several of the provinces now have legislated tax credits which are administered by the federal government under tax collection agreements. 2) If the federal government were to cut back the unemployment insurance program (as was proposed in a commission report released in late November),[3] this action would impose costs on the provinces, which bear responsibility for providing a "safety net" for individuals in short-term or insecure employment. In turn, most of these provincial programs are cost-shared with the federal government under the Canada Assistance Plan. 3) Provincial governments have authority to alter the distribution of family allowance payments, for example, by making higher per-child payments in the case of larger families. In these and other ways, the tax-and-transfer system is in effect a joint creation of the federal and provincial governments. Changes in one component affect other components, which may be partially or wholly the responsibility of another order of government.

If the program review that is being conducted by the federal Department of Finance lives up to its advance billing, it will be the first comprehensive re-examination of the tax system since the report of the Royal Commission on Taxation (the Carter Commission), which reported in 1966; and it will be successor also to the abortive federal-provincial Social Security Review launched in 1973. But it will differ from both in several respects. First, the present enquiry takes place against a backdrop of large budgetary deficits and a failed attempt (in the May 1984 budget) to curb social spending. Second, it will look at both aspects of income redistribution together, one hopes in a coordinated way. Third, it will be conducted internally, whereas the Carter Commission held extensive public hearings, and the Social Security Review was a joint undertaking with provincial officials. Fourth, it will be conducted in an ideological climate, at home and in other industrial states, marked by neo-conservativism; indeed, the United States Congress has now enacted major tax reforms lowering rates of tax on

4

higher-income earners. (This, as Stewart remarks, will be a potent incentive for Canada to introduce similar, if perhaps less dramatic, reductions in the tax burden on the wealthy.)

The objectives for reform of the tax-and-transfer system are clear. The actions that are taken must, as a package, be equitable and politically feasible while meeting fiscal as well as broader economic goals; they must take account of the international situation and domestic budgetary difficulties; and they must engage the provinces as willing partners. These criteria imply a need to rethink relationships among income groups in the context of Canada's ties with its trading partners, principally the United States, and in the context of a federal country marked by sharp interregional differences.

Quebec's Constitutional Initiative

On 9 May 1986, Quebec's minister responsible for Canadian Intergovernmental Affairs, Gil Rémillard, announced that Quebec would recognize the legitimacy of the Constitution Act, 1982, if it were amended to take account of five fundamental requirements. Quebec, he said, acknowledges that the Act is legally binding; but it was imposed on the province in disregard of its vehement objections at the time, and no Quebec government could ever accept it in its present form. The five conditions were: (1) recognition of Quebec's character as a distinct society, (2) a veto for Quebec over future constitutional amendments, (3) added powers over immigration, (4) limitation of the federal spending power, and (5) participation by Quebec in the nomination of Supreme Court judges. In addition, Mr. Rémillard expressed his support for fuller constitutional guarantees, in the Canadian Charter of Rights and Freedoms, of the rights of linguistic minorities. All these issues are discussed in chapter 4 of this volume, and the full text of Mr. Rémillard's speech is appended to the chapter.

Quebec Premier Robert Bourassa reiterated these conditions at a meeting of the provincial premiers in Edmonton 11-12 August, and proposed that the Quebec veto be achieved by requiring that future amendments be approved by at least two-thirds of the provinces (as at present) containing at least *three-quarters* (rather than, as at present, one-half) of the population of Canada. In July, Prime Minister Mulroney – without endorsing Quebec's proposals, but suggesting receptiveness toward them – had written the premiers recommending their serious attention to Quebec's constitutional initiative. The premiers agreed to give the five items priority over other constitutional matters, and not to expand the agenda of any future negotiations by linking other issues to them; this resolve was reaffirmed at a First Ministers' conference (FMC) in Vancouver late in November.

It is important not to exaggerate the significance of these developments, or to take for granted that a new accord can soon be reached. Quebec has insisted that negotiations have not yet been initiated, and that only informal pre-negotiation soundings have been made. Prior to the Vancouver meeting Mr. Rémillard had completed a tour of the provincial capitals with the goal of discovering whether or not there were good prospects for obtaining an agreement that Quebec could sign; the province took the position that it did not wish to make a formal launch unless there were reasonable assurance that the talks would be successful. By year's end, that assurance had still not been obtained; a new round of behind-the-scenes bilateral talks was under way, this time involving Senator Lowell Murray, federal minister for federal-provincial relations, and his provincial counterparts. It appeared that the declarations at Edmonton and Vancouver, which sounded upbeat, contained a certain amount of bravado. Animosity towards Quebec was building up as a result of perceived federal government favouritism towards the province in a number of policy decisions pertaining to the economy; continuing controversies over language policy in Quebec and other provinces were another factor. Equally if not more significant, the commitment to deal with Quebec's constitutional grievances first, and to address any others later, seemed shaky. Tactically, a province that wants (say) changes in the structure of the Senate, would be giving up bargaining power by agreeing first to changes in the amending formula, giving Quebec a veto. Other provinces have promised not to link their own high-priority issues to those desired by Quebec, but it is not certain their resolve will be maintained. An important factor to consider is that by the Constitution Act, 1982, all legislatures – not just the cabinets – must endorse any changes to the amending formula itself. Thus the process, even if begun behind closed doors, must eventually become a very public one.

The challenge here is obvious: to reach agreement on a revised constitutional accord, supplementing and in significant ways altering the one reached by ten governments – excluding Quebec – in November 1981. It cannot be done simply as a favour to Quebec; Quebec's Confederation partners must (as is discussed in chapter four) see a new accord as being in their own self interest. Their self interest will have to be reconciled with the conditions announced by the Government of Quebec. The Quebec government, in turn, is constrained by its electorate. Quebec nationalism, as Gil Rémillard stated when he announced the government's position on the constitutional issue, is not dead, far from it: and, he might have added, it will be a potent restraint on the position that Quebec takes in the negotiations he hopes soon to see formally launched. Nationalists are wary that the provincial government, if it is too anxious to strike a deal with the rest of Canada, may give away too much.

Coping with Falling Resource Prices

In November 1985 the wellhead price of Alberta light crude reached its all-time peak of $37.24 per barrel; eight months later (July 1986) it had plummeted to $14.54, for a net drop of 61 per cent.[4] Thereafter it recovered somewhat (by year's end, to about half its peak figure), but market specialists predicted that significant recovery would be unlikely to occur until the 1990s. One factor that is thought to militate against sharp increases for five or ten years is the expansion of productive capacity in non-OPEC countries, so that even if OPEC succeeds in disciplining its members, the effect of its doing so will be less marked than in 1973-74 or 1978-79. Furthermore, the price of natural gas – as the closest substitute energy source – is closely linked to the price of oil; western Canada has substantial surplus or "shut-in" capacity.

Oil is not the only resource product that was hit by falling prices in 1986. As a result of an agricultural trade war between the European Community (EC) and the United States, the initial price paid by the Wheat Board for wheat and other grains – mainstays of the prairie economy – dropped by 20 to 33 per cent from their 1985 levels, with the more severe price drops occurring with the lower-grade grains.[5] The EC subsidizes agricultural production through guaranteed-purchase arrangements that result in huge stockpiles of farm goods; these are subsequently dumped on world markets at prices far below what the EC pays for them. In December 1985 the United States, which increasingly was finding its own exports undercut, enacted a farm bill that reduced price supports while compensating producers by augmenting direct subsidies. These actions have depressed world prices for agricultural products while shielding American farmers against the effects of doing so. The U.S. aim is to bankrupt the EC fund that pays the subsidies, ultimately forcing the EC to abandon its policy. In the meantime, Canadian producers suffer, because Canada cannot afford to copy the U.S. policy – its export sales are too high a percentage of total production.

The federal government has committed $1 billion to cushion the blow of falling grain prices, but actual losses may well be as high as $2 billion. These "price shocks" will inevitably force many farmers into bankruptcy, following (as they have) several years' of cost-price squeeze that have eaten up cash reserves.[6]

The significance of the 1986 crash of the oil/gas and grains markets appears in combination with longer-term trends. Plunging prices accentuated an existing slide in prices for western-produced commodities in general. This stands in contrast to trends in central Canada and the Atlantic region. Edward A. Carmichael writes:

> In the mid-1970s, [non-energy commodity prices] increased fastest in the Prairie region, reinforcing the boost given by higher energy prices. Large increases in wheat and other grain prices were primarily responsible. Since 1980, non-energy commodity prices have been weaker in Western Canada than in the rest of the country [also, as noted earlier, oil prices peaked in 1981]. British Columbia experienced large declines in lumber and copper prices in 1980-81, followed by a weak and intermittent price recovery. The Prairie region has suffered a steady decline since 1980, primarily the result of stagnant or declining grain prices. Central Canada and the Atlantic region, on the other hand, have had relatively strong indexes since 1980. In Ontario and Quebec, improved prices for newsprint and for primary iron and steel have been chiefly responsible. Stronger prices for fish, iron ore, and newsprint have helped the picture in Atlantic Canada.[7]

One result of these changes in relative prices has been to reverse the shift in economic fortunes and economic power that occurred in Canada during the 1970s. As recently as November 1981 the federal government was basing its economic policies on what it saw as a long-term rise in the price of primary products relative to manufactures, and was predicting continued interregional migration towards the west (with migrants coming mainly, it would seem, from Ontario).[8] That this assumption was erroneous soon became clear, although federal policies did not adapt quickly to the new situation.

As David Hawkes and Bruce Pollard illustrate in chapter 7 of this volume, the sharp drop in oil and gas prices experienced in 1986 poses a dilemma for federal policy makers. From 1974 to 1985 Ottawa had held domestic prices below world levels, sheltering consumers against the price shock administered by the OPEC cartel; Hawkes and Pollard quote former Ontario Premier William Davis as saying that if trends should reverse in the future, central Canadian consumers will again – as in the 1961-73 period – be called upon to support the producing regions. (Davis conveniently ignored the difference in magnitude of interregional subsidization resulting from federal policy in the pre-1973 and post-1973 phases.) The "shock absorber principle", if we may so name the policy Davis apparently foresaw, would imply price supports or some form of public subsidization of producers to compensate for downward fluctuations in world commodity prices. So far, Ottawa has shown no inclination to do anything but alleviate the tax burden on the industry – the larger players have avoided asking for more. However, one should not focus on this case alone, fascinating as the intricacies of the oil/gas industry may be. The larger question is whether the federal government should routinely underwrite the risks inherent in resource production, acting as agent for interregional transfers of wealth, and smoothing out the bumpy ride of primary products on world markets.

The shock-absorber principle, an idea that is capable of application both to commodity markets and to the fortunes of economic regions, provides a rationale for the $1 billion that Ottawa has committed itself to spending for the support of prairie grain farmers. How far should this principle be extended? The most vulnerable segments of the petroleum industry have requested the federal government to establish a floor price for oil and gas. Others, less interventionist and well within historical Canadian norms for government-business relations, have called for price guarantees in the case of major development projects (oil sands, the Beaufort Sea, the Atlantic offshore). For example, Husky Oil proposed in early December that Ottawa underwrite some of the risk involved in launching major projects. Husky suggested that the federal government enter into long-term contracts to purchase oil at an agreed price, although production will not come on stream until the 1990s.[9] Depending on whether prices are higher or lower than expected, the public treasury will receive windfall gains or losses; in the meantime the government's guaranteed price will have ensured that the projects do actually go ahead, contributing both to employment and to future security of supply.

A federal government that acts as an insurer and shock-absorber necessarily shapes relations among economic regions. Indeed, if it declines to play this role, it implicitly opts to allow relations among economic regions to be recast every time there is a major shift in relative prices, particularly between resource products and manufactures. But whatever it does, one would wish it done consistently, for if the federal government protects consumers (and thus consuming regions) against increases in resource prices, as in 1974-85 with oil and gas, but does nothing to help producers when prices slump, its action is transparently predacious.

While the preceding discussion has focussed on the potential or actual role of the federal government as shock-absorber, the provincial governments may play this role too, at least to some extent. This is the idea behind the "heritage funds" established by Alberta and Saskatchewan, in which these provinces stashed away a portion of the windfall gains of the 1970s when resource prices soared; the idea was that in the downswing, the funds could be used (as indeed they are) to dampen its recessionary effects. Thus, even if a choice is made (implictly or explicitly) by government to act as shock-absorber, the function may be performed by the federal government interregionally, or by provincial governments – at least to some extent – inter-temporally. Which (if either) of these choices is made goes a long way to defining relations among economic regions and the respective policy roles of federal and provincial governments. Thus they will help determine whether citizens direct their political loyalties primarily to Canada as a whole, or to the province; the balance of "divided loyalties"[10] will affect the future shape of Canada.

Bilateral Trade

Through 1986 Canada played the ardent suitor to a broadly indifferent United States on trade matters. The Prime Minister had written President Ronald Reagan 1 October 1985 proposing that the two countries explore "the scope and prospects for a bilateral trade agreement," to which the President had replied that he believed "our objective should be to achieve the broadest possible package of mutually beneficial trade barrier reductions.... I want to see this process moved as promptly as possible." However, it was not until 23 April 1986 that the President cleared the necessary Congressional hurdles to open negotiations towards an agreement to be implemented by legislation under the so-called "fast track" procedure.

Bills considered under the fast-track procedure cannot be amended during their passage through Congress; Congress is committed to voting on them expeditiously, and to accepting or rejecting them as presented. Under the Trade Agreements Act, as modified in 1984, the fast track rule is available until 2 January 1988 for the approval of bilateral trade agreements with Israel and Canada. The effect is to prevent Congress from reopening a package deal. But the 1984 Act also stipulates that the President must give 60 days notice of his intention to open negotiations, and that he must consult regularly with the relevant committees of Congress during the course of negotiations. If, within 60 days of receiving the advance notice, either the Senate Finance Committee or the House of Representatives Ways and Means Committee disapproves, the President cannot proceed.

Thus, in the spring of 1986, the Senate Committee on Finance had an opportunity to kill negotiations for a trade agreement with Canada even before they started. The committee, in a preliminary vote, appeared poised to do exactly that, unless several outstanding trade disputes had been settled first. The most important of these concerned Canadian softwood lumber exports, which in 1985 amounted to $Cdn 4 billion and which industry spokesmen claimed to be subsidized by the provinces through their timber-leasing practices (low royalty charges, or stumpage dues) and other policies. Key senators on the Finance Committee voiced these concerns, but withdrew their objections after interviews with the President; and the committee, by splitting evenly on the vote, allowed negotiations to go ahead. However, the incident appeared ominous to Canadians for two reasons: first, it revealed the extent of real opposition, within a Congress known to be in a protectionist mood, to bilateral free trade with Canada; and second, it was suspected that the President had promised the recalcitrant senators a deal, perhaps on the lumber issue.

Talks opened between Canadian negotiator Simon Reisman and his American counterpart Peter Murphy 21 May 1986. However, eight months later the two men were still publicly and somewhat acrimoniously contradicting each other on the scope of an eventual agreement. Murphy had insisted, before discussions began, that all forms of subsidy or potential subsidy to Canadian production, including medicare and regional development incentives, might have to be looked at in order to ensure that Canadian producers would not enjoy unfair advantages against their American competitors;[11] and in January 1987 he warned that the 1965 Auto Pact might have to be put on the table too. This prompted a riposte from Reisman, that Murphy was either being foolish, or was a knave. Whereas Murphy seemed deliberately to be trying to unsettle the Canadian negotiators with his off-the-cuff public pronouncements, U.S. Ambassador Thomas Niles was much more reassuring, for example in insisting that social policies were not within the purview of the talks. The net effect on the Canadian debate was to give both the supporters and the opponents of a trade agreement lots to worry about, and lots of ammunition.

The fact that negotiations were under way did not impede the application of American trade laws, which allow domestic producers to seek the imposition of countervailing duties if products entering the United States are shown to be subsidized. (The "countervail principle" is that the duty will neutralize a foreign subsidy, so foreign producers will not enjoy an unfair advantage over their American competitors.) On 22 May 1986, catching the Canadian government by surprise, the U.S. imposed a countervailing duty on Canadian exports of cedar shakes and shingles, prompting an uncharacteristicly angry outburst from the Prime Minister. More significantly, a threatened countervailing duty on softwood lumber was avoided only by virtue of an agreement reached 30 December, whereby Canada promised to impose a 15 per cent export duty on softwood lumber pending possible upward revision of provincial stumpage dues. Predictably, these two actions provoked unbridled denunciation in Canada, and the Mulroney government's decision to seek a political settlement in the case of softwood lumber was hotly contested. Opponents, including industry spokesmen and the Government of Ontario, said it surrendered sovereignty. Supporters, especially the Province of British Columbia, considered that the deal was the only possible way of keeping an estimated $600 million in duties in Canada. It appeared to be a foregone conclusion that if Canada did not levy the charge, the United States would do so; and the Mulroney government promised to return the money to the provincial governments.

The softwood lumber dispute carries broad implications for both Canadian-American and federal-provincial relations, particularly in the context of a possible free trade agreement between the two countries. Trade Minister Pat Carney insisted that the dispute, forcing Canada into negotiations (in which, though she avoided saying so, the United States obviously held the upper hand), demonstrated why a trade pact is necessary: Canada does not want to be placed in so unfavourable a position again. The argument assumes that a trade agreement would grant Canada immunity from similar proceedings in the future. This is a dubious supposition since the report of the U.S. Senate Finance Committee recommending passage of the 1984 trade law stated that neither the Israeli nor the Canadian trade agreements, if successfully negotiated, would hinder the imposition of countervail: "The agreements would make clear that they will not affect the normal operation of the domestic trade laws; for example, procedures for domestic industries to seek relief from unfairly traded imports would operate without regard to such agreements."[12]

One significant fact about the softwood lumber case is that by threatening countervail the U.S. levered Canada into an agreement that Ottawa and the Government of British Columbia said was the only alternative to a legal challenge which we could not hope to win, and that left the U.S. with extensive control over it implementation. With this agreement, the United States reached far into what hitherto had been regarded as domestic Canadian policy, in this instance, resource management matters within exclusive provincial jurisdiction.

Another way in which the case is important is that it may point to a new federal-provincial relationship in trade matters. Richard Simeon, in chapter 9 of this book, draws attention to many of the ramifications of the trade negotiations for federal-provincial relations. He also points to the difficulties that may be encountered in negotiating and implementing a trade agreement, because of the federal division of powers. It is therefore interesting to note that in the softwood lumber case the federal government, being convinced of its impotence to fight the threatened countervail, imposed an export tax which can only be removed if the provinces adapt their policies in ways desired by the United States. Ottawa cannot constitutionally and authoritatively tell the provinces how to manage their forests, or what stumpage dues to collect; but it can impose a tax that may force the provinces to play ball by a set of rules established through bilateral negotiation between Canada and its southern neighbour. Thus while Ottawa cannot, in an analogous cases, assure the Americans that no province will offer a prohibited subsidy, it can promise to neutralize the effect of any subsidy by taxing exports if the American authorities, through procedures laid down in domestic trade laws, determine that imports have been "unfairly traded". This is especially worrisome in the context of a list published by the U.S. embassy of 16 Canadian programs, besides those at issue in the softwood lumber dispute, "that provide slight subsidies". The list includes investment tax credits, a variety of regional development incentives, British Columbia's Critical Industries Act, Quebec's Tax Abatement Program [the Quebec Stock Savings Plan?], and export market development programs.[13] Other major industries, including pulp and paper, potash, uranium, steel, and copper, fear they may be targets of actions similar to the one on softwood lumber.

The bilateral trade talks, the two disputes concerning the lumber industry, and the possibility of similar disputes affecting other products all point to the possibility and indeed the likelihood of major changes in the U.S.-Canada relationship in 1987 and beyond. Canada's problem is, as it has always been, to find a way of interacting with its southern neighbour on a basis as nearly equal as the one-to-ten size ratio will permit. Our policy in the past has oscillated between multilateralism – for example, in trade matters, trying to invoke GATT rules to minimize the disadvantages inherent in inferior size – and "exceptionalism", or trying to strike a deal with our big friend on the assumption that when it was playing tough with the rest of the world, the fallout for Canada was incidental and could be avoided through bilateral negotiation. Now it seems that many of the grievances the United States has on the trade front are directly and even primarily with Canada. In these circumstances exceptionalism seems unpromising, and the bilateral approach in general may be of dubious value; but there is no assurance that recourse to the GATT, which has very little to say about non-tariff trade barriers, can be an effective way of defending Canadian interests.

The Intermingling of Issues

Our discussion of four basic relationships – between the relatively rich and the relatively poor, between Quebec and the rest of Canada, among economic regions, and between Canada and the United States – has revealed how, in each case, extensive interaction between the federal government and the provinces is involved. The federal-provincial dimension is much more fully explored in subsequent contributions to this volume. However, the complexity of the problems that face Canadians in rethinking basic relationships, and meeting the challenges that each implies, is even greater than has been suggested so far. All these relationships intermesh, as do the various political issues in which they are crystallized.

It is impossible in the context of this essay to explore the intermingling of relationships and issues in a way that is at all satisfying. One must be arbitrary in illustrating the interconnections. However, the following brief list may be suggestive:

- Changes in the Canada-U.S. trading relationship have different effects on different classes. Workers bear the brunt of industrial adjustment more than owners and managers: workers' financial reserves tend to be more slender or even non-existent; loss of a job is more threatening, as the prospect of finding alternative employment is often more remote or uncertain; workers cannot, as capital can, shift to new products or locations with relatively little physical or psychological disruption. Thus it is not surprising that the trade unions are broadly hostile to a trade agreement whereas business groups are divided but, in general, favourable.[14]

- Regional interests, too, are bound up in the debate over bilateral free trade. Provinces whose economies would encounter relatively little adjustment in employment patterns or industrial structure, but would (or so they wager) obtain more assured access to the U.S. market, favour a trade agreement. Thus, all the Atlantic provinces and the three westernmost provinces are favourable, while Manitoba and Quebec are more ambivalent, and Ontario (which, perhaps incorrectly, anticipates the mose severe adjustment problems) is most negative, without having declared forthrightly against it.

- Those who are in an economically insecure situation, both employees and employers, tend to rely more on the federal government's role as economic shock-absorber and equalizer. Accordingly, while federal actions affecting the viability of resource industries (and other sectors too) may have significant regional consequences, one should not neglect to note divisions within each industry and region. In the case of the oil and gas industry, it is significant that the firms most vulnerable to the effects of declining prices – those with the lowest ratio of equity to debt – are those most inclined to ask for government intervention. Firms, whether large or small, that have been long-established and have built up large capital reserves, can better survive a slump and even profit by hard times in the sense that they can consolidate their position, buying out firms that are unable to meet fixed debt payments. This situation has implications for Canada-U.S. economic relations, because the better capitalized firms tend to be the American-owned "majors". A shakeout in the industry is likely to diminish Canadian ownership ratios.

- Changes in the tax-and-transfer system will obviously affect rich and poor in different ways, but they will also have implications for the relationship between Quebec and the rest of Canada. Policies for income support and redistribution have cultural as well as economic impact. Quebecers regard themselves as forming a distinct society, characterized not only by the prevalence of the French language but by a far wider range of cultural attributes. It is assumed that modes of expression and communication (like language, art, and music) are only the most visible features of a culture, which may be described as the collective personality of a people. One feature of a distinct society, or culture, is a particular "public philosophy" that defines mutual obligations between the individual and society at large; these values are reflected, in part, in policies affecting income distribution. Thus the Quebec government has always been leery of federal initiatives in welfare-related fields, wanting to retain control over program design (for more on this, see chapter 4, below).

- The relationship between Quebec and the rest of Canada involves a mix of cultural and economic issues. Cultural differences may reinforce economic regionalism, yielding a potentially explosive situation. When the federal government takes decisions that, unavoidably, favour one region over another, a "neglected" or disfavoured region may see the decision as ethnic favouritism or prejudice, if Quebec interests are involved. When a decision favours Quebec one cannot always disentangle regional rivalries from suspicions of "French power"; conversely, if a decision works to Quebec's disadvantage, Quebecers may interpret it as a manifestation of supposed dominance by the anglophone majority.

As noted, the foregoing cases are merely illustrative of how difficult it is to compartmentalize the four basic relationships that have been the focus of this essay. I have argued that current issues and those now visible on the horizon will require Canadians to re-think these relationships. It would be convenient if the tensions inherent in them, or the policy issues that highlight them, could be dealt with one by one. However, such simplicity is unattainable. Issues overlap each other; basic political relationships are interwoven. This makes it essential for our political leaders to balance each element in this complex situation with the others, and to recognize that preoccupation with a single issue or problem risks, through inadvertance or neglect, aggravating our overall situation.

Notes

1. Canada, Minister of Finance: *The Corporate Tax System: A Direction for Change*, [budget paper], May 1985.

2. The tax, analogous to the value-added taxes that are a major source of revenue for countries in the European Community, and for the Community itself, would presumably be levied as a percentage of firms' gross incomes, minus the purchase cost of non-labour inputs (raw materials, energy, or semi-manufactures consumed in the production process; goods purchased for resale). In other words, it would be a tax on labour costs plus profits. An attraction over the present manufacturers' sales tax is that it does not require identifying which goods are taxable, and at what stage; in addition, it can be applied to services (such as transportation. machinery repairs, or banking transactions) as well as to the production of goods. A major question is whether it would be applied to retailers, in which case provincial governments might well consider it an intrusion into a tax field that hitherto they alone have occupied.

3. The commission was chaired by Claude Forget, and included representatives of management and labour. Its chief recommendation was "annualization" of the program, under which the amount paid in weekly benefits would depend on the individual's earned income over the previous year. A person employed for only a relatively short period of time would receive benefits, as at present, but at a considerably lower level. The effect of the proposed change would have been to strengthen the *insurance* aspect of the scheme, making it less of a general income-supplementation program, and in particular making it much less attractive to workers in seasonal industries. Such workers would have to rely more on social assistance ("welfare") or other programs administered by the provinces. The labour representatives on the commission denounced the report even before it was released late November, and appended a lengthy dissent. The government, recognizing the unpopularity of the recommendations, promised that the program

would remain intact until at least 1988, or presumably until after the next election.

4. Data supplied by the Department of Energy, Mines, and Resources, Government of Canada.
5. *Globe and Mail*, 9 April 1986, *Regina-Leader Post*, 26 April 1986.
6. I am grateful to persons in farm organizations with whom I have discussed these matters.
7. *New Stresses on Confederation: Diverging Regional Economies* (Toronto: C.D. Howe Institute, 1986), "Observation No. 28," 10.
8. Canada, [Minister of Finance]: *Economic Development for Canada in the 1980s* (budget paper), November 1981. The "regional dynamics" of economic development are discussed on pp. 3-5. The paper refers (p. 5) to an expected influx of people into the west, particularly Alberta, but does not say where the migrants could be expected to come from. It is said that the authors of the white paper believed Ontario would be the major source.
9. *Calgary Herald*, 3 December 1986.
10. The phrase is E.R. Black's. See his *Divided Loyalties: Canadian Concepts of Federalism* (Montreal: McGill-Queen's University Press, 1975).
11. *Globe and Mail*, Toronto, 20 May 1986.
12. United States Senate, Committee on Finance: "Authority for Trade Agreements with Israel and Canada." Ninety-eighth Congress, Second session, Calendar No. 976 (Report 98-510), 12 June 1984, p. 6.
13. United States Embassy, Ottawa: News Release 86-181, 16 October 1986.
14. For a brief discussion, see Peter M. Leslie: "The State of the Federation, 1985", *Canada: The State of the Federation 1985*, ed. Peter M. Leslie (Kingston, Ont.: Institute of Intergovernmental Relations, 1985), 13-18.

II

FOCUS ON THE PROVINCES

2 B.C. IN CONFEDERATION

Donald E. Blake and
David J. Elkins

The past three years have been eventful ones in British Columbia. The Social Credit government used its 1983 re-election mandate to make major changes in government spending priorities, labour-management relations, human rights legislation, and protection of the disadvantaged all in the name of economic recovery. As the battle between the government and its opponents unfolded, governments and political observers at all levels across Canada looked to the province for insights as to what might happen if restraint of the B.C. variety were attempted in their jurisdictions, and even to forecast what might happen if the Progressive Conservatives replaced the Liberals in Ottawa.

Of course the Liberals were replaced, an event which itself deserves consideration as marking a major change in the province's relations with the federal government. For the first time in over a decade, most British Columbians had voted for the party which formed a majority government in Ottawa. And this time (unlike 1968), that government seemed to be on the same ideological wavelength as the government in Victoria. The ending of feelings of alienation and powerlessness which had developed during the Trudeau era may be at hand. The election of the Conservatives also eliminated a source of opposition to restraint in B.C. although apparently it did not provide an ally. While the Mulroney government flirted with restructuring social programs and launched a major inquiry into the delivery of government programs,[1] it displays no signs of following B.C.'s path to social spending cuts or massive reductions in the bureaucracy. However, it has made free trade, advocated for many years by Premier Bennett, a crusade of its own.

But from the province's point of view there are clouds on the federal-provincial horizon. The federal commitment to free (or at least freer) trade has not prevented a major blow to the province's forest industry in the form of a huge U.S. tariff on shakes and shingles, or the resurrection of attempts by U.S. producers to reduce B.C.'s share of the softwood lumber market. While not so large a cloud, the native land claims issue has been a major source of disagreement between the two governments, and complicates attempts by the province to increase access to marketable timber.

Because the political agenda in British Columbia has been so dominated by the issue of financial restraint, and because the government's actions may have served as an object lesson, positive as well as negative, for other governments in Canada, it seems appropriate to review the genesis of the battle over restraint and to explore the impact it had (and is having) on the province – especially now that Bill Bennett, the man responsible for it, has left the premier's office. There are several interrelated themes: What did the government believe its restraint program would accomplish? Was government "downsized"? How do megaprojects such as Northeast Coal and Expo 86 fit into a program of restraint? What are the implications for federal-provincial relations?

We also assess the change of government in Ottawa for what it tells us about the province's relationship to the national political community. The shift in emphasis from cultural and language issues to economic issues was welcomed by the provincial government, and gives the federal government a chance to appear as a benefactor rather than a villain to the province's voters.[2] The free trade initiative represents a major symbolic shift in the direction of support for economic priorities established by the western provinces, including British Columbia, rather than the central provinces, but its handling as well as its final outcome could conceivably drive Ottawa and Victoria as far apart as they were during the Trudeau era.

Related to the last point, but worthy of comment in its own right, is the situation regarding native rights, land claims and aboriginal title. As we mark the 100th anniversary of the railway promised by the terms of union, this major piece of unfinished business threatens to tarnish the splendor of the occasion, and the two governments pursue strategies which seem antithetical to one another.

Finally, we want to speculate about the future. To what extent will the bitterness produced by the restraint battle and the attempt to tame the unions affect the pattern of political conflict in British Columbia? Does the existence of a philosophically congenial government in Ottawa augur for a peaceful era in federal-provincial relations or will the aboriginal rights issue, the province's insistence on a direct role in free trade negotiations, and Ottawa's apparent reluctance to launch a neo-conservative crusade of its own drive the two governments apart?

22

Restraint and the Role of Government

The recession of 1981-82 hit British Columbia particularly hard. Between those two years the provincial unemployment rate rose from 6.7 per cent to 12.1 per cent. An anemic growth rate of 2.0 per cent in 1981 was followed by a decline of 5.9 per cent in 1982, the year leading up to the last election. The cause seemed obvious enough – the markets for the province's natural resources had virtually collapsed. Provincial revenues from natural resources plummeted from $862 million in the fiscal year 1980-81 to $597.6 million in 1981-82 to $542.5 million in 1982-83, declines of 30.7 per cent and 9.2 per cent, respectively.

The Social Credit government entered the campaign for the May 1983 election committed to a recovery program based on restraining government expenditures and encouraging job creation in the private sector. A prominent feature of the campaign was the government's promise to continue public sector wage controls and to reduce the size of the public service, citing, among other justifications, the principle of fairness. They argued that public sector employees should not be immune from the effects of the recession which had been visited primarily on private sector workers.

The election campaign had prepared the province for some action to deal with economic decline, but not for the dramatic steps which followed. After the election, Social Credit gave every indication that it now believed the "crisis of capitalism" was at hand, that and even stronger steps must be taken to arrest and reverse the province's economic decline. When Finance Minister Hugh Curtis introduced his post-election budget on 7 July 1983, he outlined a neo-conservative diagnosis of the province's economic ills and proposed remedies which set the stage for a dramatic confrontation between the government and key groups in society.

Curtis called for reducing public expectations regarding the role of government. Government growth was blamed for strangling the private sector through its sheer size and the "regulatory web" it had woven. Public sector strikes were blamed for disrupting the private economy and wage gains by public employees for bidding up the price of labour in the private sector, thus threatening the province's survival in international markets. Efficiency considerations dictated that some government services be privatized and that regulations limiting the freedom of action of businessmen, and thus economic recovery based on the private sector, be abolished. Since the recession had robbed the government of sufficient revenues to meet all its financial commitments without resorting to deficit financing or tax increases, "ability to pay" became a prominent part of the government's rhetoric.

The ideological position underlying the course the government was to follow was clearly stated by the finance minister:

> ... I remain committed to a government role in the economy which supports private initiative, which provides permanent and rewarding jobs and which builds a secure and prosperous economic future. No country, no region, has achieved enduring prosperity through expansion of overbearing government bureaucracy. Those governments which lean too heavily on the taxpayer suppress individual initiative and in fact mortgage the future, and that will inevitably precipitate economic decline.[3]

The restraint program consisted of a package of budgetary changes, cancellation of discretionary programs, and legislative changes incorporated in 26 government bills. The government proposed to cut the public service by 25 per cent over two years and change the basis for bargaining with government employees. This was to be accomplished by passing legislation eliminating provisions against layoffs in labour agreements with government employees and by freeing public sector managers from restrictions regarding firing, promotion, and transfer.

Costs of government were to be further reduced by eliminating a number of discretionary social programs and grants to a variety of community groups dealing with seniors, women, and the handicapped, freezing welfare rates, and placing ceilings on education and health spending. The planning functions of the province's regional districts were to be eliminated (which would reduce the numbers of governments whose permission was required for development projects), and bills were introduced to abolish the Human Rights Commission and to eliminate rent controls and the office of Rentalsman.

Organized extra-parliamentary opposition began to form within a week of the budget speech and announcements of the government's legislative intentions. Operation Solidarity, an alliance of trade unions backed by the B.C. Federation of Labour, was formally created on 15 July. On 3 August, they proposed an alliance with a variety of groups representing opponents of social program cuts, human rights activists, women's rights groups, and advocates for senior citizens and the handicapped who had already mobilized. The result, the Solidarity Coalition, was formally constituted on 30 August representing approximately 150 community groups and all the labour unions represented by Operation Solidarity.[4]

During the summer and fall the Solidarity Coalition and Operation Solidarity tried a variety of tactics including rallies, conferences, and conventional lobbying techniques, in an effort to get the government to withdraw its legislation and restore programs eliminated in the name of restraint. Neither side was prepared to compromise since Solidarity demanded negotiations with the premier based on the entire legislative agenda and the premier insisted that groups affected by the restraint program should meet with the cabinet ministers responsible for individual programs and areas of concern.

Opposition within the legislature was met by government use of closure (18 times between 19 September and 12 October), all night sittings, ejection of Opposition Leader Dave Barrett for the balance of the session and finally adjournment of the legislature on 20 October for a "cooling off period". However, conflict outside the legislature continued to escalate culminating in a strike by the B.C. Government Employees Union and the announcement by Operation Solidarity that it was prepared to organize a series of strikes culminating in a province-wide general strike of public sector and private sector workers.

In the end, after protracted negotiations and a province-wide teachers' strike, the labour component of the Solidarity Coalition, Operation Solidarity, struck an agreement with Premier Bennett which resulted in withdrawal of legislation restricting the right of government employees to negotiate crucial working conditions, and allowed public sector unions to negotiate job protection based on seniority in place of the guarantee against layoffs which had been eliminated by the Public Sector Restraint Act. The only satisfaction gained by the non-labour members of the Solidarity Coalition was a vague promise to negotiate and a pledge to restore to the public school system funds saved during a short teachers' strike.

The "Kelowna Accord", as the agreement came to be called, both reflected and exacerbated incipient divisions between private and public sector unions, and between labour and community groups. In the end, the only concrete concession by the government had simply been to restore some collective bargaining rights for public sector unions. Apparent victories for the non-labour side, such as the withdrawal of legislation to weaken protection for human rights and tenants' rights, proved fleeting since passage of the Human Rights Act and the Residential Tenancy Act in May 1984 largely accomplished what the government desired in the first place.

Organized labour's defenses were further tested by passage in May 1984 of Bill 28, The Labour Code Amendment Act, which made it easier to decertify trade unions and enabled the Cabinet to designate "Economic Development Projects" open to non-union labour and exempt from strikes. The first effects of that legislation were seen in the confrontation with construction unions at the site of Expo 86 which resulted in a victory for non-union contractors. However, the likelihood of a repeat confrontation with the government was virtually eliminated by provisions of the Bill restricting the ability of trade unions to strike over political issues.

Critics of the 1983 restraint budget could be forgiven for questioning the government's stated objectives. Growth of bureaucracy was alleged to be a problem, yet British Columbia already had the lowest level of public employment (government, hospital and educational employment combined), 16 per cent of the labour force, in Canada. Only one province, Ontario, had proportionately fewer hospital workers (2.1 per cent vs. B.C.'s 2.2 per cent), and none had fewer employed in government service or education sectors.[5] The restraint budget called for an increase of 12.3 per cent in government spending, one of the largest year-to-year increases in Canada. The effective result was a reduction in the budget share for health, education and welfare from 68.5 per cent in 1982-83 to 68.2 per cent in 1983-84. That trend has continued with 65.1 per cent in 1984-85, 64.6 per cent in 1985-86, and a projected 64.2 per cent in 1986-87.[6] Within the social policy sphere, education and health spending have lost ground to welfare spending, costs for which were driven up by the recession and continue to reflect the province's high unemployment rate (over 14 per cent).

Conflict over educational spending has continued unabated. Legislative changes introduced in 1983 removed the power of local school boards to tax commercial and industrial property and allowed the provincial Department of Education to set ceilings on school board budgets, ceilings which did not allow salary increases for teachers. Dozens of school boards threatened to submit budgets which ignored provincial guidelines, but in the end only two did so. The Minister of Education responded in the spring of 1985 by firing the school boards involved, in Vancouver and Cowichan, a district on southern Vancouver Island.[7]

Operating grants to universities were virtually frozen by the 1983 restraint budget, cut by 5 per cent in the 1984 budget, and by a further 5 per cent in 1985. The 1986 budget provided essentially the same amount for university base budgets as was granted in 1985. Any extra funds have been awarded at the discretion of the provincial cabinet for "adjustments", special programs, and "excellence". Because provincial cuts have coincided with increases in federal transfers for Established Programs Financing, in a sense the entire burden of post-secondary funding is met by the federal government. Assuming 32.1 per cent of Established Programs Financing transfers are intended for post-secondary education, the $489 million transferred by the federal government in 1985-86 exceeded the total amount spent in that sector by over $6 million.[8] The provincial government rejects the argument that

EPF transfers are earmarked in the case of post-secondary education or should be in the case of transfers for health, and continues to incur financial penalties linked to its user fees for hospital visits.

It is unlikely that the federal government will take on the provinces over educational spending in the way its predecessor did over health care funding. In fact, British Columbia is the only province which supports the federal government's decision to scale down the rate of increase in EPF transfers. The educational funding issue remains a significant part of the provincial political agenda, but seems destined to fade from view as an issue in federal-provincial relations.

The role of the state more generally remains an issue at both levels, with its significance heightened by the focus of the Macdonald Commission, and federal government pledges to reduce government spending.[9] While the Canadian state appears somewhat less developed than other, particularly European, nations (it ranks 12th out of 20 among OECD nations on total government spending as a percentage of GDP),[10] the trend is clearly upward and the consensus seems to be that governments can do little about it. Does the British Columbia experiment with restraint constitute an exception?

From the outline of events and budgetary record, it should be clear that the size of government did not diminish significantly in this period. Of course, government employment was reduced and many specific programs were scaled down or eliminated, but these were apparently more than fully compensated by increased spending on megaprojects. In other words, the government simply made a major effort to change spending priorities.

In a sense, government has become more visible – whether growing or shrinking – to the extent that its opponents have elicited heavy-handed responses. Abolishing the Rentalsman's Office, replacing the Human Rights Commission with a less potent Human Rights Board, and failing to re-appoint the Ombudsman have each engendered vitriolic denunciations on both sides. In that way, it has become difficult to assess the long-term effects of the Socred restraint package.

When the rhetoric subsides and when calmer tempers prevail, will there be "less government", a different kind of government, or more of the same? Although we are of the opinion that there may be a slightly altered role for the provincial government, it is really too early to offer any conclusion with confidence. A sincere and competent effort to "get government off the back of the people" cannot succeed in the short run. Not only are governments large and unwieldy contrivances – like oil tankers on the ocean – whose direction can be changed only slowly and with great effort; they are also organizations which have over a period of decades built up expectations of services and benefits which few groups or individuals wish to see disappear. The Mulroney government in Ottawa learned that lesson in regard to "universality" of social services in 1984-85, and the Bennett government may have come up against the same obstacle even earlier. Although government in B.C. has not been significantly reduced yet, expectations may have been curtailed, an objective announced by the finance minister when he introduced the restraint budget, and may be further decreased as time passes.

Has the restraint program been an exercise in cynicism? Strictly speaking, such a question can hardly ever be answered unequivocally, since it entails an assessment of the motives of decision makers. On the basis of statements and actions, however, cynicism seems quite appropriate for some aspects of the program and quite inappropriate for others.

Regarding several social programs and institutions designed to protect individuals, cynicism may be the correct evaluation. There is little doubt that downgrading and then eliminating the Rentalsman has not been accurately portrayed by the government. For example, to say, as they have, that the office could be better replaced by action through the court system is misleading. It is true that the provincial government can show a saving of a few million dollars by closing the office of the Rentalsman, but this has two kinds of hidden costs. For one, the courts themselves become more costly as more cases are brought to them which were previously handled elsewhere. For another, individuals must pay more for court services and lawyers than before. In evaluating the last point, it is essential to recognize that the cost is not borne by tenants alone; landlords found the Rentalsman useful. Now a landlord must go to court to evict a troublesome tenant or recover damages, whereas for the previous decade a visit to the Rentalsman was sufficient – cheaper, quicker, and less bother.

There is no point in recounting in detail the many ways in which false economies have been achieved. The Rentalsman is only one example. Freezing of welfare payments is another, in this case shifting the costs to charitable organizations such as churches and the Food Bank (now serving over 3000 families or individuals each week in Vancouver alone). One cannot help concluding that the government has been less than candid about its motives and about the actual effects of its actions.

When one turns from social services, however, a different conclusion may be warranted. Not that the actions were less contrived or controversial, but the motives have not been disguised. Take the field of labour relations as a case in point. There has never been any serious doubt that the government has had at least two goals. One was to weaken the ability of unions in general to dictate costs and conditions of work. We noted above that the battle over non-union contractors' right to work on Expo 86 projects was settled – in Bill 28 – by allowing the Cabinet to designate "Economic Development Projects" which would be open to non-union labour (as well as unionized labour) and which would be exempt from strikes. This is a powerful tool, openly acknowledged as essential to economic recovery and restructuring. Likewise the efforts – unsuccessful so far – to create "free enterprise zones" beyond the ken of federal import duties, the Labour Code and certain taxes, were not disguised as anything other than opportunities to create a better climate for businesses rather than labour. They were, of course, publicly also justified as being of benefit to workers insofar as they might create new and permanent jobs.

Another goal – less openly heralded but certainly real – was the exploitation of the division between public sector and private sector unions and their members. As we have noted above, this is a growing and significant cleavage in B.C.. Most of the public sector unions have primarily "white collar employees" or at least the active and leading elements are of that type. We have in mind not only the civil service employees in line departments (clerical and professional staff), but more significantly hospital employees, public school teachers,[11] college and university employees (though not university professors, who are legally debarred from forming unions), and employees of large government agencies such as the Insurance Corporation of B.C..

Although traditionally the NDP built its strength – as did its predecessor, the CCF – on blue collar unions and their members, its growth in the past two decades derives mainly from public sector unions and from the middle class groups who favour social services, quality education, and expanded health services. The blue collar unions, to the extent that they can be lumped together, may be seen as coming around to the view that their members' wellbeing depends on the health of the resource industries which the Social Credit governments have fostered.

The role of government – if not its size – may therefore be interpreted in light of the changing economic forces partly beyond its control. As traditional industries – especially forest products and mining – have become more capital intensive, their share of the labour force has declined. Concurrently, the service sectors of the economy have grown absolutely and even more proportionately; they constitute in B.C. as elsewhere a vast new segment of the labour force.[12] Both Social Credit and the NDP must face these changing circumstances, either by hastening the changes and welcoming the beneficiaries into their fold, or trying to capture each other's traditional supporters. This accounts in part for the decline in support for the Liberals and Conservatives (provincially but not federally), although polarization has other roots as well.

This situation is ironic. Precisely because so many aspects of economic change lie beyond the control of the provincial government, it must try harder to control what lies within its realm. Thus, the role of government – this provincial one, at any rate – must both grow and decline. It must exert ever larger efforts, it feels, for the megaprojects and withdraw from regulation or control of "free enterprise" in the sense of the small and large businesses in the province.

If Social Credit is to succeed in breaking out of the web of expectations surrounding the welfare state and government direction of the economy, it will have to confront obstacles facing every modern state. As Alan Cairns put it:

> The contemporary state manoeuvres in an ever more extensive policy thicket of its own creation, interacting with a society that is tied to the state by a complex network of benefits, dependent relationships and coercions. From this perspective the state, in confronting society, confronts its own past, and the society that seeks to influence the state directs its efforts to transforming the multiple linkages that interpenetrate and affect almost every facet of its functioning.[13]

Federal-Provincial Relations

B.C. is part of the West, and as such it has often been alienated from the central government in Ottawa. Its disputes have sometimes been shared by other provinces, but often it has had its own reasons to resist Ottawa's blandishments. It shares the feelings of powerlessness regarding federal institutions associated with its relatively small population share, but unlike the other western provinces has never had to fight for control over its own resources – that came with entry into Confederation. Its principal resource industries, forestry and mining, are clearly under provincial jurisdiction although federal taxation and tariff policies as well as federal jurisdiction over the ports obviously affect those industries. While, unlike the Atlantic provinces, British Columbia has acquiesced to federal control of the fishery it no longer makes a major contribution to provincial GDP.[14] Thus, "the historical record provides little support for basing grievances on a quasi-colonial past or federal obstacles to provincial prosperity,"[15] and since the provincial government has blamed international forces beyond its control for the province's contemporary economic difficulties, it can hardly lay them at Ottawa's door.

For the most part we will ignore those aspects of federal-provincial relations which B.C. shares with other provinces, except for passing references, and concentrate on a few which put B.C. in a class by itself.

Two will occupy us most of all in this section – trade issues and the externalities of the B.C. restraint program. In the next section we turn to native issues, which also have a federal-provincial aspect as well as aspects peculiar to B.C. itself.

To put B.C. in context, it must be recalled that this province was a member of the "gang of eight" which opposed Prime Minister Trudeau's attempt to patriate the Constitution unilaterally. That gesture was typical of the relations with Ottawa which were usually stormy during the Trudeau era, as they were for most provinces. In common with several others, this province was chastised by the Liberals, and since 1984 by the Conservatives in Ottawa, for allowing user fees in hospitals. Despite all of the past grievances and despite some on-going sore points, federal-provincial relations have entered a more amicable – or at least quieter – phase since the election of the Mulroney Government in September 1984, as has been true generally with all provinces.

In part, better relations were inevitable. The removal of Trudeau, the man everyone "loved to hate", was bound to help, if for no other reason than a new broom sweeps clean. In addition, however, one must recognize that Social Credit under Bill Bennett became less of a "third party" and more like a traditional version of the Conservatives at the provincial level. Thus, on the grounds of ideology and potential supporters, one would expect an improvement in relations with Ottawa. Whether that situation will last depends on future events, of course, but several accomplishments show that relations can be civil. After recounting them, we will deal briefly with some aspects which could become contentious issues.

On ideological grounds as a business-oriented government, and for pragmatic reasons due to its resource-based economy, the government of B.C. has always been concerned to foster freer trade. In particular, it wants the federal government to allow the provinces greater scope in this area. The province's emphasis on trade issues is understandable. Fully 40 per cent of manufacturing trade shipments go to destinations outside Canada, the highest level in Canada, whereas only 15 per cent, the lowest in Canada, go to other regions of the country.[16] In 1983, the value of exports as a percentage of GDP was 28.1 per cent, the highest in Canada.[17] Nearly half (47 per cent in 1984) of the province's exports go to the United States, but a substantial (and increasing) percentage (36 per cent) go to the Pacific Rim.[18]

Thus, Premier Bennett applauds Prime Minister Mulroney's efforts to negotiate free trade with U.S.,[19] since it will help the forest industry in B.C.. He has in mind, however, a broader range of trade initiatives which are being pursued in several ways. For one, the province has had for several years a Minister of International Trade, whose efforts have been focussed on the Pacific Rim more than on Europe or the U.S.

Arrangements have also been concluded with the federal government to post B.C. trade representatives in several Canadian Embassies and Consulates abroad.[20] Although more are planned, the first four postings are significant: Hong Kong, Seoul, Dusseldorf, and San Francisco. Half are in the Orient, only one in the U.S.. The location of one officer in San Francisco is, of course, logical, since the B.C. government plans postulate the export of hydroelectric energy to California, as well as the possibility of water exports some day. Thus, the government announced a desire to re-negotiate the Columbia River Treaty,[21] which was a bitterly contested issue in the reign of Bennett's father in the 1950s. Likewise, as we will argue below, the plans for the Site C dam hinge on long-term contracts for energy exports to the west coast grid of the U.S..[22]

The B.C. government had put forward plans for "export zones" in B.C. which would have required federal legislation and approval. When Ottawa proved less than enthusiastic, these plans were quietly – rather than angrily – abandoned in favour of "special enterprise zones."[23] As envisioned, they will be regions (perhaps even as small as a single building) designated by the B.C. Cabinet to get relief from all provincial sales tax and for ten years, relief from provincial corporate income tax. Since that would still leave them subject to federal taxes, to import duties, and to export regulations, it remains to be seen whether they will induce new enterprises to locate in B.C. and if so whether they will prosper. The federal government's proposal to designate Vancouver as an international banking centre can be seen as a response to the province's aspirations.

A trade-related issue which may also involve Expo 86 and the restraint program leads us to turn our attention to some "external" effects of B.C. restraint. This issue – the merits of exporting logs rather than lumber – is inordinately complex and contentious. Does the restriction on log exports (mainly to China and Japan) help or hurt the province?[24] If the logs would not be used domestically, because of low demand in the recession, why not export them as surplus? Does such exporting also, in effect, decrease employment since the "value-added" component accrues to foreign mills? Is this practice necessary because of different customs about house construction in Japan?[25]

What gives this issue its particular poignancy are the rumours that it involves a "deal" with Jack Munro, international vice-president of the International Woodworkers of America to ensure labour peace at Expo.[26] The speculation has been fueled by the fact that Munro has stated publicly that he favours the restrictions even at the expense of loss of jobs. Since Munro and the premier were the architects of the

"Kelowna Accord" in 1983 which ended the threat of a general strike, the rumors have been taken seriously in some circles. They may be groundless, of course, since legislation subsequently has made political strikes at Expo illegal, as noted above.

The restraint program has had repercussions for federal-provincial relations in several domains. For example, some people feel that the federal decision to locate Canada Place, the federal contribution to Expo 86, on a site not in the False Creek area but on Coal Harbour was a blatant attempt to "distance" Ottawa from Expo. Other views are that the decision to build the pavilion and convention facilities a mile from Expo was made before plans for Expo were complete. This has plausibility, since Senator Jack Austin had towards the end of the Trudeau era been trying to create a visible presence for Ottawa in Vancouver.

The federal government has apparently gone some way to help make Expo 86 a success, even if its own pavilion is not on the Expo site. For example, two off-the-record interviews with federal civil servants have verified that the Canadian International Development Agency (CIDA) has poured money into the construction of pavilions representing several Third World countries. In addition, the federal government has helped to fund SkyTrain, the lower mainland's new high tech rapid transit system, directly and indirectly. Despite that aid, the B.C. and federal governments got into a squabble when it became known that the B.C. logo would be prominently displayed on the sides of each SkyTrain car whereas the federal logo would be smaller and only visible on the inside of cars.

Many aspects of federal-provincial relations must be passed over here, but two deserve some comment to round out this section. As part of its drive to reduce health costs, the B.C. government, perceiving a surplus of doctors, froze the issuance of new billing numbers. Subsequently, they promulgated regulations which "rationed" the billing numbers so that they could insist on new doctors moving to rural communities which had too few or no doctors and thus spread the services more evenly. This practice was quickly challenged in the courts on the grounds that it violated the Charter of Rights and Freedoms. The B.C. Supreme Court ruled that it did violate these rights to mobility and declared the regulations unconstitutional.[27] The matter is being appealed to the Supreme Court of Canada, and in the meantime the B.C. government is exploring other means of ensuring an adequate supply of doctors to rural areas.[28]

The issue of billing numbers is only part of the confrontation with the federal government over health services and their financing. User fees such as the $10 charge for visits to hospital emergency wards are defended by the B.C. government on the basis that they deter frivolous usage. Polling suggests that B.C. residents prefer them to higher taxes or lower level of services,[29] and one suspects that many federal Conservatives feel the same way. But the federal government insists on penalizing any provincial government for their use, penalties amounting to about $88 million so far. This could become an interesting issue over the next year since the province will get a refund on the penalties if abolished by 31 March 1987, although they do not have to return the fees to individuals who paid them.[30]

Finally, one can speculate more broadly about the restraint program in B.C. as the harbinger of a neo-conservative revolution. While Premier Bill Bennett argued repeatedly that all governments will have to take steps similar to his as we move into the new realities of the late twentieth century. He welcomed the departure of Trudeau and the election of Mulroney as a harbinger of such a change in attitude in the federal government. There is some truth in this, of course, as seen in the federal efforts to negotiate free trade and to "privatise" crown corporations. The abortive attempt to restrict "universal" social payments might be seen in the same light. Prime Minister Mulroney, however, criticised the Bennett restraint program when first introduced, while he was Opposition Leader, and it seems unlikely he will tread the same path now, especially since it has engendered so much opposition in the province.

There is another sense, however, in which Bennett and Mulroney together may herald a change in federal-provincial relations. For a long time – and certainly throughout the Trudeau era – federal-provincial relations were portrayed as "zero-sum": what one government gained, another lost. Hence, Trudeau's oft repeated claims and efforts to regain some of the powers lost to the provinces, and the premiers' unstinting attempts to resist these "encroachments" as devious and dastardly.

What requires serious consideration is the possibility that both sides were misguided. During the 1960s and 1970s, both federal and provincial governments grew – in expenditures, in regulatory powers, and in proportion to the private sector.[31] The major change was not a shift of power to one or the other level, but a generally expanded use of existing powers by both levels of government. Since 1983 in B.C. and since 1984 in Ottawa, what we witness is the rhetoric – and perhaps a real attempt – to "downsize" both levels of government. If that happens, and it is not clear that it will, one could still not conclude that the Bennett restraint program caused the shift in attitudes. After all, Margaret Thatcher and Ronald Reagan were saying and doing some of these things before 1983. But Mr. Bennett will no doubt try to claim a leadership role.

Who Owns British Columbia?

Related to federal-provincial relations but going far beyond it is the set of issues surrounding native rights in Canada and B.C.. In part, this derives from inclusion of reference to these (undefined) rights in the new Charter of Rights and Freedoms, but in greater part it stems from three features of recent events in B.C. For one, B.C. has a higher proportion of natives than any other province (nearly 3 per cent of the population), and a substantially higher proportion who have never signed treaties about their lands and rights (roughly 90 per cent lack treaties). For another, it was the Nishga land claims in B.C. which established the legal basis for aboriginal title, first in a B.C. Supreme Court decision in 1970 and then in the Supreme Court of Canada in 1973, which led the Trudeau government to take these claims seriously and to open negotiations. Finally, the culture of B.C. natives has been revitalized in the past two decades. Especially significant has been the blossoming of artistic endeavours among many Northwest Coast groups (led by Bill Reid and now encompassing scores of distinguished carvers and print-makers). In some cases, languages near extinction are being used more extensively.

This is not the place to review the whole history of natives in B.C., but several recent developments should be mentioned. In particular, an experiment in local self-government is underway; confrontation over land use has become more common and visible; and negotiations have been delayed by federal-provincial disagreement over who is responsible for compensation, if anyone.

Natives have long had a form of self-government under the Indian Act, in the form of an elective band council system. Two problems are especially prominent. For one, the band councils have never had the degree of autonomy and control of resources characteristic of municipalities, let alone provinces. They do not control school or hospital funds, for example, or a police force. More seriously, the band council has followed a majoritarian model, whereas aboriginals claim the heritage of an informal and consensual style of government. As one commentator put it, "Aboriginal communities have not allowed individualism to prevail over community to the extent that we [whites] have."[32]

In the period covered by this chapter, a significant step has been taken to change this system towards more meaningful self-government within Confederation.[33] In October 1985, Indian Affairs Minister David Crombie announced his intention to provide enabling legislation to turn the Sechelt Indian band in B.C. into the first experiment in native self-government. Such legislation would allow the band to opt out of the Indian Act and thereby gain title to reserve lands and cease to be wards of the government. The concept has engendered disagreement among native groups, since it can be seen as avoiding or undercutting the issue of title to lands outside the reserves. It would also, of course, be a government subject to provincial jurisdiction, as all local governments are. (Similar negotiations regarding self-government for the Nishnawbe Aski in Ontario are underway but less advanced.)[34]

A federal task force reported in early 1986 and recommended further progress along the lines of self-government.[35] One of the most significant of their comments concerned self-government as a compromise between natives as wards of Indian Affairs and complete settlement of claims. For example, the task force argued that the government should provide rights to natural resources and abandon the idea of extinguishing aboriginal rights. As the chair of the task force, Murray Coolican, said, "What needs to be extinguished are not aboriginal rights, but dependency on outside institutions and financial support."[36]

Such moves towards self-government are not the only development in this area. The Gitksan-Wet'suwet'en tribal council in northern B.C. has begun trying to set up its own government over about 55,000 square kilometres of northwestern B.C.. It is an extremely bold gesture, because the group rejects the concept of compensation for lands and rights; they instead want the land itself, but without necessarily displacing any non-natives living in the area. It is too early to predict the outcome, but conflict and protracted negotiations are likely, since the B.C. government has expressed disapproval.[37]

Attracting the most attention, locally as well as nationally, the conflict over the logging of the South Moresby islands is more typical of the way federal and provincial matters intersect. The B.C. government has given lease and logging rights in several parts of this group of islands; and the Haida have responded with claims to control the area as sacred areas. In addition, the federal Minister of the Environment has recommended that the area be declared a park; the Minister of Indian Affairs has offered to mediate; a B.C. Member of Parliament was arrested and fined for participating with the Haida in blocking a road leading into the logging area; and a special task force set up by the provincial government recommended limited logging and then letting the natives have the land.

The public – not just governments – is involved. Church groups and environmentalists have been active; newspaper editorials and commentary abound; and celebrities such as Pierre Berton have got into the act. A poll commissioned by *The Vancouver Sun* (in November 1985) found that about three out of five British Columbians support the negotiation of native land claims, and half support the Haida in their campaign of civil disobedience on Lyell Island (in the South Moresby area).

As if these issues were not complicated enough, innocent suggestions often elicit new aspects. For example, there have been suggestions that the federal government should transfer title to Stanley Park to the City of Vancouver as part of its Centennial celebrations in 1986.[38] This aroused the ire of the Burrard, Musqueam, and Squamish bands, who argued that they own the land; and thus no government can dispose of the area without their consent.[39]

Although much federal-provincial conflict revolves around claims by each level that they alone have the power and duty to do something, in the case of B.C. natives the reverse seems to be the case. The federal Minister of Indian Affairs has stated that B.C. must participate in negotiations and compensation, since the federal government cannot do it all by itself and besides "It's B.C. land."[40] The position of B.C. is complicated. The provincial government believes that aboriginal title was extinguished at Confederation, but that if it still exists, the federal government must deal with the matter. For one thing, the B.C. government argues, Indian affairs is a federal jurisdiction. For another, by the terms of union when B.C. joined Confederation in 1871, the federal government assumed all debts and obligations extant at that time.

The positions are clearly polarized, and the rhetoric is commensurate with the gravity of the issues. In 1983, at a federal-provincial conference on natives, James Gosnell, Chief of the B.C. region of the Assembly of First Nations, laid down the gauntlet: "Now ... if you want me to put it like lock, stock, and barrel or total ownership, whether it is the mountains, inside the mountains, up in the air, the snow, the sea, you name it .... Our definition is as I have said it: we are the true owners of B.C., even at this moment."[41] Premier Bennett, as expected, responded by saying that there will be no talk until natives give up the concept of aboriginal title, especially of the "lock, stock, and barrel" variety.[42] Brian Smith, the Attorney-General, was equally explicit in the legislature last year: "Our position has been that if Ottawa wishes to acknowledge, recognize, and reimburse for such claims, that is within their purview to do so. We would prefer that it were not so, but if they wished to do that, that was their responsibility."[43]

By the spring of 1986, B.C. ministers had reached the point of talking to native leaders. Some discussions took place in 1985 concerning the self-government experiment in Sechelt mentioned above. Further discussions followed the civil disobedience campaign by the Haida on Lyell Island. The federal and provincial governments have exchanged a series of letters about legal challenges to ownership, about each government's policies on title and other matters, and about the responsibility for compensation in light of B.C.'s terms of union. Where they will go from here is anyone's guess.

Where do we go from here?

The restraint program was advertised as something new, and portrayed by the government's friends and foes alike as an attempt to impose a neo-conservative vision on the province. But in retrospect it may appear as little more than a contribution to the continuing rhetorical battle between left and right in British Columbia. Spending cuts have had little effect on government's share of the economy,[44] and the government has begun to loosen its purse strings (but not the political strings) for educational spending. Candidates to succeed Bill Bennett as party leader and premier tried to outdo each other with their pledges to replace confrontation with consultation. After exhorting its citizens to prepare for a high tech future, the sun supposedly having set on the forest and mining industries, the provincial government has returned to its traditional faith in resource exports and megaprojects.

The Northeast Coal project was launched before the initiation of restraint, but the government has proved unwilling to abandon the massive subsidies to B.C. Rail required to sustain it. Spending on transportation and highways increased by 38 per cent in the 1985-86 fiscal year, and, with the help of the federal government, B.C. will spend $300 million to restore the province's forest base between 1985 and 1990. The government is also looking to markets for hydro-electricity in California to justify proceeding with expansion of power development on the Peace River. In the short run, it has staked the province's economic future and the government's political future on the hope that Expo 86 will provide a stimulus to desperately needed investment, and is prepared to incur a huge Expo deficit to that end. Each of these economic development strategies requires federal cooperation, but not federal initiative, so whether they succeed or fail it is the provincial government's reputation for economic management which is on the line.

While we seem to have returned to business as usual on the economic front, the restraint battle may have intensified divisions in the province's political culture between proponents of individualistic and free market solutions to economic and social problems and those endorsing collective responsibility and activist governments. Attacks on the wisdom and motives of public sector employees, the efficiency of public bureaucracies, and the degree of government responsibility for seniors, welfare recipients and the unemployed go to the heart of the most prominent attitudinal division between Social Credit and NDP voters. Even in 1979, well before the implementation of restraint measures, differences of opinion on these questions cut across class lines and proved to be the most powerful predictor of provincial voting choice. However, unless public attitudes have shifted dramatically since then, most British Columbia voters gravitate towards the ideological centre. They expect polarized politics, but do not endorse them.[45]

Another crucial feature of the politics of the seventies and eighties in British Columbia was the emergence of a new electoral coalition supporting the NDP. The slow but steady growth of NDP support from roughly one-third of the electorate to approximately 45 per cent was closely associated with the unionization of public employees, and the growth of employment associated with the health, welfare, and educational services provided by government. As the party with the strongest official beliefs in the rights of workers to bargain collectively, and in the benefits of state intervention to achieve equality, the NDP, solidly supported by organized labour in traditional private sector occupations, was a natural home for public sector workers generally. In its battles with the Solidarity Coalition, the government was able to exploit latent divisions between public and private sector workers which could ultimately weaken the electoral coalition on which the NDP's new found competitiveness depends.[46] However, in doing so it may have weakened its hold on its own middle class and professional supporters who were offended by a resurgence of Social Credit populism and disruption of the educational system.

The NDP victory in the 1984 Okanagan North by-election provides partial confirmation for this hypothesis. The Okanagan has been a Conservative stronghold for generations. W.A.C. Bennett spent virtually his entire political career representing the region, and Bill Bennett succeeded his father as member for Okanagan South. However, it is also a region which has shown a marked increase in support for the NDP since the mid-sixties, linked to expansion of public employment and modest industrialization. As we have shown elsewhere, a straight line extrapolation of election results in the region from 1966 to 1983 would have led one to expect more close races and even NDP victories within one or two elections.[47] Dissatisfaction with the government's handling of restraint may have hastened the process.

Memories of restraint will likely have dimmed by the time of the next election, but the basic ideological and structural factors associated with the relative strength of the province's two main parties have not altered significantly. However, despite this, and despite the transfer of the NDP leadership from Dave Barrett to Bob Skelly (thus distancing the party from its record in 1972-75), and the replacement of Bill Bennett by Bill Vander Zalm (perhaps reducing the salience of the restraint battle), the outcome of the next election is by no means obvious. Counterbalancing negative aspects of government handling of restraint are the strains it produced between public and private sector components of the labour movement and between working class and middle class supporters of the NDP. The Socreds have been embarrassed by resignations from the cabinet for violation of conflict of interest legislation, but the NDP has suffered defections of two of its own MLAs – one to Social Credit and one who became an independent, formed a one-man party, then became the first Progressive Conservative member of the legislature since 1979. If the economic recovery program succeeds the government will have been vindicated. If it fails, the voters will still have to decide whether the NDP is the party to turn to in bad times.

Relationships with the federal government will be dominated by the free trade issue for some time, with native rights and transfer payments intervening from time to time. Unlike the case in provinces such as Alberta, issues of federal-provincial relations rarely appear as major sources of division in provincial politics. The free trade issue has the potential to become an exception, since it has been portrayed by labour leaders as another attempt to undermine union agreements and drive down wages, and is opposed by the federal New Democratic party.

The province must be on guard lest the traditional political clout of the central manufacturing regions reassert itself, or that Mulroney's eagerness for a free trade pact result in major concessions to the U.S. which will damage the province's forest industry. The irony of the free trade issue is that while British Columbia has finally succeeded in getting the federal government to adopt one of its economic priorities, the outcome could be unfavourable to the province. From Ottawa's point of view, keeping B.C. onside will be critical to federal Conservatives standing in the province. Our research strongly suggests that Conservative support in B.C. is not based primarily on ideological affinity, but on rejection of a Liberal record which was perceived to be insensitive to the province's economic needs and too attentive to those of the central Canadian provinces, especially Quebec. When we again hear references in the premier's speeches to the iniquity of the terms of union and the favouritism shown the central provinces, we will know that we have returned to business as usual in this area too.

Notes

1. For highlights of the subsequent report see *The Globe and Mail*, 12 March 1986. Unlike the case in British Columbia where the restraint program was prepared hastily and implemented with virtually no public input, the 21 volume Nielsen Taskforce report seems destined to occasion many months of discussion.

2. See Donald E. Blake, "Managing the Periphery: British Columbia and the National Political Community", in R. Kenneth Carty and W. Peter Ward (eds.), *National Politics and Community in Canada* (Vancouver: UBC Press, 1986) for a detailed analysis of federal actions which have alienated British Columbians and possible actions which could strengthen attachment to the centre.

3. B.C. *Hansard*, 7 July 1983, 160.

4. A detailed account of the formation of the Solidarity Coalition, the structural problems which plagued it and its activities is contained in Patricia Nelson, *Solidarity Coalition: The Struggle for Common Cause* (unpublished M.A. Thesis, University of British Columbia, 1985). For a briefer account and a series of essays by critics of the restraint program see Warren Magnusson, *et al.*, *The New Reality: The Politics of Restraint in British Columbia* (Vancouver: New Star Books, 1984).

5. See Sharon L. Sutherland and G. Bruce Doern, *Bureaucracy in Canada: Control and Reform* (Toronto: University of Toronto Press and the Royal Commission on the Economic Union and Development Prospects for Canada, 1985), pp.139-40, Table 3.28.

6. All figures are from the 1986 provincial budget. The 1985-86 figures are based on revised estimates. It should be noted that the budget share for social spending in the 1981-82 fiscal year was still lower (62.8 per cent according to figures in the 1985 provincial budget).

7. Voters in those districts were allowed to vote in special elections to restore local school boards. The result reflected the province's customary polarization. A left leaning slate swept all seats in Vancouver, and a pro-government majority was elected in Cowichan.

8. These figures include tax points as well as cash transfers and are based on federal assumptions about the balance between health and education. For detailed calculations and estimates of the effects of the cuts which take inflation into account see Neil Guppy, "Education under siege: financing and accessibility in B.C. universities," *Canadian Journal of Sociology*, 10 (1985) 295-308.

9. See Keith Banting (ed.), *State and Society: Canada in Comparative Perspective* (Toronto: Royal Commission on the Economic Union and Development Prospects for Canada and the University of Toronto Press, 1986).

10. David R. Cameron, "The Growth of Government Spending: The Canadian Experience in Comparative Perspective," in *ibid.*, p.24, Table 2-1.

11. School teachers are restricted to bargaining over salaries, and do not have the right to strike.

12. For details see Rennie Warburton and David Coburn, "The Rise of Non-Manual Work in British Columbia," *B.C. Studies* 59 (Autumn 1983), 5-27.

13. Alan Cairns, "The Embedded State: State-Society Relations in Canada," in Banting (ed.), *State and Society*, p. 57.

14. In 1983, fishing represented 0.8 per cent of GDP compared to 8.5 per cent for forestry and 6.9 per cent for mining. See British Columbia Ministry of Finance, *Financial and Economic Review*, August 1985, Table 6.1, p. 71.

15. Blake, "Managing the Periphery...," p.173.

16. J. Terence Morley, *et al.*, *The Reins of Power: Governing British Columbia* (Vancouver: Douglas and McIntyre, 1983), Table 11, p. 274. The figures are for 1974.

17. Wendy L. Carter, "What Makes B.C. Tick: A Profile of British Columbia," draft paper, Office of the Federal Economic Development Coordinator, Vancouver, B.C., April 1985, p. 24.

18. British Columbia Ministry of Finance, *Financial and Economic Review*, August 1985, p. 3.

19. After refusing to make a presentation to the Macdonald Royal Commission which came up with the recommendation!

20. *The Globe and Mail*, 17 January 1986.

21. *The Globe and Mail*, 15 October 1985.

22. The first step in that direction has been taken with the signing of an agreement with U.S. utilities to study legal and technical issues associated with the proposal. See *The Globe and Mail*, 13 June 1986.

23. *The Globe and Mail*, 8 March and 7 June 1985.

24. *The Globe and Mail*, Report on Business, 21 April 1986.

25. These issues are reviewed by David Lloyd-Jones, *The Globe and Mail*, 8 March 1986.

26. *The Globe and Mail*, 21 April 1986.

27. *The Globe and Mail*, 23 March 1985.

28. See *The Globe and Mail*, 9, 14, 17 and 24 March 1985.

29. See Vaughn Palmer, *The Vancouver Sun*, 20 March 1986.

30. *Ibid.*

31. R.A. Young, P. Faucher, and A. Blais, "The Concept of Province-Building: A Critique," *Canadian Journal of Political Science*, 17 (1984), 783-820.

32. Noel Lyon, *The Globe and Mail*, 21 May 1985.

33. *The Globe and Mail*, 25 October 1985.

34. *The Globe and Mail*, 29 November 1985. The relevant legislation covering the Sechelt Band was passed in June, 1986.

35. *The Globe and Mail*, 20 March 1986.

36. *Ibid.*

37. *The Globe and Mail*, 21 April 1986.
38. *The Vancouver Sun*, 10 February 1986.
39. *The Vancouver Sun*, 19 February 1986.
40. *The Vancouver Sun*, 20 March 1986.
41. Quoted by Vaughn Palmer, *The Vancouver Sun*, 16 November 1985.
42. *Ibid.*
43. *Ibid.*
44. Current provincial government expenditures as a percentage of Gross Domestic Product from 1981 to 1984 were 16.7 per cent, 17.1 per cent, 17.3 per cent, and 17.8 per cent, respectively. In contrast, both Alberta and Ontario witnessed reductions between 1983 to 1984, from 19.4 per cent to 19.0 per cent in the case of Alberta and from 16.2 per cent to 15.8 per cent in Ontario. See Statistics Canada, Provincial Economic Accounts, 1969-84, Catalogue No. 13-213, 1986. Calculations are based on figures in tables 1 and 3. However, assuming the growth projections for 1985 and 1986 are accurate (6.2 per cent and 7.7 per cent, respectively, unadjusted for inflation), government in B.C. must have begun to shrink since provincial spending grew by only 3.9 per cent between the 1984 and 1985 fiscal years, and is estimated to grow by 5.7 per cent in 1986.
45. For further details see Donald E. Blake, *Two Political Worlds: Parties and Voting in British Columbia* (Vancouver, B.C.: University of British Columbia Press, 1985), esp. chaps. 4 and 5.
46. See Donald E. Blake, "The Electoral Significance of Public Sector Bashing," *B.C. Studies*, No. 62, (Summer 1984), 29-43.
47. See Donald E. Blake, Richard Johnston, and David J. Elkins, "The Modern Party System," in Blake, *Two Political Worlds*.

3 NOVA SCOTIA: OPTIMISM IN SPITE OF IT ALL

Agar Adamson

Alexander Hamilton in *The Federalist Papers* wrote: "It is, therefore, as necessary that the State governments should be able to command the means of supplying their wants, as that the national government should possess the like faculty in respect of the wants of the Union."[1] Hamilton, if he were alive today, would be disturbed to learn that this particular principle was no longer operative in Canada, especially in the Atlantic region. In the Atlantic provinces, including Nova Scotia, the operative principle today might appropriately be described as "dependent federalism".[2] Indeed, it may well be that Hamilton's principle has never been operative in Canada, as all provinces have been recipients of federal funds since 1867.[3]

While Nova Scotia is less heavily dependent upon federal fiscal transfers than the other Atlantic provinces,[4] it is estimated that during the 1986-87 fiscal year, $1.2 billion or 40.9 per cent of its revenues will come from the federal government (see Table 3.1). This figure does not include federal government spending in the province, comprised of such items as federal defence and coastguard establishments, penal institutions, harbour construction, the Cape Breton Development Corporation (Devco), fisheries, and grants from the Department of Regional Industrial Expansion (DRIE), as well as programs having a legislated scale of benefits such as transportation subsidies or social security payments. When all such expenditures are taken into account, the total amount of funds channelled either directly or indirectly to Nova Scotia in the current fiscal year may top $2 billion, or $2250 per capita. But even this does not take account of tax expenditures, or exemptions and abatements benefiting industry and individuals.

Table 3.1
Federal Fiscal Transfers to Nova Scotia

	1983-84	*1984-85*	*Forecast* *1985-86*	*Estimate* *1986-87*
Federal Sources of Revenues (thousands of dollars)	1,093,647	1,145,569	1,144,245	1,211,361
Equalization	606,516	622,744	621,338	625,275
Established Programs Financing	305,872	334,610	337,608	356,424
Shared Cost Programs	177,887	184,912	182,281	227,080
Other Federal Sources	3,382	3,303	3,018	2,582
Federal Sources (as a per cent of Total Gross Revenues)	45.2	43.8	41.3	40.9
Equalization	25.1	23.8	22.4	21.1
Established Programs Financing	12.6	12.8	12.2	12.0
Shared Cost Programs	7.4	7.1	6.6	7.7
Other Federal Sources	0.1	0.1	0.1	0.1

Source: Nova Scotia Budget 1986-1987, 18 April 1986

Provinces that have relied heavily on federal transfers have reacted in dissimilar ways to dependency. At times, for example, Newfoundland has acted aggressively, initiating litigation to claim its constitutional rights and denouncing the federal government for policies that, in its view, disadvantaged Newfoundlanders.[5] In contrast, Nova Scotia's Premier John Buchanan (a Conservative) has followed a practice of "quiet diplomacy" with both Liberal and Conservative governments in Ottawa, and has enjoyed a record of success.[6] Like many other Nova Scotia premiers and especially his Liberal predecessor Gerald Regan, Buchanan has cultivated good relations with sympathetic federal cabinet ministers – and therein lies a dilemma, appropriately seen against a historical backdrop.

Nova Scotia's economic history has been marked by a series of disappointments and it is not surprising that this province was the first to preach separation from the federation. It was also the first to use the cry of secession and provincial rights to obtain financial concessions from Ottawa.[7] In 1867 Nova Scotia was a "have province", but because of changes in technology (steam replaced sail, oil and natural gas replaced coal), it soon became a province dependent upon federal government fiscal transfers.

Furthermore, if the West was said to have a handicap, so has the East.[8] Transportation costs coupled with Macdonald's national tariff policies made it not only difficult for Nova Scotian products to be competitive in the central Canadian markets, but at the same time, they lost many of their pre-confederation foreign markets. Changes in climate and technology, as well as politics, led to the decision to keep the St. Lawrence River open year round to Montreal, thus harming the economies of Halifax and Saint John. The construction of the St. Lawrence Seaway also damaged the provincial economy. Nova Scotia, as well as the other two Maritime provinces, did not benefit from the opening of the northern and western lands.

The growth of the Canadian population, especially because of immigration to the provinces west of the Ottawa River, meant that Nova Scotia's "voice" in Ottawa lost much of the strength that it had in 1867, particularly in the House of Commons, but also in the Senate, the Supreme Court of Canada and the public service.

Nova Scotia, despite these economic, geographic and demographic setbacks, has frequently sent strong voices to Parliament. These include Joseph Howe, Sir Charles Tupper, Sir John Thompson, W.S. Fielding, Angus L. Macdonald, J.L. Ilsley, Sir Robert Borden, Clarie Gillis, George Nowlan, Robert Stanfield, and the irrepressible Allan J. MacEachen. These men, each in his own way, articulated Nova Scotia's desire for further federal fiscal assistance. They gave Nova Scotia a national stature, which was perhaps greater than the province deserved. The election of September 1984 was, therefore, a double-edged sword for Nova Scotia. On the one side, there was the fact that the Progressive Conservatives were now in power both in Halifax and in Ottawa, a fact that John Buchanan used very effectively during the campaign for the 6 November 1984 provincial election. Brian Mulroney had attended university in Nova Scotia and a number of his senior PMO advisors are Nova Scotians. The Conservatives won nine of the 11 federal seats and Mulroney, like Trudeau and Turner, has two Nova Scotians in his Cabinet.

On the other side, Nova Scotia, especially Cape Breton Island, lost Allan J. MacEachen, the man who almost singlehandedly kept the economy of Cape Breton afloat with massive transfers of federal funds and patronage grants. Worse still for Nova Scotia, there does not appear to be anyone in the new Mulroney government who has MacEachen's economic "clout". Robert Coates tried, but his time in Cabinet was all too brief for him to make a major impact. For a year following Coates' resignation, the Maritimes did not even have a member on the Cabinet's

Planning and Priorities Committee, the so-called "inner Cabinet". Many Maritimers continue to be concerned that none of the major economic or other senior portfolios are held by Maritimers.

Of the various federal cabinet positions, perhaps the most important from a Maritimes perspective is the holder of the regional development portfolio, currently the Minister of Regional Industrial Economic Expansion. He is "the minister of hope" for Nova Scotia, and indeed, for all of Atlantic Canada. The minister is charged with the unenviable task of pumping scarce federal funds into a province which has experienced all the uncertainties of the Canadian economy, plus the blandishments of innumerable federal and provincial politicians who have for years preached that Eldorado is just around the corner. Indeed, it is scarcely an exaggeration to say that one way of looking at Nova Scotia's relations with Ottawa during the first year and a half of the Mulroney government could be described as "waiting for Sinc."[9] The resignation of Sinclair Stevens from the Cabinet on 12 May 1986 was not well received in Nova Scotia. Stevens was highly regarded, particularly in Cape Breton, for his efforts in bringing new industries to the province. Several Cape Breton commentators pointed out that during the parliamentary debate on "the Stevens loan issue", it was Ontario Liberals and New Democrats who raised the issue, and not Liberals from Cape Breton, the inference being that the MPs who pursued the matter were more interested in scoring political points than in jobs for hard-pressed Nova Scotians. The Nova Scotians who made these comments saw the "Stevens issue" as another example of the lack of knowledge and understanding of the economic plight of the Atlantic region by those who live in "Upper Canada".

The replacement of Stevens, who was not from a region where the Department of Regional Industrial Expansion (DRIE) is an important actor in the economy, with Michel Côté from Quebec has caused some ripples of concern in Atlantic Canada. It is feared that Côté will be more interested in looking after Quebec, and and thus, by inference less interested in the problems of Atlantic Canada than was Stevens, who had shown a remarkable concern for Atlantic regional issues, particularly those of Cape Breton. For the first time in many years Nova Scotians, instead of looking to one of their own in the Cabinet for assistance from Ottawa, must look to an "Upper Canadian" minister for help.

Stevens turned out to be a good consolation prize; Nova Scotia is more nervous about Côté. A Nova Scotia Deputy Minister went so far as to say privately, " . . . it's got to the point that if you want anything you call Fred Doucet in the PMO [Prime Minister's Office]." Hence the dilemma for the province: if quiet diplomacy, formerly aided and abetted by strong cabinet representation proves less effective without it, ought the

48

province to cut down its expectations, or should it decide to take the risky route of stridency?

So far there is no indication that Nova Scotia will emulate the sometimes confrontationist style of Newfoundland. It would not only be out of character for Premier Buchanan, it may be unnecessary or counterproductive. There are various reasons for thinking so. For one, Nova Scotia has been more fortunate than have the other three Atlantic provinces during the last decade. In 1984 this province led the nation in economic growth, and it also weathered the recession of 1981-1982 more successfully than did some other provinces. Much of the credit for this economic strength must be given to the now defunct National Energy Program (NEP); its economic leadership in 1984 appears to have been a "blip" for which the offshore energy developments must be given credit, rather than an indication of sustained growth.

Within Atlantic Canada, Nova Scotia (particularly the Halifax-Dartmouth area) is seen as the service centre for the region. Consequently, there has been a marked growth in the economic importance of these cities, which has had an impact on the region and not just the province. This growth has underlined Nova Scotia's continuing position as the economic leader of Atlantic Canada. However, leadership of the second division is of small consequence when there is little hope of promotion to the first division.

When the Mulroney government assumed office in September 1984 it faced a number of crucial public policy issues affecting Nova Scotia. The first of these was the "offshore". Nova Scotians for the past decade have been told, not only by Buchanan, but also by his predecessor Gerald Regan, that prosperity is just around the corner. The reason for this optimism was the discovery of hydrocarbons (principally natural gas) on the Scotian shelf and the worldwide increase in energy prices. Nova Scotians had visions of their province returning to its prior economic status of a "have province".

The Buchanan government was so certain that the economic climate was about to change that it has produced a succession of budgetary deficits since coming to power in 1978. In that year the accumulated provincial debt was half a billion dollars. By March 1987, it is predicted to be $3.5 billion.[10]

Nova Scotia, unlike Newfoundland, had entered into an agreement with the Trudeau government to develop the province's "offshore" resources.[11] The agreement did not deal with the question of the ownership of these resources, but only how they should be developed. The question of ownership has never been the emotional issue in Nova Scotia that it has been in Newfoundland, principally because Nova Scotia's claim was not nearly as sound in law. This does not mean that

Nova Scotia has given up its claim to outright ownership of the resource, only that Nova Scotia will fight this battle at some time in the future, and on a political rather than a legal plane. The Nova Scotian approach was obviously the correct one, as not only did the courts rule against Newfoundland, but more importantly, in the early 1980s Nova Scotia benefited economically from development, while Newfoundland's economy remained stagnant. Politically, Buchanan's approach was better than Peckford's.

That agreement, in effect, gave the government of Canada control of the Canada-Nova Scotia Offshore Oil and Gas Board, which oversees the development of the resource. However, the government of Nova Scotia obtained Ottawa's consent that the waters surrounding Sable Island are part of the province's territorial sea. There were also other safeguards to protect the province's interests.

The final article of the agreement stated that if another province obtained a more favourable agreement, Nova Scotia could, if the province so desired, adopt this new agreement in its entirety.

The Liberals' National Energy Program with its Petroleum Incentive Payments (PIP grants) was popular in Nova Scotia.[12] If it had not been for the creation of the NEP, and particularly the PIP grants, there would have been far less activity in the Nova Scotia offshore with its resulting "spin-offs" onshore. Nor would the province's economic growth have been as marked as it was during the lifetime of the NEP.

The Buchanan government even took a leaf out of the federal program and established a Crown Corporation, Nova Scotia Resources Limited, which, like Petro Canada, is permitted to become involved in the ownership of the hydrocarbons discovered within the province.

The Mulroney government signed the Atlantic Accord with Newfoundland in February 1985,[13] and also agreed to open negotiations with Nova Scotia based on the terms and conditions of the Accord. These discussions culminated with the signing, on 26 August 1986, of the Canada-Nova Scotia Offshore Petroleum Resources Accord.

The major changes from the 1982 agreement are: the resource will be jointly managed, Nova Scotia will have control over revenues and other fiscal instruments as if the hydrocarbons were onshore, the $200 million development fund described in the previous agreement becomes a gift rather than a loan, and Nova Scotia is compensated for the loss of the Crown share found in the 1982 agreement.

Insofar as Nova Scotia is concerned, the 1986 agreement is an improvement over that signed in 1982. However, the federal Minister of Energy still has the authority to veto decisions made by the five-member jointly appointed Canada-Nova Scotia Offshore Oil and Gas Board. The Board is primarily responsible for decisions such as the collecting of royalties, approval of technical aspects of development plans, exercising emergency powers, and regulating good oil field practices. Certain Board decisions, such as the call for bids on exploration licenses and setting the terms and conditions of production licenses, must be approved by the two governments. Two members of the Board are appointed by each government and the chairman is jointly appointed by both governments.

Not only is the $200 million loan of 1982 transferred to status of a gift, but Nova Scotia Resources Limited, the provincial Crown corporation which is licensed to participate in exploration as well as in pipeline construction, will receive a one-time $25 million grant from Ottawa. Finally, the question of equalization which has been unanswered since 1982 is clarified. Basically, the new Accord ensures that there will not be a dollar-for-dollar loss of equalization payments as a result of Nova Scotia receiving royalties from the offshore hydrocarbons.

Certainly, the 1986 agreement is an improvement over the 1982 agreement for the province. However, in times of conflict the veto given to the federal Minister of Energy means that Ottawa retains the upper hand in controlling the development and exploration of Nova Scotia's offshore hydrocarbons.

Perhaps all of this is academic, given the recent deterioration in world oil prices. Certainly, the Nova Scotia offshore cannot be profitably developed if prevailing world oil prices remain below $20 (U.S.) a barrel.[14]

The replacement of PIP grants with federal corporate tax incentives, which are less advantageous to the industry, has not been well received by Nova Scotia . However, given the fact that world prices have collapsed and with the exception of the Cohasset A-52 well, the rate of hydrocarbon discoveries has not been outstanding, making it difficult to predict the impact of these new federal policies.

Nova Scotia's "Eldorado" is still some years away, and the province will remain dependent upon Ottawa for aid for some time to come. For the first time in a number of years, the offshore was not even mentioned in the provincial budget, brought down on 18 April 1986.

The fishery is a perennial issue in this province. The major governmental dispute is between the province, which is principally interested in jobs, and the federal Department of Fisheries and Oceans, which is concerned not only with jobs, but also with conservation of the species. Fisheries policy as an aspect of intergovernmental relations is a paper in itself. The debate in the fishery centres around the questions of modernizing and improving the product versus custom, convention tradition, and jobs. There is also the question of the inshore versus the deep sea operators. In 1986 there have been a number of additonal disputes over the employment of freezer trawlers. Ottawa, after considerable procrastination, has opted for modernization and approved the implementation of freezer trawlers, much to Nova Scotia's pleasure and Newfoundland's annoyance. The fishery is an area which is going to need far greater federal-provincial cooperation, not only between the politicians, but also between the bureaucrats. Disputes between Nova Scotia and Newfoundland, particularly over access to northern cod stocks, are going to require more strenuous umpiring by the Minister of Fisheries and Oceans than has been the case as of late.

The fishery, however, does present another example of Nova Scotia's strength within the region. As the report of the Kirby task force on the Atlantic fishery illustrates, Nova Scotia fishermen, and especially those from the South Shore region of the province, are relatively well off, some having a net annual income in excess of $60,000 as compared to certain Newfoundlanders who may be fortunate to net $4,000 per year from the fishery.

The two levels of government did work harmoniously to try to prevent the implementation of duties on fish exports to the United States. That they were unsuccessful should not be seen as a failure of their efforts, but an example of American misunderstanding of Canadian social support programs.

Perhaps the most notable federal policy outputs of recent years affecting Nova Scotia – certainly those best illustrating its state of dependency – are those concerning the island of Cape Breton, which prior to 1820 was a separate political entity. Cape Breton is separated from the mainland by the Strait of Canso, which is three kilometers wide.[15] But more than water divides Cape Breton from the mainland! Many provinces have their cultural, political, and geographical divisions: in Newfoundland, the Avalon Peninsula from the reminder of the province, the north from the south in Ontario, and the lower mainland from the remainder of British Columbia. Certainly the divisions within Nova Scotia are as great as these, and in fact, they may even be more pronounced.

David Lewis, among others, has written about the political divisions between Cape Breton and the mainland. These political divisions continue to exist as illustrated by the recent attempt to found the Cape Breton Labour Party.[16] Similarly, there are differences amongst trade unionists because the labour movement has always been stronger and more militant in Cape Breton. Nova Scotians are divided sociologically, just as the Strait of Canso divides the province geographically.

For years, Cape Breton has suffered from chronic economic problems: massive unemployment, a lack of economic development, and the demise of the industries that did exist. It has become a virtual vassal state of both levels of government, propped up by government aid, including that provided by the Laird of the Island, Senator Allan J. MacEachen.

In 1967, for example, the province was forced to become the owner of the Sydney Steel Plant because Hawker-Siddeley, the previous owner, had decided to abandon the plant as it was no longer economically viable. Since 1967 both levels of government have pumped millions of dollars into this aging plant, which basically produces only rails. In 1986-1987 the province will spend $13,476 million to help pay off the debts of the plant,[17] while the total debt is now estimated to be $300 million.[18] Add to this amount the $150 million Ottawa (70 per cent) and Halifax (30 per cent) have agreed to spend between now and 1990, and the total is $450 billion. By 1990 the plant may, with luck, be employing between 800 and 1000 Cape Bretoners.

During the past year Ottawa consented to assist with the construction of a new arc furnace. John Buchanan, who as a university student had worked in the steel plant, had publicly desired a more expensive oxygen furnace, which would have employed more people. However, as Ottawa was paying 70 per cent of the costs, Buchanan, despite his public pronouncements and private lobbying, had to back down.

All over the world, steel plants younger than Sydney's are being closed by private and public sector cost conscious management. The question arises, Why keep Sysco open? The answer is that with an "official unemployment rate of 25 per cent" there are no other jobs available for those who would be displaced. When one considers the entire social welfare shock of closure and the total impact on the community, it may well be cheaper to keep the plant open, at least until 1990, as a social welfare measure than pay welfare directly to those who would lose their jobs. Also, one must remember that Sysco is a market for Cape Breton coal.

The same situation exists concerning the coal mines, which are now owned by the federal crown corporation Devco. The increase in world energy costs have given the coal mines a new lease on life and new mines have been opened. The two principal purchasers of Cape Breton coal are Sysco and the provincially owned Nova Scotia Power Corporation, the province's electrical utility. Despite this increased production, Devco lost $16.9 million in 1985.

Nova Scotia is dependent on steam generation for almost all of its electricity. Coal has replaced oil as the principal fuel to turn the Corporation's turbines. The coal used in the power plants also produces acid rain, a fact which the provincial government refuses to discuss. (They have great faith in the prevailing westerly wind blowing the acid out to sea.) Perhaps, the most acrimonious dispute between Ottawa and Halifax in 1986 concerned the environmental impact of the Sysco tar ponds. Environment Canada demanded that these ponds be cleaned up as they are a known health hazard. The province and the local citizenry argued that jobs were more important than the cleanup and refused Ottawa's request. However, as the Government of Canada is paying the lion's share of Sysco's modernization program, Environment Canada's views prevailed and the tar ponds which are filled with carcinogenic wastes from the steel plant are now to be removed and the land revitalized.

The federal and provincial governments have in the past decade poured millions of dollars into Cape Breton, yet the local economy appears to be a bottomless pit. All sorts of "wonderful" ideas have been tried by Devco, such as car assembly plants, the reconstruction of Fortress Louisburg, sheepherding, oil refineries, pulp mills, and the manufacturing of heavy water, all with little or no lasting success. Changes in technology and in world economic conditions continue to keep Cape Breton in economic servitude, dependent upon Governmental largess. Even the province's offshore "boomlet" only benefited the Halifax region.

Cape Bretoners, many of whom are descended from Highland Scots who came to Nova Scotia following "the clearing of the Highlands", remain a clannish and loyal community. They do not all wish to take the advice of the 1958 Royal Commission on Canada's Economic Prospects (The Gordon Report) and "go down the road" to Boston or Toronto or Calgary.

Since the 1984 federal election, life in Cape Breton has been in a greater state of flux than usual. For years Allan MacEachen had persuaded his Cabinet colleagues to keep Atomic Energy of Canada's two heavy water plants open, even though there was no market for their product, his argument being that it was cheaper to keep the plants open than to pay the workers unemployment insurance.

The federal budget of May 1985 brought this Alice in Wonderland situation to an abrupt end: "Continued operation of AECL's two heavy water plants on Cape Breton Island can no longer be justified."[19] To replace these plants, Ottawa introduced a number of tax incentives. These included a 50 per cent tax credit to enhance job creation in such industries as farming, tourism, fishing, manufacturing, and processing. Finance Minister Michael Wilson prophesied that no new enterprise in Cape Breton would have to pay federal income tax for ten to fifteen years because of these tax changes.[20]

The February 1986 federal budget went even further, establishing the Atlantic Enterprise Programme, which stated in part:

Under this Programme, guarantees of loans totalling up to $1 billion and interest rate buy downs of up to 6 percentage points will be made available to stimulate and support productive new private investment in the region. To avoid duplication with the existing federal and provincial programs, the Programme will be limited to term loans of a minimum of $250,000. The sponsors of eligible products will be required to share the risk. The normal level of government guarantees will be set at 85 per cent of the principal amount of the loan. The Programme will apply not only to manufacturing and processing, but will also complement existing programs in related service sectors, tourism, and primary industries, in recognition of the important role played by these sectors in the Atlantic economy.[21]

This program, which applies to all four Atlantic provinces and also to the Gaspé region of Quebec, is designed to create jobs in the private sector. The Government of Canada will guarantee loans for business start-up as well as expansion expenses. These are in addition to certain income tax incentives. The budget also liberalized some of the specific Cape Breton programs introduced in the May 1985 budget. For instance, the minimum investment required was lowered from $50,000 to $25,000, and some tax credits were raised to 40 per cent from 20 per cent regardless of the size of the business.[22]

It is too early to assess the impact of these budget incentives on Nova Scotia, and particularly on Cape Breton. Several firms have been attracted to the region, most notably Magna Industries. One German firm, Thyssen, wishes to build a plant on Cape Breton to make military equipment for export to the Middle East. The provincial government favours this plant as it would employ 400 people. However, the Mulroney Cabinet is split on the issue, and as of August 1986, no decision has been reached.[23] This matter could become an issue of some magnitude between Ottawa and Halifax in the future. On the other hand, excessive DRIE bureaucracy has prevented some local firms from expanding in Cape Breton; one even moved to Ontario.

Through all these policy changes, the Government of Nova Scotia put on a brave face. Naturally, it welcomed the positive steps taken by the Mulroney government in the 1985 and 1986 federal budgets. It did not protest the closure of the two AECL heavy water plants. The handwriting had been on the wall for some time and Ottawa did a more than adequate job of privately advising Buchanan and publicly preparing Cape Bretoners prior to the budget. In other areas too, Nova Scotia has avoided public opposition to federal policies that have affected it adversely. A striking illustration is the decision, announced in the May

1985 budget and implemented in 1986 in Bill C-96,[24] to cut back the rate of growth in grants to the provinces under the Established Programs Financing [EPF] Act. At the November 1985 meeting of First Ministers in Halifax, the federal decision was condemned by all provinces except British Columbia (which agreed to it, *provided* it was part of a larger deficit-reduction package, thus accepting the federal argument that grants to the provinces should not be immune to overall spending cuts) and Nova Scotia.

John Buchanan had at first decried Ottawa's action. However, after meeting with Brian Mulroney the day before the conference opened, Buchanan underwent "a conversion on the road to the conference." He announced that he "... had secured a guarantee for the first time that transfer payments would not be reduced and that the province can expect a substantial increase in next year's payments."[25] In actual fact, the 1986-1987 provincial budget shows that the province will receive $11 million less during the current fiscal year in EPF grants than would have been the case had the federal government not curtailed the increases established in the 1982 EPF legislation.

Buchanan's actions remain a mystery. Did he fail to understand the proposals as some of his opponents claim? Did he "sell out" as some of the other premiers alleged? The matter remains an arcanum, although rumours of a federal appointment continue to swirl through Halifax political circles. No matter what the truth is, Nova Scotia's deficit has increased because of the May 1985 federal budget.

The province also had to incur additional costs of $7.9 million during the current fiscal year as a result of the The Young Offenders Act.[26] This federal Act is not in keeping with the theory of interdependent federalism. With the passage of this single piece of legislation, no matter what its merit, the Parliament of Canada unilaterally shifted the cost of incarcerating young offenders from Ottawa's books to those of the provinces.

The province, using its typical "quiet diplomacy", tried to persuade Ottawa to postpone implementation of the Act for one year. It was so certain that its lobby had succeeded that it had no institutions available to incarcerate young offenders when the Act was proclaimed. The Solicitor General at the time was Elmer MacKay, a Nova Scotian MP. Obviously, quiet diplomacy is not always effective.

The history of The Young Offenders Act and of the 1985 budget illustrate a major deficiency in contemporary Canadian federalism: there is no intergovernmental machinery, save for First Ministers' conferences, which scarcely assure amicable resolution of the issues brought before them, to resolve fiscal and other conflicts between the two levels of government. There is no constitutional requirement for the federal government to consult the provinces before Parliament enacts legislation which will have a major, adverse, impact upon provincial budgets. Its practice of imposing costs on the provinces violates the principle of federalism enunciated by Alexander Hamilton in *The Federalist Papers*, quoted earlier.

If Ottawa would only consult the provinces more frequently on fiscal matters, it is just possible that the party in power nationally would not see its provincial counterparts defeated so frequently in provincial elections. Also, the nationally disruptive tactics of provincial premiers running against Ottawa might not be as prevalent as they are currently. The "fallout" from recent federal fiscal actions has undoubtedly scared the provincial Tories. The national parties should realize that in Nova Scotia, as elsewhere in the Maritimes, it is the provincial party which manages the national campaigns. A party in office provincially is a much greater electoral asset than one in opposition. Yet both Liberal and Conservative governments of Canada fail to take this simple political fact into consideration when dealing with the province.

If in this respect the federal government often appears neglectful even of its own political interests, in another it seems remarkably indulgent. This year, as already indicated in Table 3.1, which is based on provincial budget figures, Nova Scotia will receive $1.2 billion directly from the federal treasury. This means that on a pro rata basis, $233,793 or 19.3 cents of every dollar the province receives, will go to service the public debt. Only the departments of Health ($899,585), Social Services ($318,518), and Education ($847,791) will spend more than this amount, while the total number of dollars required to service the debt is $673,104 million.

These figures deserve some comment! Canada, as Ursula K. Hicks points out, " . . . has always been interested not only in general assistance to correct the inherent federal/provincial imbalance, but also in a policy of discriminatory aid to the poorer provinces."[27] Equalization payments, which are unconditional grants, permit Nova Scotia to have services available to the citizenry, which are equal to those who live in provinces with more fortunate economic conditions. Equalization is part of the Canadian federal concept and is now, on the initiative of Nova Scotia, enshrined in the Constitution Act [1982].[28]

The province can use these funds as well as those from EPF to please its electorate, while the federal government receives little or no political credit from the taxpayers for raising these funds.

All of this is well known to students of Canadian federalism. However, is it not a duty of the province to be frugal with these funds? Should Ottawa have some authority to bring a province into line if its spending and budgetary practices are out of line with the national norm?

Ottawa is attempting to cut the federal deficit; Nova Scotia, despite statements to the contrary, is not seriously attempting to cut its own deficit. Last year's provincial budget promised to reduce the deficit to $184 million. Instead, the deficit increased to $245.3 million. In 1986-1987 it is predicted to be $233 million.

The April 1986 budget does not give the impression that the government is serious about deficit reduction. The major spending cut, which was not in the budget, cancelled the subsidy on electrical rates, saving the treasury $36.7 million in 1986-1987.

Even though it is not compatible with the current theory of federalism, surely the national parliament should have some authority to pressure a province, which obtains 40.9 per cent of its revenues from Ottawa to practice prudent fiscal management. Of course, sound economic management is not necessarily good politics, as the Clark government found out when William Davis, then Premier of Ontario, would not support the gasoline tax increases proposed in the December 1979 budget. Federalism requires unit-centre cooperation if it is to be effective. Furthermore, federal parties need the support of the provincial party at election time. The Mulroney Tories have attempted to establish harmonious intergovernmental relations to replace the confrontational system which existed during the Trudeau years. Nevertheless, the Parliament of Canada has a duty to the taxpayers of Canada to see that the funds, which it votes for payment to the provinces, are used prudently. Perhaps one way this could be carried out would be to depoliticize the issue by the establishment of a federal-provincial grants council which could oversee the whole question of federal-provincial fiscal relations. Another possibility could be through public opinion. For instance, will the taxpayers of Alberta be content to continue to see their taxes used in a questionable manner by "have not" provinces?

Fortunately, Nova Scotians are slowly becoming concerned over the size of the provincial deficit. The Buchanan government maintains that it cannot act on the deficit without reducing services. One wonders if this really is the case, or if they are more concerned about the political ramifications of cutting services. The size of the Nova Scotia debt does illustrate the economic situation the province faces and the need for the programs outlined in the recent federal budget to assist the province, but it also gives one a picture of John Buchanan. Buchanan is a populist and an effective campaigner. He is a marvelous electoral asset for his party. He is also an impulsive spender. It is very difficult for the Management Board, the budgetary control body, to oversee expenditures when the Premier goes about, as he has in the past, handing out funds wherever and whenever the spirit moves him.

Internally, Nova Scotia needs to find ways to cut expenditures. Two possible answers are, first of all, municipal reorganization to curtail the existing expensive duplication of services, and secondly, a reform of the public service.[29] A glance at the 1986 Estimates shows that the province could save money by restructuring municipal boundaries. Savings could also be made by reorganizing such municipal services as police and social assistance.

Nova Scotia is a province beset with social-welfare problems. One example is housing. In order to please tenant voters, the provincial government has virtually given these inhabitants permanent tenure in their residences. The result of this policy is that developers refuse to build any new rental accommodations. In the rural areas, there is often a shortage of adequate housing for the rural poor. The whole issue of rural poverty is one that is only now coming to light because of recent criminal convictions for incest and child abuse. Nova Scotia's social and economic problems, like the fiscal ones which are closely related to them, are real. Nevertheless, the large sums transferred to the province by the federal government continue without any meaningful federal-provincial public policy debate, even though – or perhaps partly because – both governments are formed by the Progressive Conservative Party. "Bandaid policies", instead of long range planning, is an appropriate way to describe the current situation. Unless there is a drastic change, not only in the price of hydrocarbons, but also in the province's reserves, Nova Scotia is going to be dependent upon Ottawa for much of its direct and indirect revenues for years to come. The problem of unemployment and underemployment will continue to be a source of concern. Good relations with the federal government will continue to be important no matter who is in power in Halifax and Ottawa.

Despite its size and small population, Nova Scotia has benefited from federal policy. Reference has been made to the NEP and PIP grants. These may have been seen as a negative factor but not in Nova Scotia. The closing of AECL's heavy water plants may indeed prove to be a blessing in disguise, provided business continues to make use of the special grants put forth in the Wilson budgets of 1985 and 1986.

Recent changes in fisheries policy, particularly the licensing of freezer trawlers, has been an economic benefit to the province. The Mulroney government's interest in reviving the Navy cannot help but be a benefit, particularly to Halifax. Sysco has been given yet another chance to survive.

One potential problem lies in the field of federal-provincial relations. Here the Buchanan government will undoubtedly continue to be a reactive rather than a proactive government. The premier is his own minister of intergovernmental affairs, and has used his own office staff as the departmental staff, rather than the members of the Policy Board, who in the past prepared Nova Scotia's position papers for intergovernmental conferences. This apparent change has caused some public servants in other provinces to ask their counterparts in Nova Scotia, "What is going on?" Recently Nova Scotia did not attend a lower level federal-provincial conference because the premier neglected to tell anyone that it was taking place. Buchanan nevertheless has effectively handled relations with Ottawa and the province has benefited favourably from federal policies. To say that there are no irritants or policy differences between Halifax and Ottawa would be incorrect, but on the other hand, relations between the two governments are more harmonious than are those between Ottawa and certain other provinces. Of course, as the February 1986 Nova Scotia Progressive Conservative Party's annual meeting illustrated, Nova Scotians still think they deserve better and they would like to see more assistance from the Mulroney government.[30]

The Buchanan government does support Mulroney's trade initiative with the United States, although they have yet to develop any concrete policy proposals. Apparently, the province believes that certain of the irritants concerning the export of fish products to the United States would be removed with free (or freer) trade. However, as a recent study points out, Atlantic Canada could fare badly in bilateral trade talks because of the various governmental support systems which are already being criticized in New England. Regional interests are going to have to be well-guarded by regional politicians if Atlantic Canada is not to suffer in any free trade agreement. A recent poll states that support for free trade is higher in Atlantic provinces than in any other part of Canada, with the exception of Alberta.[31] Although one can aptly describe Nova Scotia's current policy towards both federal-provincial relations and domestic issues as reactive, and can criticize the government for a lack of meaningful policy development and planning, one cannot fault it for the lack of a social conscience. Buchanan and most of his cabinet are "Red Tories" and have shown a concern for social issues.

Nova Scotia's future is cloudy. With an official unemployment rate of 13.5 per cent (25 per cent in Cape Breton) and few natural resources other than the fishery and, perhaps, hydrocarbons, the province is dependent on the development of service industries for the Maritimes and financial assistance from Ottawa. The size of the provincial budgetry deficit remains a major concern. Will Ottawa continue to pour federal funds into this province and, particularly, into Cape Breton if the province fails to deal with its deficit?

Harmonious relations and general support of Ottawa's proposals at federal-provincial conferences remain a necessity for any government of

Nova Scotia, no matter what its political colour. It must always be remembered that Nova Scotia's voice within the federation is numerically weak. There are only 11 Nova Scotia MPs and 10 Senators. Federal elections are not won or lost in Nova Scotia, thus the general thrust of federal policy is not directed to the voters of the province. Although Nova Scotia is over represented in the Senate, as compared to the West, the Senate has seldom acted as a protector of provincial rights.

All of the Atlantic provinces would benefit from a reformed Senate, which would have equal representation of all of the provinces despite their population, plus greater authority to protect the provinces as a true house of the province rather than the current situation in which the Senate is just a house of patronage.

Given Nova Scotia's numerical weakness at the federal level, it is a credit to both levels of government that Nova Scotia's place in the federation is as secure as it is and that Ottawa, with the tacit consent of the "have" provinces, is prepared to assist the province's economic and social development.[32]

Joseph Howe might have been able to flirt with separatism; John Buchanan certainly cannot. Both his personal future and that of his province are tied to economic decisions made in Ottawa.

Notes

1. Alexander Hamilton, *The Federalist Papers XXXI*, Clinton Rossiter (ed.) (New York: Mentor, 1961), p. 195.
2. This term contrasts with the "interdependent federalism" proposed by R.L. Watts to indicate that federal and provincial governments rely on each other in making policy, but that legally neither level of government is subordinate to the other. See his *Multi-Cultural Societies and Federalism,"* a *Study for the Royal Commission on Bilingualism and Biculturalism* (Ottawa: Queen's Printer, 1967).
3. See The Constitution Act [1867] Section 118, and The Constitution Act [1907] as evidence that the provinces were never fiscally independent of Ottawa.
4. For figures on per capita cash transfers by province in 1984-85, see Peter M. Leslie: "The State of the Federation 1985", in Leslie (ed.), *Canada: The State of the Federation 1985* (Kingston, Ont.: Institute of Intergovernmental Relations, 1985), p. 28.
5. Bruce Pollard: "Newfoundland: Resisting Dependency", in Leslie (ed.), *Canada: The State of the Federation, 1985*, pp. 83-117.
6. Buchanan has been very successful in claiming federal policy announcements as his and has obtained considerable political "mileage" from federal announcements made in Nova Scotia. On

one occasion, Allan MacEachen's office was so annoyed that Buchanan was to have a federal announcement made in Province House and that the federal public servants had readily acceded to Buchanan's request of venue that MacEachen refused to have the announcement presented until the meeting and the subsequent press conference were moved to a federal government building. Buchanan, however refused to attend the conference in a federal government building; consequently, the announcement was made in a Halifax hotel room (neutral territory).

7. R. M. Dawson, *The Government of Canada* (Toronto: University of Toronto Press, 1964), p. 86.

8. See W. L. Morton, *The Progressive Party in Canada* (Toronto: University of Toronto Press, 1967).

9. Jeffrey Simpson, *The Globe and Mail*, 29 January 1986.

10. Nova Scotia Budget, 18 April 1986.

11. For details, see Canada-Nova Scotia Agreement on Offshore Oil and Gas Resource Management and Revenue Sharing, 2 March 1982.

12. In March 1984 John Buchanan publicly disassociated himself from statements made by Mulroney in Calgary concerning the Conservatives promise to end the NEP when they obtained office.

13. For details see Bruce G. Pollard, "Newfoundland: Resisting Dependency", in Peter M. Leslie (ed.), *Canada: The State of the Federation 1985*.

14. *Halifax Chronicle-Herald*, 25 April 1986.

15. Geographically, the two parts of Nova Scotia are similar, although geologically, Nova Scotia does differ from the rest of Canada. J.T. Wilson, convocation address, Acadia University, May 1976.

16. For details on the rise of the Cape Breton Labour Party, see Agar Adamson, "Does MacEwan's Real Ale Give the NDP Heartburn?", Atlantic Provinces Political Studies Association Annual Conference, Wolfville, 24 October 1985.

17. Nova Scotia Estimates, 18 April 1986.

18. Jeffrey Simpson, *The Globe and Mail*, 31 January 1986.

19. Michael H. Wilson, Budget Speech, The House of Commons, 23 May 1985.

20. Wilson, *Budget Papers*, 23 May 1985, pp. 18-19.

21. *Ibid.*, 26 February 1986, p. 14.

22. *Ibid.*

23. *The Globe and Mail*, 14 February 1986.

24. Editor's note: References to this legislation are contained in articles published elsewhere in this volume. See Gil Rémillard, "Speech to the Mont Gabriel Conference, May 1986" and R.L. Watts, "Financing Post-Secondary Education and Research".

25. *Halifax Chronicle-Herald*, 24 November 1985.

26. See The Young Offenders Act, Statutes of Canada, proclaimed April 1984.

27. Ursula K. Hicks, *Federalism Failure and Success: A Comparative Study* (London: Macmillan, 1978), p. 188.

28. See The Constitution Act [1982], section 36.

29. For an examination of this issue, see Agar Adamson, "Politics Without Policy", in *Policy Options*, Vol 6., No. 6, 1985.

30. See *Halifax Chronicle-Herald*, 1 February 1986, "Party Faithful Blast Tory MPs". See also *The Gazette*, Montreal, 28 February 1986, "We Went From the Frying Pan into the Fire."

31. *The Globe and Mail*, 4 July 1986. The report in question is published by the Institute for Research and Public Policy. The poll was published in *The Gazette*, Montreal, 5 July 1986.

32. One of the major continuing irritants of Canadian federalism is Ottawa bureaucrats' lack of knowledge and understanding of the provinces. For the State Dinner at the Spring 1986 NATO Foreign Ministers' Meeting, External Affairs flew place-settings for 300 to Halifax. Such condescending attitudes by federal bureaucrats is not new, but that they continue to exist is a problem of Canadian federalism. It appears that we can integrate the politicians, but not the public servants.

4 QUEBEC AND THE CONSTITUTIONAL ISSUE

Peter M. Leslie

Introduction

"Government by consent" is generally acknowledged to be an essential characteristic of a free society. Violation of this principle offends against democracy and imperils the political stability of a country whose people are committed to democracy. It should therefore be of great concern to all Canadians that Quebec, alone among the provinces, has never assented to the present groundrules of Confederation. Those rules were significantly changed by the Constitution Act (1982) over the vehement objections of the Parti Québécois government. And the present Liberal government, which is explicitly federalist, also finds parts of the Act unacceptable.

The constitution delimits the powers of the federal and provincial governments both in relation to each other and (since 1982) in relation to the individual. Thus it sets out procedures through which the Canadian people and the various provincial communities shall order their affairs. In so doing it helps determine how those communities shall relate to each other and to the whole. What concerns us here is that the constitution helps establish the character of the relationship between Quebec and the rest of Canada.

At stake is the province's ability to pursue a preferred course of economic, social and cultural development. During the 1960s a set of rapid, far-reaching changes in Quebec society called into question the then-existing relations between francophones and anglophones, between Quebec City and Ottawa, and between Quebec and the other provinces. Constitutional reform was demanded to facilitate and extend the desired realignment of traditional relationships. Not that the constitution itself defines how language groups and the regions are situated relative to each other, but it does establish a framework within which those relationships evolve. In the end, Quebec's initiative – in a sense – bore fruit; but it was bitter. The framework was modified, on federal initiative, by the Constitution Act (1982); and while the other provinces accepted the new rules, Quebec did not.

The Constitution Act (1982) is based on an accord reached in November 1981 between the federal government and the nine provinces having an English-speaking majority. In the preceding year, Quebec had worked closely with seven other provinces to block the federal government's proposals for constitutional reform. Their alliance, however, broke apart when a compromise agreement that was unacceptable to Quebec was worked out. The process by which this result was achieved was traumatic for the Quebec participants, who felt betrayed by their former allies. The Quebec government reacted by reinforcing its isolation. It suspended normal relations with the ten other governments, its Confederation partners.

Since the proclamation of the revised constitution in April 1982, considerable progress has been made towards rebuilding a good working relationship between Quebec and the other governments. However, to some Quebecers (an unknown percentage) the 1982 Constitution Act stands as an unhealed sore and a symbol of the province's exclusion and defeat, "a second Conquest". In substance, the Act is also unacceptable – indeed, no leading figure in Quebec provincial politics has ever endorsed it – because it provides (in the view of the provincial government) an insecure framework for Quebec's continued social and cultural development along lines of its own choosing. For these reasons the Government of Quebec wants to modify the framework imposed upon it in 1982, and to solidify on a new basis its relations with its Confederation partners.

Outside Quebec, however, many people resent what they regard as the province's disproportionate influence within the federal government; and most Canadians probably assume that the partial accord of November 1981 resolved the constitutional issue once and for all. There is no sign of public enthusiasm for reopening constitutional talks.

This situation points to continued uncertainty about Quebec's place in Canada today. Part of the uncertainty is about the prospects for a constitutional settlement acceptable to the Quebec government. But there are also other issues of a less tangible character, especially the future of Quebec nationalism, and the evolution of Quebec's working relationship with the federal government and with the other provinces. These matters must be seen in context with changes in the Quebec economy, changing cultural patterns, and changes in how Quebecers view their own situation in Canada and North America.

A cross-section of informed opinion on these matters, providing a broad survey of the basic issues concerning Quebec's place in Canada today, was presented at a conference held at Mont Gabriel, Quebec, 9 to 11 May 1986. The conference, entitled "Rebuilding the Relationship: Quebec and its Confederation Partners", was organized by the Institute of Intergovernmental Relations in conjunction with the Montreal newspaper *Le Devoir* and *l'Ecole nationale d'administration publique*. Of the 65 participants, half were from Quebec and half from the rest of Canada; there was roughly equal representation from government (senior officials from the Government of Canada and from most of the provincial governments attended), from the universities, and from a variety of other organizations.

The remainder of this chapter is a summary of discussion at the Mont Gabriel conference. The conference report seems a useful vehicle for outlining the scope and content of unresolved constitutional issues between Quebec and the other ten governments. The report serves this purpose mainly because Gil Rémillard, Quebec's Minister of International Affairs and Minister responsible for Canadian Intergovernmental Affairs, gave the keynote address, setting out Quebec's conditions for participating in a new constitutional accord (for a full text, see Appendix). Mr. Rémillard's speech, which was a constant point of reference for the entire conference, was followed by a session exploring changing political attitudes and priorities in Quebec, with special emphasis on the values, behaviour patterns, and concerns of youth, for whom the Quiet Revolution of the early 1960s, the October Crisis (1970), and perhaps even the election of the Parti Québécois (1976) are historical events rather than personal experiences. In this session participants discussed, among other things, the strength and the character of Quebec nationalism, a topic which was to be a recurrent theme in other sessions as well. The first day of the conference concluded with an address by the Honourable Benoît Bouchard, Secretary of State of Canada.

The second day consisted of three sessions dealing with the federal and provincial governments' policy roles and responsibilities – first in language matters, then in social affairs, and finally in matters of economic development and the control of economic institutions. This order of topics was chosen because it follows major shifts, over time, in the focus of Quebec nationalism. This seemed appropriate for a set of sessions the overall purpose of which was to explore the political implications of linguistic and cultural dualism in Canada. In the past, Quebec has wanted to pursue goals toward which its Confederation partners appeared indifferent, or even opposed; and the other ten governments seemed (to Quebec) to agree on objectives that threatened the province's autonomous development. Duality of purpose seemed to extend across the whole policy spectrum. What is the situation now? Do Quebecers continue to see dualism where other Canadians see a more complex pattern of diversity? It did not appear useful to ponder such questions in the abstract. Instead, three sessions – the whole of the second day of the conference – were set aside for discussing government roles and responsibilities in specific policy fields: language, social affairs, and economic development.

The final session, held on the third day of the conference, focussed on constitutional issues. Discussion crystallized around Mr. Rémillard's list of five conditions for Quebec's acceptance of a revised Constitution Act, plus constitutional guarantees of the rights of linguistic minorities (endorsed by Mr. Rémillard, but not stated as one of the five conditions).

Rebuilding the Relationship: A False Problem?

Let's start with the most basic question of all. Was the conference based on a mistaken premise? In three different ways, the organizers or the participants were admonished that they were grappling with a false problem.

The first such suggestion came well before the conference from someone (a provincial government official) who wrote:

> In terms of the overall theme of the Conference, I think it over-emphasizes the differences between Quebec and other governments in Canada. Of course, it would certainly be useful to gain a fuller understanding of Quebec's position and "mood" on social, economic and constitutional issues, but I do not think it has to be set in terms of "re-establishing normal ties between Quebec and its Confederation partners."

Since this comment was made by letter and not at the conference, others were unable to respond to it, and one cannot judge how many shared this opinion. Probably some did – especially some of the those who were invited but who (unlike the letter-writer) decided not to attend. The more this happened, the less representative the group that assembled at Mont Gabriel. This is troubling, but even more troubling is the fact that most non-Quebecers may view "rebuilding the relationship" as an already-accomplished task, whereas most Quebecers may see it as incomplete. It is therefore significant that at the conference, almost all the Quebec participants appeared to take for granted that "normal ties" cannot be deemed to obtain until there has been a constitutional settlement.

A second warning that the conference theme mistook reality was voiced by Thomas J. Courchene, whose presentation to the conference has subsequently been published.[1] Courchene warned:

> Quebec is not interested in "rebuilding" the traditional relationship at either the economic or the political level. Rather, the province is dedicated to building a strong financial and economic base in order to look outward to the rest of the world.

Participants did not query this. All recognized the economic vitality of Quebec – its forward-looking and outward-looking stance. But most of those present also evidently recognized that to build a new economic relationship with the rest of Canada and with the rest of the world demands that Quebec have a wide range of economic powers, giving it a degree of control over economic processes and institutions. In other words, Quebec's economic goals have a political and constitutional dimension. (This is the case also with other provinces.) The very fact that the goals are new ones gives pertinence to rebuilding Quebec's political and constitutional relationship with its Confederation partners, though necessarily on a different basis than was acceptable in the past.

The most serious challenge to the overall conception of the conference came from those Quebecers who asserted that the public mood in the province would not tolerate a return to constitutional issues, any more than would the public mood in the rest of Canada. A Quebec businessman said:

> Just when exhaustion [caused by the intense and fruitless political debates of the past few years] is giving way to stability and enthusiasm, you invite me to come and participate in reopening the dossier of our collective insecurity. I'm not interested. Recalling the two solitudes is outdated. The presumed isolation of Quebec is an abstraction. The re-emergence of Quebec is going on, not in the Ministry of Intergovernmental Affairs, but in the universities and the factories of the province....The state is giving way to the individual, it is privatising, deregulating, rationalising, leaving to private enterprise responsibility for wealth creation....I don't want a new constitutional debate and especially not a new election or a new referendum on the subject. Our job now is to contribute to material well-being.

These sentiments were given added force by reports of survey data showing that Quebec youth today are largely uninterested in politics, federal-provincial relations, and relations between language groups. They are preoccupied by personal goals; they want most of all to feel good about themselves (*"se sentir bien dans sa peau"*). They want peace and harmony, they want material well-being. Family relationships, personal friendships, and work matter most to them. Among public issues, the public as a whole (i.e., all ages) gives top priority to peace (75 per cent), pollution (70 per cent), unemployment (70 per cent), and inflation (65 per cent); next come the future of the French language (59 per cent), federal-provincial relations (35 per cent, with younger respondents showing much less interest than older ones), the future of English in Quebec (30 per cent), and Quebec independence (25 per cent).

One participant, a specialist in the communications media, stated his belief that the constitutional debate would not again become a priority in Quebec in the near future. When and if it does, the "scenery" [*"le décor"*, the cultural context] will have changed. To understand Quebec youth, one must see what television they watch and what radio stations they listen to, he said. The music that dominates is rock, and the rock is in English. Young people listen mainly to English stations; young francophone performers sing 90 per cent of the time in English. He went on:

> Soon it could happen that in Quebec there is no distinct society; and the constitutional debate presumes that Quebec society is different ["spécifique"]...Canadian unity could come about through the United States, as both groups [anglophone and francophone youth] listen to American rock and immerse themselves in the cultural products that come to us from the United States....In this context, the debate on cultural sovereignty takes on full meaning, becomes more significant than a mere slogan. What is at stake here is much more important than a veto power for Quebec, or any opting-out clause.

In the discussion that followed, several participants expressed doubts, not about the accuracy of such observations concerning the public mood in Quebec, but about the inferences that non-Quebecers might be tempted to draw from them. Most of the comments were about the latent strength of Quebec nationalism, as will be reported below. One comment, though, was along quite different lines:

> It is perfectly fine to pursue private goals. But there is a relationship between personal goals and the political structure, or between non-alienation and the make-up of collective institutions. Most of us at the conference are probably aware of this, but many people are not. What is appalling about [the Quebec

businessman's] presentation is that it makes a virtue of avoiding debate on political structure, political culture, and political formations. This is not "perfectly fine" for Quebecers, or for anyone. I am concerned to show how political organization is important to the sense in which we enjoy life, and get out of it what is important to us. It is good to be aggressive, as Rémillard was, about describing political structure as something within which to create something of value.

The response: "I agree 90 per cent with what you say. But let's have bread and butter for a while, then we may come back later and touch up the political structure."

Quebec Nationalism

Nationalism remains a vital if hidden force in Quebec society; it can be expected to thrust itself forward again, giving impetus to a major political movement if francophone Quebecers feel themselves threatened by events within or outside the province. Such was the consensus among conference participants; some were more emphatic about it than others, but none voiced disagreement. The consensus was (appropriately enough) articulated mainly by the Quebecers – anglophone as well as francophone – but it was obvious that many others were very receptive to their message.

Can people be bored with politics and the constitution, and still be susceptible to nationalist appeals? Many particpants affirmed, in effect, that this exactly describes the Quebec situation today. Over the past quarter century, Quebecers have reordered their life as a collectivity. They take pride in their accomplishments. They have adopted policies and created institutions that express a distinctive set of values and further their collective goals. They feel moderately secure about these things now, but any challenge to what they have created, whether in the cultural field or in economic affairs, would touch off a sharp reaction, bringing to the fore again "the national question" and the constitutional issues that crystallize it. A few quotations will illustrate this.

A former union leader:

I do not think that constitutional issues are a priority for the unions. However, there is something underneath that's smouldering. If anything threatens the rights of the unions, or of the citizens, nationalism will reawake. If an attempt were made to remove Quebec's control over the language of education, or if there is an attack on the provisions of Bill 101 [Quebec's language law, passed in 1977] regarding French-language signs, there will be a new mobilization of opinion on national questions.

A business consultant:

I am concerned that people outside Quebec will think there is no more nationalism here....Nationalism is viewed by Quebecers as a positive force. It can take many forms. Young entrepreneurs are branching out, buying anglophone firms, spreading across Canada and internationally. When the federal government introduced Bill S-31 [in 1982, a bill proposing to limit provincial ownership of interprovincial transportation firms], seeking to attack the Caisse de Dépôt, a group of francophone businessmen launched a campaign against the legislation, forcing the government to drop it. The business community in Quebec has assumed responsibilities formerly exercised by government, in defending the interests of Quebec. If ever in the future there is an attack on fundamental Quebec institutions, like the Caisse, these [business]men will react.

An anglophone Quebecer:

The moment Quebec feels its capacity to be different is attacked, it will react.

These are only three of many statements of a similar character. Throughout the discussion of policy roles and responsibilities in language matters, social affairs, and economic development – and of course in the discussion of the constitutional agenda – awareness of the continuing importance of nationalism was ever-present. As one participant put it: "Quebec nationalism has evolved to a considerable degree....I don't think nationalism has receded, it has changed character and focus."

Language

A lone voice challenged the whole thrust of federal language policy, for which there is constitutional support in the Canadian Charter of Rights and Freedoms. The essence of the criticism was that whereas more than 90 per cent of anglophones are unilingual and 80 percent of francophones too are unilingual, language policy in Canada is defined by bilinguals. The present language regime is one that responds to the needs of minorities, but a sensible language would serve, instead, the needs of *le Québécois majoritaire.* (A *majoritaire* was described as a person who has never been forced to choose between his culture and his career, has never had to earn his living in a second language, and has never learned that to speak his own language means to be reprimanded, ineffectual, or marginalized; he is a person who requires only his own language to satisfy all his daily needs; for him, a second language is a hobby.)

It would be reasonable, said the critic, to have a language policy the goal of which was to avoid imposing minority status on the more than 20 million Canadians who are now unilingual. In this context it makes sense not to maximize bilingualism, but to minimize it. Canada does not need institutional bilingualism, but a *bilinguisme touristique*, to facilitate the exchange of bad English and bad French across the country. Instead, the aim of federal policy has been to help out the linguistic minorities (but only the anglophone and francophone ones), by declaring French and English official, and eligible for subsidies. But these policies cannot fundamentally change the position of the francophone minorities outside of Quebec, who are an endangered species; for them, French is less and less important as a means of earning one's livelihood and making one's career. The only place where this can occur is in Quebec, and even there a policy of official support is needed. Dignity demands that big business in Montreal should welcome *le Québécois majoritaire*; any other goal for language policy would be a *trompe l'oeil* or delusion. The Pepin-Robarts Commission (the Task Force on Canadian Unity, 1979) understood this, and made timid steps in this direction, but was denounced on the grounds that a minority cannot afford to leave its fate to the whims of a majority. Conclusion: national reconciliation is a desirable policy, but if it does not occur through a language policy that gives *le Québécois majoritaire* his rightful place, it will last only a short time.

No one supported these arguments, but they deserve attention because they summarize the case for the language policy of the Parti Québécois as implemented through Bill 101, passed in 1977. Certain provisions of that law were subsequently invalidated by Section 23 of the Charter of Rights, dealing with language rights in education. Present Quebec policy, as Mr. Rémillard made clear, is to strengthen and extend Section 23. In this respect it represents an about-turn from PQ policy. The Liberal government does not regard language guarantees benefiting Quebec anglophones, as well as francophones in other provinces, as something that would weaken a fundamental policy aim, namely to support the use of French as the primary (but not the exclusive) language of work within the province. This aim is one that is shared by the Liberals and the PQ. Unfortunately no one at the conference challenged the contention, implicit in the critic's attack on federal policy, that stating and protecting the rights of linguistic minorities is inconsistent with a policy geared to the needs of *le Québécois majoritaire*.

This surely is the nub of the continuing controversy over language policy in Quebec. But conference participants ignored the controversy. Only two persons offered a rejoinder to the criticism of policies to support bilingualism. One said that if policy reinforces unilingualism the two groups could scarcely interact with each other, and certainly not on a basis even approaching equality. The other, a Quebec anglophone, gave a much fuller response:

> Why should Canadians support the minorities? The answer is, we are engaged in "rebuilding the relationship" between the language groups. That is, we are engaged in a process of nation-building. Constitutional talks are a nation-building exercise and should reflect not only the existing situation but also where we want to go, our aspirations. As a Quebecer, I'm aware of the problem of two solitudes, where the groups interact through their elites when they have to. Then no real relationship develops, people interact on the basis of stereotypes. Sure, we are concerned about trade and economic development. But if this is all that concerns us, Quebec may decide its real relationship is with the United States. Quebecers may take the attitude, "Let us do what we want to within our borders, to the extent we can, and minimize our relationship with the rest of Canada." The challenge here is to English Canada. Do they want to address our situation [in Quebec]? Quebecers must want to feel part of Canada; the rest of the country has to offer Quebecers a sense of belonging.

One thing that became abundantly clear at the conference is that the Quebec anglophones and the francophone minorities in other provinces have nearly identical interests. They are cooperating in an effort to obtain stronger constitutional guarantees for minority language rights. The Quebec anglophones can no longer rely, as they once did, on their economic power to ensure protection of the rights they have acquired within the province. Thus, although their situation is less precarious than that of francophones outside Quebec, they are now among the most articulate proponents of administrative, legislative, and constitutional action to extend the provision of public services (especially education) to linguistic minorities.

Most of the discussion on language policy focussed on the condition of the minorities and on steps to be taken to improve it. Several participants were obviously delighted at Mr. Rémillard's proposal to clarify and strengthen Section 23 of the Charter, both by guaranteeing linguistic minorities administrative control over their own school systems, and (more tentatively) by eliminating the phrase "where numbers warrant", which narrows the right to education in the minority language. Participants also welcomed a declaration by the Secretary of State, the Honourable Benoît Bouchard, expressing extended support at the policy level, perhaps especially through the use of the spending power, for the rights of linguistic minorities; these plaudits were, however, qualified by noting the shortcomings of federal administrative action. Finally, focussing on the provinces, Ontario's recent extension of French-language services was seen as a very positive step, counterbalanced to some extent by developments in other provinces. Recent court decisions gave cause for concern. *Overall, the most strongly argued view was that improved constitutional guarantees for minority language rights are a priority item, and that constitutional declarations must be followed through with appropriate legislative and administrative action.*

There was fairly widespread recognition that, even though progress has been made in relation to minority language education rights, Section 23 of the Charter remains to some extent unapplied. One participant asked what steps should be taken to ensure that it is fully put into effect. Is there a role here for the federal government to play? There were various responses. One was that while Ottawa cannot act authoritatively in the field (as the questioner had recognized), perhaps it can supply financial assistance. (It is not clear whether the suggestion was that the federal government should extend its subsidies to the provinces for minority language education, or should support litigation under the Charter to get favourable court decisions.) Another suggestion was that the federal government could refer the matter directly to the courts, in order to get an early ruling. Another proposed step toward putting Section 23 into effect – this time involving interprovincial negotiation rather than federal action – would be for Quebec to bargain for fuller application of Section 23. (Here, however, the interests of the Quebec anglophones and the francophones in other provinces might diverge. Part of Section 23 will not come into effect until assented to by Quebec. The province might conceivably promise to give that assent – but only if the other provinces applied the clause more effectively. In other words, Quebec might make certain anglophone rights in Quebec conditional upon recognition of francophone rights elsewhere.)

Social Policy and the Federal Spending Power

Debates over social policy – mainly income security and health care – are difficult to disentangle from controversies over the spending power. The reason is simple: conditional grants are a major device through which the federal government becomes involved in fields that are primarily or exclusively under provincial jurisdiction. Social policy is a case in point. Thus, at Mont Gabriel, when the conference agenda focussed attention on social policy, participants spent much of the time debating the spending power.

All those who contributed to the discussion recognized that present patterns in social policy are being challenged by fiscal contraint and will increasingly be so in the future. One said:

> The mechanisms of fiscal federalism that we have in place are all expenditure-oriented, entitlement-oriented, and carry an upward bias. They are not designed to reduce costs, control expenditures, bring entitlements into line with the economy.

This speaker concluded that deconditionalizing the grants system would be desirable. However, others favoured a strong federal presence in social affairs through the spending power, precisely because they thought that in its absence the provinces would cut back levels of service. It appears to be a fair generalization that those whose primary goal was to support the income security and health care systems defended conditional grants, while those who were visibly more worried about program costs opted for provincial responsibility and federal withdrawal.

One may reasonably ask how (or whether) this debate has anything to do with rebuilding the relationship between Quebec and its Confederation partners. The answer may have been given by a speaker who outlined some of the major steps Quebec had taken to establish a set of social policies that conformed to its own value-system or culture. He pointed out that the federal government became heavily involved in social policy, partly through constitutional amendment (unemployment insurance, 1940; old age pensions, 1951; and supplementary powers in the pensions field, 1964), and partly through conditional grants. None the less, while the welfare state was being constructed, Quebec had sufficient latitude to go its own way to some extent. Administrative arrangments were made (pensions, family allowances) that gave Quebec an opportunity to adapt federal programs to its own needs; and some of the reforms initiated in Quebec eventually influenced policy design in the rest of Canada (social assistance, income security, health care services, and social services). In short, Quebec was an innovator, and as long as federal fiscal transfers were growing, Quebec was able – in spite of Ottawa's often unwelcome interventions in the social policy field – to follow its own lead.

Now, however, (the speaker suggested) the situation has changed. In a climate of financial constraint, earlier conflicts may easily be exacerbated. The federal government is simultaneously tightening the conditions attached to some of its fiscal transfers, as in the case of the Canada Health Act (1984), and disengaging itself financially from the programs that it had initiated at an earlier time. The debate on universality has yet to be engaged in earnest. The speaker appeared to suggest that as the federal government attempts seriously to come to grips with emerging fiscal problems related to social policy, which sooner or later it cannot avoid doing, it is likely to take decisions that will disrupt the system of income security, social services, and health care that Quebec has been able to build up over the years. As long as enough money was available for Quebec to adapt and complement federal policies in ways that gave expression to its specificity, or cultural uniqueness, Ottawa's presence in an area of primarily provincial responsibility was tolerable even to Quebec; but in an era of reduced fiscal room for manoeuvre, better protection against federal incursions into areas of provincial jurisdiction may be essential.

Quebec participants took for granted that the field of social affairs illustrates Canadian dualism. In other words they assumed that cultural differences between Quebecers and other Canadians gives that province a much stronger incentive to assert control over the social policy field than is the case with other provinces. As the session chairman pointed out, one cannot grasp the essence of the subject (social affairs) unless one recognizes to what an extent Quebec's institutions are distinctive ("*originales*"). No one at the conference challenged this assumption, but anglophone participants paid little or no attention to it. The discrepancy illustrates what Quebecers call "a dialogue of the deaf". The anglophones talked about fiscal problems, about citizens' entitlement to income security and public services, and about ways of sorting out the conflict between them. By contrast, the francophones were preoccupied by cultural distinctiveness, the extent of Quebec's capacity to respond to public demands reflecting needs and preferences specific to Quebec, and how fiscal constraint may make this problem more acute than in the past.

One has to ask whether, if anglophones and francophones more or less routinely talk past each other on social policy and the spending power, this tendency is likely to stand in the way of rebuilding the relationship between Quebec and its Confederation partners. Conference discussion may be a fairly good guide on this question. The discussion demonstrated that controversies over the exercise of the spending power have shifted focus in the past few years, and that the more recent concerns are ones where the provinces can be expected to take a common stand. Depending on the position taken by the federal government, this may augur well for reaching a constitutional settlement – at least on spending power issues.

To explain this, it will be useful to note that three main concerns were interwoven in conference discussion on social affairs and the spending power, as follows.

- One was the traditional concern over the introduction of new programs that may not fit provincial priorities, and the procedures that should be observed (whether constitutionally required or not) when the federal government undertakes a new initiative in the field.

- A second concern was the extent or specificity of conditions that, constitutionally, can be attached to federal transfers to provincial governments, an issue that has been highlighted by the Canada Health Act.

- Finally, participants discussed what can be done to ensure that the federal government does not unilaterally reduce its financial commitments to programs it has launched in the past.

Conference discussion did not clearly distinguish these three aspects of the subject, but it will be helpful to separate them here.

New Programs

When the participants spoke of the introduction of new programs, the debate on the spending power had a very traditional ring to it. Francophone participants were far more likely to oppose, on principle, the use of conditional grants. Anglophones were, as the stereotype predicts, much more inclined to take a "flexible" or "pragmatic" view. While several of them argued against conditional grants as being inappropriate to the needs of the day, few if any wanted to prohibit them altogether, or for all time. One, referring to Mr. Rémillard's desire to limit the spending power, said he hoped that the Quebec position would not go so far as to cripple the way in which Canadians have been able to achieve, within a somewhat restrictive constitutional structure, the advancement of social welfare policies and programs. He noted that several factors – among them the thrust for a free trade agreement with the United States – threaten standards already achieved in the social policy field, and he explicitly welcomed a continued federal presence through conditional grants. Not only this person, but some others too, supported a relatively or entirely unrestricted spending power on the basis of several overlapping arguments: that all Canadians should, as an element of citizenship, be entitled to a high standard of public services; that nation-building considerations justify the federal government's inducing the provinces to provide services up to a defined national standard; that fiscal disparities among the provinces require an extensive system of federal payments to provincial governments including conditional grants, equalization grants alone being inadequate to the purpose; and that "client groups" would be nervous if the federal role were restricted to making unconditional grants such as equalization payments.

Responding to this line of argument, one participant (an anglophone) said that conditional grants, while arguably necessary in the past, have probably outlived their usefulness. They are not a good control mechanism, because there are always ways to get around them; money can be diverted to other purposes unless a very rigid set of conditions is set up. Is it not time to ask whether we need conditional grants any more? The immediate rejoinder, also by an anglophone, perfectly illustrated the pragmatic approach.

> My answer is yes: it's *always* time to ask if we should get rid of conditional grants. It is also always time to ask whether we should reconditionalize certain grants. To constitutionalize these things is to place the dead hand of the past upon us. Duly elected governments should negotiate every three or five years with each other, for example on the application of the principles contained in Section 36 of the Constitution Act (1982) [the equalization clause]. Judicializing equalization formulas, or any other aspects of fiscal relations, is something about which I have very grave doubts.

Another said:

> I don't believe in "constitutional determinism". Socio-economic factors should determine not only what our social policies are, but who makes them. Canada faces three problems in this field: a fiscal challenge (the deficit), a demographic challenge (the elderly will make up an increasing percentage of the population), and a technological challenge (new methods or techniques are devised; our social programs must adapt). The constitution has to allow us to set the right social policies; no one pattern is satisfactory. Provinces must be able to experiment. These three challenges will [should?] shape our social programs, not the constitution.

These interventions strikingly illustrate the approach, or style of argument, adopted by the non-Quebecers. By contrast, the Quebecers (among whom only francophones participated in the discussion of social policy) evinced no interest in arguments suggesting that conditional grants might be useful or appropriate in some circumstances but not in others. They took the view that if citizens want certain kinds of public services or insist upon the observance of certain standards, they can and should address their demands to their provincial governments. Canada is a federation, not a unitary state, precisely because preferences vary by region or province. If a province cannot meet its residents' demands because it is poor relative to other provinces, the appropriate remedy is equalization, not centralization. Conditional grants may be tolerable – that will depend on how specific the conditions are, and how much money is available – but never desirable.

The difference in approach between Quebecers and others has a very practical consequence. While at any moment in time, or in relation to a specific issue or program, Quebec and other provincial governments make take a common stand, the latter are likely to formulate their position on an issue-by-issue basis. Thus, from Quebec's point of view, they are unreliable allies against federal incursions into areas of provincial jurisdiction. To Quebecers, it is much safer to constrain the spending power through constitutional prohibitions enforced by the judiciary.

The importance of having provincial powers clearly set out in the constitution was underlined by a francophone who argued that political agreements or administrative arrangements are an inadequate basis for provincial autonomy. The fragility of such arrangements was illustrated, he said, by the federal government's introduction of the child tax credit in 1977-78. The tax credit, while inoffensive in itself, had the effect of reducing the proportion of the family allowance payments that the provinces could redistribute among recipients according to family size. An agreement was in place allowing the provinces – in practice, only Quebec – to do this. However, a large part of the principle contained in the administrative agreement was nullified by the introduction of the child tax credit. This could not have happened if the scope of provincial powers had been set out in the constitution, as Quebec had sought to have done at Victoria in 1971. *This case may also explain, the speaker said, why Quebec would like to constitutionalize the "Cullen-Couture" administrative agreement on immigration (1978).*

Non-Quebecers may be against conditional grants, and at Mont Gabriel many of them were; but the conference also showed that non-Quebecers tend to prefer political mechanisms over constitutional and judicial ones as devices for determining the structure of the grants system. A new constitutional accord, if one had been drafted at Mont Gabriel, would probably not have included a blanket prohibition against conditional grants, or even have set up many procedural hurdles for the introduction of new shared-cost programs.

In brief, when discussion focussed on the traditional problem relating to the spending power – the introduction of new programs – Quebecers and non-Quebecers approached the subject from different angles even when they preferred unconditional grants over conditional ones. On this aspect of the constitutional agenda, the two groups seemed far apart. However, the discussion also revealed that new areas of controversy relating to the spending power have opened up and have even to a large extent supplanted the traditional concerns over its exercise. Attention now focusses much more on prohibiting the attachment of stringent conditions to federal transfers, and on finding some device to lock the federal government into its fiscal commitments to the provinces, at least for some fixed period of time. On these two aspects of the spending power issue – if conference discussion is a reliable guide – divisions between Quebecers and non-Quebecers scarcely exist.

Stringency of Conditions

There was quite a lot of discussion about the legitimacy and indeed the constitutionality of shared-cost programs that attached very detailed or restrictive conditions to fiscal transfers. The tighter the conditions, the more doubtful their constitutionality; indeed, it was noted, litigation is now under way, challenging the spending power. It was suggested, apparently with regret, that this had occurred because the federal government had recently been too aggressive in exercising powers having a doubtful constitutional basis. Developing the point, the same person who had referred to the child tax credit and the family allowances went on to say that the design of conditional grants schemes, notably in health care, had formerly sought out a very narrow line between uniformity and diversity.

As initially formulated, the conditions were fairly general in character. But to the four conditions originally applying to medical insurance (universality, accessibility, portability, and administration by a public agency) the federal government had added a fifth, comprehensiveness, in 1977, when introducing Established Programs Financing. And with the Canada Health Act, 1984, Ottawa began to oversee the administration of medical care.

Adding a fifth condition broke the delicate balance. I was surprised at the decision to do this, because predictably it would provoke a challenge, whether by the Ontario Medical Association, or by a provincial government. There is the danger that with a court decision, where there will be a winner and a loser, one will throw out the baby with the bath water. While I understand the desire to have a workable sanction, in imposing it Ottawa went much too far. It took a big risk, stretching the elastic of federal power to the breaking point. I am aware that for some people, Section 36 of the Constitution Act (1982) was intended to support both equalization payments and conditional grants. This illustrates the same tendency to stretch federal powers to the limit.

It would be incorrect to say there there was a consensus view on these matters at the conference, but opinion did seem preponderantly against shared-cost programs with conditions as specific as those in the Canada Health Act. Even so, it is doubtful that a constitutional amendment prohibiting the attachment of such conditions would have been supported. One person said:

I wonder if it would be wise to restrict the federal power to make conditional grants. The courts are about to rule on their constitutionality; we should wait for the courts' decision. In any case, have we not been well served by governments' reticence to challenge the spending power, and to seek clarity? Where the constitutional basis of action is doubtful or uncertain, governments usually seek to reach agreement.

Another, responding to the suggestion that a decentralized system is more efficient than a centralized one, because the provinces can experiment more with program design, said:

The problem with regarding the provinces as laboratories for social experiments is that too often the technicians come in the image of William Aberhart. There are indications of what would happen if we did make all grants unconditional. Alberta is adopting the U.S. practice of having private commercial hospitals; several provinces might move in that direction. Extra-billing still exists in some provinces, suggesting that the conditions written into the Canada Health Act are not stringent enough.

In the case of post-secondary education, the provinces are underfunding, and are not carrying out their responsibilities. Several provinces now spend no money of their own on post-secondary education. There should be sanctions against provinces that underfund. We should re-conditionalize the federal grant. One reason for doing so is that the anglophone population (at least) is highly mobile among provinces; this produces externalities in the sense that provinces think they can import the talent they need, or conversely if they do educate the population, some of these people will move to other provinces. Quebec, though, is a special case. There are sensitivities here that are not parallelled elsewhere, and there is also less tendency for people to move out. This means that special arrangements may be required, perhaps opting out.

These were dissenting views. Most participants apparently regarded the attachment of very specific conditions to fiscal transfers, as in the Canada Health Act, as an abuse of the spending power.

Federal Back-Out

Mr. Rémillard was especially emphatic in his condemnation of the federal government's tendency to reduce its financial contribution to programs that had been initiated through conditional grants. In particular, he criticized Bill C-96 (subsequently passed by Parliament), which cut back the rate of growth in federal payments under the Established Programs Financing scheme, covering health care and post-secondary education. His comments underlined a very basic fact about the spending power: the problem now, from the provinces' point of view, is generally how to keep Ottawa in, not how to keep it out.

Surprisingly, relatively few of the participants at Mont Gabriel dwelt on this. However, it was recognized that from a provincial perspective, the worst situation is one where the federal government attempts to impose national standards and simultaneously cuts back the level of transfers. This can, as one person noted, raise a legitimacy problem:

> Conditional grants formerly covered half the cost of the programs concerned. With the current arrangements, financing is divorced from levels of service [and fiscal transfers]. To what extent can Ottawa impose standards when its financial contribution drops? Or rather, how far can its contribution drop, and national standards still be defined and applied? Is there a breaking point?

No one attempted to answer this question; perhaps it was too obviously rhetorical. However, it pointed to a problem that one would be irresponsible to ignore. It is also evident, even if no one at Mont Gabriel made a point of saying so, that Quebec and the other provinces are in an identical situation when the federal government backs out of its financial commitments. All would be happy to see some way of ensuring that Ottawa cannot walk away from an intergovernmental agreement. It would have been interesting if participants had discussed alternative ways of achieving this goal, for example through a constitutional amendment providing for formalized accords that neither party could unilaterally pull out of, or amend prejudicially to the interests of the other.

Economic Policy and the Legitimacy of Federal Power

The session on economic policy was the one that had least to do with constitutional issues, but was also the one that demonstrated most clearly the changed – and still rapidly evolving – relationship between Quebec and the rest of Canada. The other sessions focussed on how to wrap up the old agenda of Quebec's relations with its Confederation partners; the session on economic policy pointed to the existence of a new agenda, even if its main features are still difficult to discern. It was evident to all that Quebecers' attitudes towards business, the thrust of Quebec's economic policies, and the structure of the provincial economy – its place in the Canadian and North American economies – have all been transformed in recent years; but the group assembled at Mont Gabriel had great difficulty in coming to grips with the institutional and constitutional implications of these developments. It was also apparent that, in addition to such implications, there are some policy issues giving rise to a potential legitimacy problem for the federal government, in view of the regional impact of its economic policies.

The Quebec Economy and Economic Policies

It was repeatedly said at Mont Gabriel that the Québécois of the 1980s have a new, positive attitude towards business. As one person put it, it's no longer the archbishop or even the deputy minister who is held up as a model to emulate, but the entrepreneur, especially the entrepreneur who has "made it" in external markets. But one participant viewed these changes from a different perspective:

> I don't think Quebec is playing by new rules now, or that Quebec has changed gods. Rather, the Quebec francophones have renounced an economic structure containing two economies having little relationship to each other. Around 1960, for example, there was a "Quebec economy" – the economy that occupied the whole territory of the province except the western part of Montreal – and there were the remnants of the economy of Montreal as the metropolis of Canada. The latter was an economy in decline, a

structure that was very difficult for francophones to penetrate. Provincial policy had the effect of accelerating the decline of the Canadian economy in Montreal, and this had negative effects on the province as a whole; but it also permitted the province to reconstruct the rest of the Quebec economy, and to transform Montreal into the headquarters of a Quebec economy integrated with the rest of Canada, and not viable within Quebec alone. The effect of these changes has not been to recapture for Montreal the position it had in 1920 or even 1950, but to make it into a regional metropolis of considerable importance. I wouldn't say that now, for the first time, the Quebec francophones have discovered that they have to be competitive; previously, they had no opportunity to enter the competition; now they do.

In other words, behavioural changes match structural ones, and adapt to the opportunities at hand. But policy helps too. This was recognized by participants who shared a common interpretation of the economic role of the Quebec government today. The most thorough treatment of this subject was by Thomas J. Courchene, who stated:

The Parti Québécois became, after the referendum, the most business-oriented or market-oriented government in Canada. The designation is not fully appropriate, since the state is also playing an important role. Perhaps incentive-oriented, entrepreneurial, or peoples' capitalism more accurately reflects what is going on. Moreover, this new political economy is decidedly nationalist in nature, since it represents an integrated strategy for economic development and for the control of economic institutions by Québécois and from a location within Quebec, namely Montreal....It is probably safe to assume that the Liberal government will continue with the new political economy and perhaps even advance it in measurable ways.

Not everyone was willing to describe the policy as "nationalist", because nationalism (one person suggested) implies giving privileges to people on the basis of ethnicity. This person did not consider that linguistic bias was a feature of Quebec's economic policy. Others, however, described the policy as nationalist for precisely this reason. Indeed, the role of the provincial government in promoting the "francisation" of Quebec business – for example through the language law – was generally recognized by the group.

The idea that nationalism was a feature of Quebec's economic policy came up also in a different context, where there was obvious disagreement among participants. Courchene described the thrust of policy as "market nationalism", its goals being "to build a strong and viable economic base, ... to open up the economy, and at the same time to use the instruments of the state (subsidized share-ownership [through the Quebec Stock Savings Plan or QSSP] and the Caisse [de Dépôt]) to complement and enhance this process." The "nationalism" here related to territory rather than ethnicity or language. But, Courchene added, it is not province-building in the usual sense of the term, because it is not directed against anyone else in Canada: "They are building a strong base not in order to be able to get a BC market from Ontario; they are looking vertically or outward to the US instead of horizontally. This will only hurt Ontario if Ontario continues to look inward. Ontario should follow Quebec's lead." On the other hand, Courchene acknowledged, "The QSSP is a clear barrier to the national flow of capital because Quebecers do not get [a tax] credit for investing in new issues of firms outside the province. Other provinces cannot put it in because they don't have their own personal income tax. This is a discriminatory move, inconsistent with an internal common market. I don't know what to do about that – one thing to do is to nationalize it, let Ottawa do it for everybody."

Institutional and Constitutional Implications

Even though there were differences of nuance and emphasis, the group at Mont Gabriel shared basically the same interpretation of changes in the structure of the Quebec economy, changes in attitudes, and changes in policy. Participants experienced difficulty, however, in identifying what all these changes may signify or portend for Quebec's relationship with its Confederation partners. Discussion in this area touched upon common market issues; the extent of economic powers required by Quebec to reinforce Quebec's character as a distinct society, or to support cultural development; the flexibility of present constitutional arrangements; and the idea of creating a national securities market.

A Quebec businessman squarely addressed the common market issue. Noting the tendency of Quebec entrepreneurs to look outward, he added:

The absence of an integrated Canadian market and the existence of too many non-tariff barriers among the provinces are the most serious economic problem we have in Canada. Our constitutional experts should concentrate on this. The free trade debate has underlined once again this fundamental problem. The Quebec economy, five or six million persons, is too small to have allowed our firms to take the fundamental decisions they needed to take over the past few years to become competitive. They have to take radical decisions, to specialize, to merge with other firms, or to buy them out. The Canadian market is too balkanized to permit rationalization. Our industries must be able to count on having access to a bigger [domestic] market, in order to become more efficient, bigger, and less numerous – as we must do to be competitive not only in the United States, but also in Asia and Europe.

Some participants considered that all this was overblown, that the costs of internal non-tariff barriers (NTBs) have been exaggerated in the past. Another response was that eliminating all internal NTBs would not significantly increase east-west trade, unless Canadian industry has poor access to the American market. While there was general support for trade liberalization, opinion at Mont Gabriel appeared divided between two approaches: (1) to concentrate first on ensuring effective integration of the Canadian market, in order to rationalize and become internationally competitive, or (2) to open up internationally and let the domestic problem solve itself (which it would do, because domestic producers faced with foreign competition would not tolerate the retention of internal barriers).

On the subject of Quebec's economic powers, one participant expressed the following opinion:

What Quebec needs, as far as its economy is concerned, is enough constitutional room for manoeuvre to permit it to determine how it will adapt to shifts in the international economy and also to the strategic choices made by the federal government for the Canadian economy as a whole. The size, the resource endowments, and the industrial structure of the provincial economies vary considerably. Each province therefore has an economic situation peculiar to itself; and each must have, correspondingly, a certain capacity to adapt to external forces. But the linguistic and socio-cultural distinctiveness of Quebec often imposes upon it sharper, or greater, adaptations than are required elsewhere. The history of the past quarter century demonstrates that Quebec's room for manoeuvre is considerable, but is it sufficient?

Those who argue that on the whole Canada is already decentralized enough, often are of the view that it is decentralized in the wrong way. In economic affairs, evaluations are often made applying a single criterion, that of efficiency....I think a different form of evaluation, using the cultural security of Quebec as a guide, might be useful.

This person did not identify, however, the changes in the distribution of economic powers that might come about if the criterion of cultural security were applied. Indeed, no one argued that Quebec now lacks essential powers in the economic field. Quite the opposite was said by at least one person, and his assertion was not challenged.

If there was consensus at Mont Gabriel on the division of powers in the economic field (given the small number of people who addressed the issue, a judgment on this matter is difficult to make) it would probably be that the constitution as it stands now is flexible enough to accommodate fundamental changes in economic conditions as well as in the economic aspirations or strategies of the various provinces. Here Quebec is no exception. It was recognized that Quebec has certain powers in "non-economic" fields, for example regarding language and social affairs, that have a distinct economic relevance. One person suggested if one were looking for an "omnium gatherum" or unifying principle lying behind Quebec's policy initiatives across a wide range of areas, including in economic affairs it would be to promote the interests of *le Québécois majoritaire*, the francophone Quebecer who need never choose between his career and his culture. Some of the participants seemed uncertain whether, to serve this purpose, Quebec needed more control (or absolute possession) of policy instruments now lodged in Ottawa, or shared with it; but no one made the case that it did.

Indeed, one of the surprising things about the session on economic affairs, or about the conference as a whole, is that there was scarcely any reference to specific instruments of economic policy, or to which order of government should wield them, or to whether Quebec has needs that – because of its culturally and socially unique situation – are either more extensive than those of other provinces, or different from them. The one area that was referred to by several speakers was securities regulation and the idea of a national securities market. Courchene asserted that regulatory powers in this area are provincial, but that this in no way prevented the creation of a Canada-wide market. Three others also referred to the matter, one suggesting that while the provinces now are the active order of government in the field, Ottawa has adequate constitutional authority to impose rules or controls of its own (in which case federal law would prevail if there were any conflict with provincial law). He saw advantages in this, without specifying what they might be; the other two also seemed sympathetic. One imagines that if ever there were new federal initiatives in this area, it could easily become a federal-provincial battleground.

Some of the discussion on economic policy had less to do with the activities of the Quebec government than with those of the federal government. Both, obviously, are relevant to redefining Quebec's place in Canada, or to building a new relationship between Quebec and its Confederation partners. The problem: do Ottawa's policy decisions risk undermining the legitimacy of federal power?

The issue was placed before the conference by a participant who observed that francophone businessmen who are trying to break into export markets tend to avail themselves of the provincial government's help and advice, not Ottawa's. In many instances the federal Department of External Affairs ought to be better placed to help, but Quebec businessmen prefer to deal with Quebec agencies such as the *Société de développement industriel*. This person did not allege that federal policies, or the attitudes and behaviour of federal officials, are inadequate or unhelpful; he simply made the observation that this is what francophone businessmen do, and said that the matter ought to be of concern to the federal government.

The question of legitimacy also came up in the context of federal policies having regionally discriminatory effect. One participant, noting that Courchene painted a picture of strong social consensus in Quebec for entrepreneurial, market-oriented, competition-enhnacing policies, added: "Those who live at the other end of the country sometimes see an equally strong consensus for decisions such as Petromont, Domtar, the Western Grain Transportation Act, and dairy quotas. How do you fit that into your model?" There ensued the discussion about "province-building", referred to above; thus attention was shifted again to provincial policy; but several people were evidently deeply concerned about the actions of the federal government over the years, and about what a federal government, of any party, can do to strengthen its own legitimacy. One said:

> In the last election, in the west there was a feeling that at last we're getting rid of Trudeau and his preoccupation with Quebec. We'd had enough of the Quebec issue. Now Mulroney too seems mesmerized by the problem of Quebec. That would be OK if the economy of the West were in good shape, but it's not, it's in collapse. Oil and gas prices, agricultural prices, and mineral prices are in trouble and will remain so. This causes emotional and fiscal strain on Confederation. If Ottawa remains transfixed with the problems of Quebec, then obtaining reconciliation with the West will be difficult.

Similar thoughts were expressed by others, one of whom emphasized that all regions must have an economic stake in being part of the federation. This applies equally to Quebec and to the other provinces or regions. Quebec, which is determined to strengthen its export performance both in the United States and around the world, must have confidence that membership in the federation will support these endeavours or aspirations, and federal policy must justify such confidence. Similarly, provinces that depend heavily on resource production must perceive an economic benefit to their resource industries; too often, in the past, the net effect has been negative. This presents a challenge to federal policy makers; continued failure to meet the challenge would erode the legitimacy of federal power. The conclusion was that rebuilding the relationship between Quebec and its Confederation partners involves more than finding appropriate responses to linguistic and cultural duality; it involves also restructuring relations among economic regions.

There is also another dimension to the legitimacy problem, although in this case the problem is not Ottawa's alone but equally that of the provincial governments. That dimension is income distribution and the economic security of the worker. Only one person referred to these matters. Amid the many references that others were making to the new horizons and go-getting behaviour of Quebec's francophone businessmen, he said:

My reaction to the discussion is that this Alice-in-Wonderland approach can only be found among economists. When we're facing the worst crisis that I've lived through, they're convincing us that we are living in the best of all possible worlds. I'll take the message back to [the working-class neighbourhood] where I live. My whole reaction is, you are celebrating the insecurity of the working class because of so-called gains in entrepreneurship whose results are not reaching [my neighbourhood] and never will.

These remarks earned no applause. A couple of people responded by saying that the working class needs a competitive economy to maintain and improve its standard of living. However, this participant touched on a problem of wealth distribution that none of the others addressed. Ultimately, the political problems and dilemmas involved in rebuilding a satisfactory relationship between Quebec and its Confederation partners spill over into other areas: how to reorder relations among economic regions and among economic classes. Distributional justice – among regions and income groups – is important. A government that subordinates goals having top priority for large segments of the population cannot convince the public that another set of issues must be given top spot on the public agenda. At Mont Gabriel this was recognized when people were talking about relations among the regions. However, except in the one brief intervention cited above, participants paid no attention to class divisions in the session on economic policy and its political and constitutional significance.

The Constitution: Genie in the bottle?

The Mont Gabriel group recognized that one of the greatest barriers to reaching a constitutional settlement with Quebec was that other issues have priority for most Canadians, and that governments cannot be seen to be "wasting" their time and energies on second-order problems when the economy is in disarray. This consideration, plus the lack of certainty that the process, once initiated, could be brought to a successful conclusion, led the group to consider carefully whether the time is right for a new constitutional initiative. It was generally acknowledged that a failed attempt would have serious consequences.

Extended discussion produced apparent consensus – in the sense that any disagreement was not publicly voiced – on a number of propositions, which may be summarized as follows.

- The present situation, where certain features of the Constitution Act, 1982, are unacceptable to Quebec, must not be allowed to persist. There is bound eventually to be a resurgence of Quebec nationalism, and it would be courting disaster not to reach a constitutional accord in the interval. The constitutional issue must not be left to fester until there is some new crisis, at which time a settlement may well be unachievable.

- The challenge for the rest of Canada is to take the issue seriously enough to resolve it now, when the federation is not in crisis. If we are to "close the chapter" on the events of 1980-82, without waiting for a crisis to force the issue again upon the public mind, the time is now uniquely favourable. But to put the issue on the public agenda will require a personal, public, and vigorous commitment by the Prime Minister. No one else can do it.

- Mr. Rémillard's list of five items is a remarkably modest one, and represents a bare minimum for Quebec. In his keynote address, Mr. Rémillard had pointed out that the 1982 Act, which is binding on Quebec as on the rest of Canada, has several valuable features, notably the Charter of Rights and Freedoms. However, he had gone on to say that from Quebec's point of view, the Act also has a number of deficiencies that must be remedied before Quebec can endorse it. (1) Quebec's character as a distinct society must be explicitly recognized. (2) Quebec needs extended powers in relation to immigration. (3) The spending power of the federal government must be limited. (4) The formula for amending the constitution needs to be changed, giving Quebec, directly or indirectly, a veto. (5) Quebec must participate in the nomination of Supreme Court judges, one third of whom are (as is required by the Supreme Court Act) drawn from the Quebec bar). The group considered that Mr. Rémillard had made every effort to pare the list to the essentials, partly (one may suppose) because the Quebec government cannot be seen to backtrack in the negotiations; this would destroy its own legitimacy in the province. Implication: at the conclusion of negotiations, the Quebec government must be able to point to a satisfactory resolution of every one of the five issues. The other governments must not approach the discussions with the idea that agreement on three or four items would be enough to get Quebec to sign. In the unlikely event that Quebec were to do so, the accord would be repudiated by the electorate.

- The constitution is a genie in a corked bottle. Before uncorking it, one must be sure the genie will not grow to unpredictable proportions, or become unmanageable. One dare not expand Mr. Rémillard's list of five items. Other parties must be persuaded not to look upon the reopening of the constitutional dossier as an opportunity to air their own grievances or to win approval for whatever amendments they themselves would like to see adopted. If this happens, the agenda will expand uncontrollably, and it will be impossible to negotiate an agreement. All governments must accept – as subsequently they did at Edmonton, during the August meeting of the premiers – that the items put on the agenda by Quebec will have priority. The justification for this is that the constitutional accord of November 1981 was not acceptable to Quebec, and its moral exclusion from the constitution cannot be allowed to continue.

- Important as it is to reach a new accord, it would be a mistake to start formal negotiations unless there is a strong likelihood of succeeding. Great damage would be done, in terms of Quebec public opinion, if talks began and then failed. Thus a preliminary set of informal discussions must take place behind closed doors, and the outcome of these discussions should determine whether prospects for agreement are good enough to move the talks into a public phase. Ultimately there *will be* a public phase, because the 1982 Constitution

Act requires that all amendments secure parliamentary and legislative approval; in the case of changes to the amending formula itself, favourable resolutions must be passed by Parliament and all ten provincial legislatures.

"Distinct society", Immigration, and Supreme Court

Of Mr. Rémillard's list of five items, participants scarcely made reference to three: recognition of Quebec as a distinct society, extended powers for Quebec in the field of immigration, and appointments to the Supreme Court.

The final session of the conference focussed specifically on the desirability of entering into formal constitutional negotiations, and on the probable substance of such talks. Broadly, people were trying to identify possible snags and how the snags might minimized or avoided. Thus what was *not* said was very revealing. "How to proceed", and the related matter of preventing the expansion of the agenda, received by far the most attention. Regarding matters of substance, attention focussed on the spending power (discussed above) on Section 23 of the Constitution Act 1982 (minority language education), also discussed above, and on the amending formula. May one assume that the group broadly endorsed the remaining items mentioned by Mr. Rémillard, or thought that, on these items at least, consensus could be relatively easily reached across the country? Whatever the correct interpretation, here we we are justified merely in reporting that (1) only one person picked up on the idea of recognizing Quebec as a distinct society, suggesting that a preamble to the constitution – the 1867 Act, the 1982 Act, or a new (1987?) Constitution Act – could reasonably include such recognition; (2) only one person referred to expanded powers over immigration, and apparently he did so only to express surprise that no other division of powers items (like communications, for example) were referred to by Mr. Rémillard; and (3) one person singled out the composition of the Supreme Court as being potentially a major stumbling block, in that other provinces too might claim "representation".

Amending Formula

Resurrecting a constitutional veto for Quebec was recognized to be a potentially explosive issue. Several participants said bluntly it could not be achieved. However, in saying so they appeared to be thinking of a formula that would identify Quebec as having a role, or a degree of authority, denied to any other province, or limited to Quebec and Ontario. A number of people – perhaps half a dozen – spoke of trying to find a formula that would meet the objectives and legitimate concerns expressed by Mr. Rémillard, without singling out Quebec for special treatment. One, for example, thought that it would be useful to restructure national institutions – specifically, or mainly, the Senate – such that certain measures could be adopted only by a concurrent (or double) majority of anglophone and francophone members. Quebec would recognize that most francophone members would be from that province, giving it an effective if indirect veto power. This proposal, however, drew some criticism and no supporters.

The amending formula proposals that captured the greatest degree of attention and support were: (1) to provide for fiscal compensation in the case of amendments to the division of powers, if Quebec (or any other province) opted out; and (2) to increase, but in a minimal way, the range of amendments requiring unanimity, i.e. a resolution passed by Parliament and all the provincial legislatures. The two suggestions are complementary, making in effect a single proposal.

Unanimity is already required under Section 41 of the 1982 Act for amendments relating to a short list of matters that include the use of the English or the French language (with minor exceptions), the composition of the Supreme Court of Canada, and the amending formula itself. The general formula is that an amendment may be made by resolution of Parliament and two-thirds (i.e., seven) of the provincial legislatures representing at least one half of the population of Canada. However, a province may opt out of an amendment relating to the division of powers. Obviously, the opt-out provision cannot be invoked in the case of the following matters, to which the general formula (Section 42) applies:

- the principle of proportionate representation (by province) in the House of Commons,

- the Senate (most aspects),

- the Supreme Court of Canada, except as regards its composition, and

- extending provincial boundaries into the territories, or the establishment of new provinces.

In effect, the idea that received attention at Mont Gabriel was, first, to identify those parts of the above list of items that Quebec would have reason to be concerned about since, as repeatedly stated by Mr. Rémillard, "one does not withdraw from an institution." A second step would be to include such items – phrased as narrowly as possible – in the unanimity list (Section 41). In such matters Quebec would have a veto, but so would all the other provinces. Thus Quebec would not be singled out for "favours" and all provinces would be on an equal footing in relation to constitutional amendments, except in the percentage of the population they contained. Population, of course, is relevant to the "50 per cent of the population" rule in the general amending formula.

No one referred to the idea later embodied in a proposal made by Mr. Bourassa at the Premiers' conference in Edmonton (August 1986), that the general amending formula be changed to require the assent of two-thirds of the provinces representing at least three-quarters of the population. (Mr. Bourassa suggested 75 per cent, giving Quebec – with 26 per cent – an across-the-board veto.) The group at Mont Gabriel focussed instead on a less radical change that still appeared to meet the objectives or concerns set out by Mr. Rémillard.

Final Observations

The group assembled at Mont Gabriel was not representative of the Canadian population as a whole. However, it probably was a good cross-section of Canadians having an interest in constitutional affairs. Many of those who have since been playing an active role in informal talks towards achieving a new constitutional accord or "bringing Quebec into the constitution" were present. Thus the conference deliberations were probably a good sample of preliminary thoughts on several issues that will have to be addressed and resolved in the process of rebuilding the relationship between Quebec and its Confederation partners.

What "kept the juices going" at the conference was the strong and widely-shared conviction that national reconciliation is a national imperative. Quebec, it was recognized, had valid reasons for refusing to give its consent or support to the Constitution Act, 1982. While many non-Quebecers evidently object to reopening questions that they consider to have been settled in 1982, and in Quebec some people believe the best thing to do about the constitution is to forget about it – that is, to wager that memories of 1980-82 will fade away, so long as they are not artificially kept fresh – the conference participants insisted otherwise. They were strongly of the opinion that although Quebecers have grown tired of politics for now, and constitutional issues seem remote and outdated to the youth of Quebec, a new wave of Quebec nationalism is bound to occur sooner or later. This, they believed, makes it essential to resolve outstanding constitutional differences before a new crisis arrives.

Mr. Rémillard's keynote speech was a constant point of reference during the discussions. Participants repeatedly affirmed that the five conditions he set out for reaching a new constitutional accord made agreement "manageable", as long as the agenda was limited to these five items.

A new accord would conclude unfinished business from 1980-82. However, it would not resolve once and for all the "problem" of Quebec's relationship with its Confederation partners. Rather, it would provide a framework, acceptable to Quebecers, within which new issues – ones that are of considerable importance not only to Quebecers but to people in all parts of Canada – can be effectively tackled. Many of those issues are economic, involving relations among Canadian regions and between Canada and the rest of the world. The group assembled at Mont Gabriel was convinced that Canadians must wrap up the old agenda that in order to release themselves to deal with other problems, or to turn to other matters, for which most of them will have far greater zest.

Note

1.   "Market Nationalism", in *Policy Options*, 7:8 (October 1986), 7-12.

APPENDIX

Unofficial English-language text* of the speech by Mr. Gil Rémillard, Minister responsible for Canadian Intergovernmental Affairs, Government of Quebec, to the Conference "Rebuilding the Relationship: Quebec and its Confederation Partners", Mont Gabriel, Quebec, 9 May 1986.

17 April 1982 is a historic date for Canada. It was on this day that Elizabeth II, Queen of Canada, proclaimed the Constitution Act of 1982 on Parliament Hill in Ottawa. Thus, after more than 55 years of difficult discussions which, on some occasions, even plunged Canadian federalism into profound crisis, nine provinces and the federal government agreed not only to repatriate the Constitution, but also to substantially modify the original Constitution of 1867. This accord included a Charter of Rights and Freedoms, an amending formula, aboriginal peoples' rights, an equalization clause, and modification of the distribution of powers in matters concerning natural resources.

Little remains to be said on the fact that the Constitution Act of 1982 marked the disappearance of the last vestige of Canada's colonial status. Since the Statute of Westminster of 1931, Canada has been a sovereign country. Although the Parliament at Westminster continued to hold formal rights in constitutional matters, it never acted except at the express request of the Canadian government. Many Canadians would probably be surprised to learn that even today London could declare Canada a "colony of the British Empire". All it would have to do would be to modify the Statute of Westminster of 1931 and the Constitution Act of 1982, although as Lord Denning said in his famous obiter dictum in the Blackburn case, "Legal theory does not always coincide with political reality."

---

* This is the full text, except for a few introductory sentences of interest mainly to the conference participants. The translation, which is the responsibility of the editor, is based on the English-language text, as distributed at the conference. It takes account of additions and modifications made by Mr. Rémillard at time of delivery.

Nothing obliged the Canadian government to institute proceedings through the Parliament of Westminster to regain full sovereignty with complete international rights. Canada could just as easily have proclaimed, as a sovereign state and on its own territory, this important new part of its constitution. However, Canada opted, for one last time, to have recourse to the old colonial mechanism. By proceeding in this way it was easier for the Canadian Parliament to act without obtaining the assent of the provinces. In fact, the Supreme Court had ruled on 28 September 1981 that on the strictly legal level, nothing stopped it from changing as it wished the Canadian constitution. However, there were some restrictions with respect to the legitimacy of such an action. The Court found that according to convention Ottawa should only proceed if it had the consent of a sufficient number of provinces. Yet in referring the matter to Westminster, Ottawa could, if need be, go against what the provinces wanted. This procedure allowed it to proceed directly, without getting Quebec's consent. In the aftermath of the Constitutional proclamation of 1982, Quebec found itself isolated from major amendments to the Constitution which, in certain respects, contravened Quebec's historic rights. Four years after the proclamation of the Constitution Act of 1982, Quebec, headed by a new government, still has not adhered to the Act. No Quebec government, regardless of its political tendencies, could adhere to the Constitution Act of 1982 in its present form. However, if certain modifications were made, the Act could become acceptable to Quebec.

Therefore, the Quebec government wishes to resume constitutional discussions with its federal partners, Ottawa and the other provinces. However, essential conditions have not been satisfied for beginning serious formal constitutional negotiations. Certain points must be clarified first. Ottawa must indicate what, in its words, might be meant by signing a constitutional agreement "with honor and enthusiasm" as the Prime Minister of Canada, Mr. Mulroney, has said he hopes to do.

It should be stressed that it is not only up to Quebec to act. Our federal partners must also be active players. We expect concrete action on their part, action that is likely to steer the talks in the right direction. The ball is not only in Quebec's court but also in that of the federation, on Ottawa's side, on the side of the other provinces, the nine other provinces that isolated Quebec. We want to negotiate, but we want to negotiate with partners who first indicate to us concretely their desire to rectify the injustice that the Constitution Act of 1982 represents for Quebec.

This is not the time for listing the errors committed by one side or the other. On the contrary, it is a time for cooperation and understanding. Quebec will approach these constitutional talks firmly and with determination but also with an open mind, as required by the higher interests of Quebec and Canada. However, you will agree with me that Quebec's isolation cannot continue much longer without jeopardizing the very foundation of true federalism.

Nor is it a time for sweeping all away with the back of the hand and starting all over again. Absolutely not. Not everything contained in the Constitution Act of 1982 is bad. The Charter of Rights and Freedoms, after court interpretation, is on the whole a document of which we as Quebecers and Canadians can be proud. Its greatest merit no doubt lies in gradually giving us, as Canadians and Quebecers, a new mentality and approach with respect to fundamental rights. This is why our first decision as the new government last December was to stop systematically applying, as the former government had done, the "Notwithstanding" clause to all Quebec statutes, to exempt Quebec laws from sections 2 and 7 to 15 of the Canadian Charter. We want Quebecers to have the same rights as other Canadians.

The only valid reason that could justify the systematic utilization of this derogation clause could be as a symbol, a symbol of the disagreement of Quebec confronted with the Constitution Act of 1982. But we feel that this symbol is empty. We refuse, as a government, to take Quebecers hostage in our constitutional talks with the rest of the Canadian federation. There is absolutely no question of depriving our people of such fundamental constitutional rights as the right to life, to security of the person, to a just and fair trial, and to equal treatment under the law. These are rights intrinsic to human nature and to life in society. Hence, our first decision was to use the "Notwithstanding" clause only where necessary to protect the public interest of Quebec.

If the Canadian Charter poses few problems for Quebec, the same is not true for other aspects of the Constitution Act of 1982 which, in many respects, negates Quebec's historic rights.

On 2 December 1985, the population of Quebec clearly gave us a mandate to carry out our electoral program, which sets out the main conditions that could lead Quebec to adhere to the Constitution Act of 1982.

These conditions are:

1. Explicit recognition of Quebec as a distinct society;
2. Guarantee of increased powers in matters of immigration;
3. Limitation of the federal spending power;
4. Recognition of a right of veto;
5. Quebec's participation in appointing judges to the Supreme Court of Canada.

Quebec as a Distinct Society

As far as we are concerned, recognition of Quebec's specificity is a prerequisite to any talks capable of leading Quebec to adhere to the Constitution Act of 1982. Quebec's identity is the culmination of a slow social and political evolution. At the time of the Conquest of 1760, a unique francophone community existed with its own customs, mentality, and lifestyle, and with its own civil, religious and military institutions. These people were the true Canadians whereas the conquerors were Englishmen. The Quebec Act of 1774 and the Constitution Act of 1791, which created Lower and Upper Canada, confirmed the Canadians' unique character by giving them their first legal basis of existence and expression permitting them to conserve their civil law and their religion while also establishing a parliamentary system. Then came the Act of Union of 1840, which followed the Durham Report drafted after the Rebellions of 1837-1838. This Act united Upper and Lower Canada into a single political entity. Thus appeared for the first time, in 1840, the two designations, "French Canadians" and "English Canadians", that the British North America Act, 1867, consecrated in letter and in spirit.

It was necessary to wait more than a century before a veritable national Quebec character emerged from this French Canadian people. During one hundred years of federation, Quebecers would increasingly become aware of their identity in terms of their provincial government and in terms of a common good, a desire to live together and to share the same elements of existence, making them a specific society.

This identity must not in any way be jeopardized. We must therefore be assured that the Canadian Constitution will explicitly recognize the unique character of Quebec society and guarantee us the means necessary to ensure its full development within the framework of Canadian federalism.

Immigration

Recognition of the specific nature of Quebec gives rise to the need for obtaining real guarantees for our cultural security. Cultural security translates into giving Quebec sole power to plan its immigration. In this way it can maintain its francophone character by countering or even reversing demographic trends that foreshadow a decrease in Quebec's relative size within Canada.

Spending Power

Cultural security also signifies Quebec's ability to act alone in its fields of jurisdiction without interference from the federal government through its spending power. You are no doubt aware that this power allows Ottawa to spend sums of money in any area it wishes whether it falls under federal jurisdiction or not. At present, there is no exclusively provincial area of jurisdiction that is not susceptible in either a direct or indirect way to being affected by the federal spending power. The spending power has become a "sword of Damocles" hanging menacingly over any province wanting to plan its social, cultural or economic development. This situation has become intolerable. Bill C-96 dealing with the financing of health and post-secondary education, which is before the Canadian Parliament, is an eloquent example of this situation. This bill is clearly unjust and discriminatory as far as Quebec is concerned. It represents a shortfall in transfers totalling $82 million in 1986-87. We would be very happy if the federal government removed itself from these areas of responsibility – education, manpower, health. However, we consider it unacceptable that it should do so without granting financial compensation to provinces for the discharge of these responsibilities. Placing boundaries on the application of the spending power could be a major contribution to the amelioration of the Canadian federation. Should Bill C-96 be passed by the Canadian Parliament, the result would certainly have a serious impact on the progress of constitutional talks.

The spending power, when related to the principle of equalization, is much more acceptable. However, once again, the current situation is completely unfair to Quebec. My colleague, the Minister of Finance, Mr. Gérard D. Lévesque, had reason to denounce Ottawa's attitude in his recent budget. Ottawa unilaterally changed the rules for applying the principle of equalization which is entrenched in Section 36 of the Constitution Act of 1982. It is unacceptable for Ottawa to have acted unilaterally to change the rules of the game. The main parameters for applying the principle of equalization, as stated in Section 36 of the Constitution Act of 1982, must be written into the constitution. The application of this principle is a basic feature of our federal system; the very philosophy of our federal system, the distribution of the nation's wealth among the provinces, rests on equalization. This principle is the foundation of the country. Thus, to change it, to change the parameters governing its application, it should be necessary to employ the same formula as applies in the case of constitutional amendment. In this way the provinces would be protected from any unilateral federal action. And that is an additional reason we have to insist upon an amending formula that will respect the historic rights of Quebec within the federation, as they have existed since its creation in 1867.

Amending Formula

The present amending formula is unacceptable to Quebec because Quebec foresees the possibility of a province withdrawing from an amendment that does not suit it, and infringes on its rights, powers and property, without receiving financial compensation except in cases relating to education and culture. In all other cases, the withdrawal of a province implies no financial compensation. This means that for all practical purposes a province that takes advantage of the right guaranteed in the constitution to withdraw from amendments that abrogate its rights, and that it does not desire, will see its citizens subjected to double taxation. This is what happens when a province avails itself of the present amending formula. This is an unacceptable situation!

Secondly, although one can easily conceive of withdrawal from a field of jurisdiction, it is impossible to withdraw from an institution. This also makes the amending formula unacceptable to Quebec. One cannot withdraw from the Supreme Court. One cannot withdraw from the House of Commons. This points to a serious gap in the formula, a gap that is directly in conflict with the historic rights of Quebec because the amending formula as it now stands permits seven provinces totalling 50 per cent of the population and the Canadian Parliament to modify the Senate, certain aspects of the Supreme Court, and the base of our representation to the House of Commons, despite Quebec's objections. This is unacceptable!

While this amending formula is based on the principle of withdrawal, its drafters unfortunately did not understand that one does not withdraw from an institution. We have to repair this situation as rapidly as possible. The only way to do this is through the right to absolute or qualified veto, a right of veto which would permit Quebec to say "non" to amendments that infringe upon its historic rights in this federation. It is a security we must have and it is a major point we want to negotiate.

Supreme Court

In addition, we would also like to state precisely the role of one of the most important institutions in our federation. The Constitution is not always changed formally using the amending formula. The highest court in the land, the Supreme Court, can modify the constitution through judicial interpretation. Therefore, we would like assurances that Quebec will be a full participant in the process of selecting or nominating Supreme Court judges.

Furthermore, we would like assurances that the Supreme Court has now been constitutionalized, and is now part of the Constitution of Canada. It is a point of great importance because, as you know, it was in 1875 that Parliament decided by law to create this Supreme Court as a court of last resort in Canada. The question that arises is whether, since articles 41 and 42 of the Constitution Act of 1982 refer to the Supreme Court – to its composition, and to other features – the Court itself now has constitutional status. This is important for us as Quebecers, because if the answer is yes, that means that we have at least a guarantee that a third of the Supreme court judges, at present three out of nine, will be chosen from the Quebec Bar or Magistrature. However, if the answer is no, this means that we have no such guarantee. Parliament would have full control over its law on the Supreme Court because we know that in jurisprudence, a law is always amendable, that is, modifiable by another law. Therefore, this is a particularly important point for Quebec.

Overall Aims of Quebec, and Minority Language Guarantees

Quebec has three main objectives in opening constitutional negotiations. We want to make the Constitution Act of 1982 acceptable to Quebec, but we also want to improve it for the whole Canadian federation. For example, if we succeed in clarifying the constitutional status of the Supreme Court we shall have added precision on a matter of great importance to Quebec, but in doing so we also clarify the matter for the whole federation. The question is an important one for all the other provinces too. Thus, in the constitutional negotiations we want to improve, for the whole federation, this second historic compromise on the structure of the Canadian federation.

We also want to improve the situation of the francophones living outside the province of Quebec. This last point is especially important to us. In fact, the situation of francophones outside of Quebec will be one of our major preoccupations during the upcoming constitutional talks. Their situation could be greatly ameliorated. It would be advantageous to clarify certain ambiguous points in Section 23 of the Constitution Act of 1982, and in particular the famous expression "minority language educational facilities" found in paragraph 3(b) of Section 23. We know that members of the minority have the right to be educated in their own language, and in certain cases, in institutions that they themselves own. However, it has not been stated whether they have the right to administer these institutions. The Ontario Court of Appeal has already ruled that they do have this right, and that the power to administer the institution is comprehended in the expression of "minority language educational facilities". This is a very important element in the application of Section 23. It's one thing to be able to take courses in one's own language in a school of the majority language group; it's altogether another thing to be able to take courses in one's own language in a school that is administered in that language – and therefore to speak French not only in the classroom but also in the library, in the cafeteria, and in the schoolyard. The rights of the non-Quebec francophones would be improved considerably if it were specified in Section 23 that the expression "minority language educational facilities" signifies the right to administer these institutions.

One could also ask about the wisdom of retaining the expression "where numbers warrant" in conveying the right to minority language instruction. As the saying goes, "How many sheep does it take to form a flock?" Now, after four years of application, one must pose the following question: "Does it really make sense to include in the Constitution the concept of 'where numbers warrant'?" It is a question we must ask, in view of the problems of francophones outside Quebec.

Furthermore, these improvements to Section 23 could only benefit Quebec's anglophone community. Clearly, the problems encountered by francophones outside Quebec are not identical to those of Quebec's anglophones. However, we wish to ensure Quebec anglophones of their language rights. These rights must naturally be seen within the context of the francophone character of Quebec society and the Government's firm desire to ensure its full development.

Conclusion

Quebec's future is within Canada. This is the profound conviction of the immense majority of Quebecers just as it is the prime, fundamental commitment of this government. We believe in Canadian federalism because, within the federal system, Quebec can be faithful to its history and its unique identity while enjoying favourable conditions for its full economic, social and cultural development.

Stating our full, complete belonging to Quebec and Canada means also that we state with the greatest possible emphasis, our keen regret and feeling of helplessness about what occurred at the time of the patriation of the constitution.

As Quebecers and as Canadians, we cannot accept the fact that important amendments to our country's constitution were made without us and, in some respects, contrary to Quebec's historic rights. This is why Quebec's new government and the population of Quebec, in the interests of Quebec and Canada, would like matters to be corrected. Mention has been made of signing "with honour". Certainly, this is what we want: we are asking for the respect of the dignity and pride of the people of Quebec and respect of the province's historic rights. "With enthusiasm" – this too is possible if Quebec is once again made the major partner in the Canadian federation that it had always been.

The election of a Liberal government in Quebec in December 1985 signifies a new era for federal-provincial and interprovincial relations. Faithful to our federalist commitment, we want to guarantee Quebec its rights as a distinct society and major partner in the Canadian federation.

Quebec nationalism is not dead, far from it. It is thriving more than ever but in a different form. It is no longer synonymous with isolationism or xenophobia but rather with excellence. More than ever, we Quebecers, we French Canadians, must recall our history and remember that we owe our survival to the dangers that aroused the sense of daring and excellence in our ancestors.

Our existence as a people and our belonging to the Canadian federation is a challenge to history. Faithful to our history and confident in our future, Quebec intends to devote its efforts to continuing to meet this challenge and, within Canada, to make Quebec a modern, just and dynamic society.

III

ISSUES

5 TAX REFORM AND THE FEDERATION

Ian Stewart

Complex social systems, like complex machinery, provide abundant evidence when they are not working well. Unlike their physical counterparts, however, they give less conclusive evidence of imminent breakdown. Even when there is consensus that their malfunctioning requires address, their ministering political and social-scientific witch-doctors are less likely to agree to a common diagnosis and prescription than their mechanical engineering counterparts. But anyone who owns an appliance or drives an automobile will recognize that not even the cost-benefit analysis of mechanical engineers yields an easy and certain answer to the question of minor repair versus major overhaul or replacement. Only time can reveal whether to have been penny-wise is to have been pound-foolish.

Few Canadians, one suspects, would dispute the evidence, though they might lay varying emphasis on aspects of it, that our tax and related social welfare systems are malfunctioning. Judged against the traditional criteria of fairness (equity and neutrality), efficiency and ease of payment, and ease of understanding, the system is assailed on all fronts. Judged against two emerging and urgent criteria - contribution to economic growth and the managing of fiscal deficits - few believe that the system serves us either efficiently or effectively. And yet, until perhaps very recently, there has been less readiness to contemplate reform in Canada than is evident among many other industrial countries. Canadians have seemed to prefer the doctoring of parts rather than fundamental redesign and replacement.

A measure of this lack of interest in reform is to be found in the recent Royal Commission on the Economic Union and Development Prospects for Canada (The Macdonald Commission).[1] Only three and one-half pages of the Commission's report itself[2] are devoted to the tax system and, of the massive research underlying the report, only three papers forming parts of larger research volumes directly address issues of tax reform.[3] It must be conceded, however, that apart from the trade issue a deeply reforming zeal is absent from the Commission report in general, as it appears to be absent in Canadian society at large. Whether best thought of as a drift toward neo-conservatism, or more simply as a reaction to a decade and a half of economic strain, Canadians appear to have "shifted their involvements"[4] to private preoccupations away from the pursuit of reform agendas.

Nonetheless, recent developments make it seem likely that tax reform may yet ascend the national stage. At midsummer 1986, the publication of two important federal white papers seemed imminent: one addressing quite fundamental reform of the manufacturer's sales tax; the other, further Federal government proposals for the repair of the corporate income tax. Perhaps more dramatically, and to the astonishment of supporters and critics alike, radical base-broadening, rate reducing, tax expenditure curbing reform of the U.S. personal and corporate income tax systems seems remarkably close to achievement. If only because of competitive pressures, and not because of any robust embracing of the principles involved, it seems likely that personal tax reform, as well, must soon again preoccupy us in Canada. Increasingly editors and journalists sound the call. And even the "infamous" 1981 MacEachen budget enjoys a latter-day reprieve.[5] All of these developments persuaded Mr. Wilson, the Minister of Finance, at a late July press conference, to announce delay of the proposed white papers, and to request of the Department of Finance a survey of more comprehensive reform.

One purpose of this essay is to survey the grounds for reform and assess the issues in this emerging debate.

A second purpose is to recognize the "centrality of federalism and intergovernmental relations" to processes of reform in Canada.[6] While the workings of fiscal federalism have been subjected to intense review and scrutiny, attention has primarily been directed to the major transfer programs, equalization and the Established Programs, and to the economic union issues – impediments to the free flow of goods, capital, labour and technique.[7] Little direct attention has been paid to the tax system as a system of federalism and to the interdependence and integration issues that reside within it.

With exceptions, the tax system in Canada has reflected a strong degree of integration, with the federal government and the provinces assessing tax against a common personal and corporate base. The principal differences have existed in the sales tax field: the provinces have levied retail sales taxes while the federal government has relied on the manufacturer's sales tax and excise duties. However, in the modern age, integration or "harmonization" is losing its musical connotation of the pleasing association of parts, and is increasingly employed to imply the elimination of difference. Much of the case of those opposed to the U.S.-Canada free trade initiative and indeed, of those concerned with a world driven by competitive technological, market and exchange imperatives, resides in a fear of excessive harmonization. Indeed, the heart of federalist debate in Canada has always concerned itself with seeking a balance of centralist and decentralist forces – fears of excessive centralization or harmonization weighed against fears of "balkanization". The difficulties of tax reform, no matter how modest, are therefore magnified in our federal system. Radical tax reform and the advent of a federal value-added tax – the business transfer tax (particularly if it is to be applicable to the retail level) – will raise new issues of concertation and/or conflict.

This essay will address these matters and then, in conclusion, explore the relationship of tax reform with yet another task force report anticipated from the Department of Finance in 1987 on the reform of the country's social welfare system. It will be argued that the Macdonald Commission's failure to fundamentally address tax reform issues flawed its exploration of a guaranteed income for Canadians.

Tax Reform

It will be useful to distinguish the more pressing short-term or conjunctural, and for many the more urgent and persuasive, from the more systemic and philosophical reasons for believing that "the irresistible logic of tax reform" will have its day in Canada.[8] In a curious sense, it will be revealed, many of the issues ought not to divide left and right, though reform itself and the structure of its outcomes must inevitably invite differences of view and disrupt the status quo.

The Conjunctural

The conjunctural issues converge around four broad questions. What are the appropriate policy responses to the structural transformations in the world that have occurred with such dramatic consequences through the seventies and eighties? What are the available routes to the repair of government deficits and the seemingly inexorable rise in debt/GNP ratios which these shocks have left in their wake? What will be the necessary competitive response to a sharp revolution in taxation philosophy in the U.S.? And finally, but perhaps more controversially, what structure of policies might make the Canadian economy less vulnerable to a re-emergence of the inflation disease and with the least political, social and economic cost?

The traumas of the seventies and eighties may be characterized as the consequence of three sets of forces.[9]

The first set of forces combines all of the influences that are structural in character. It can be argued that each alone would have made the world seem less lodged on a permanent plateau of prosperity than the fifties and sixties. Combining and commingling in timing and incidence in the early seventies they proved massively disrupting. They included the real consequences of the first energy shock, which fundamentally altered the structure of input prices upon which much of post-war economic growth had been built; the emergence of new technologies based upon micro-electronics and microbiology; the emergence of new competitive sources for many of the world's raw materials; the emergence of a group of newly developing countries able to import the technologies of the industrial world and employ them with relatively highly-skilled but low-cost labour; and the rapid decolonization of the world leading to an explosion of sovereign principalities, which greatly compounded the difficulties of world economic concertation and management.

The second set of forces involved the need of industrial countries to manage and adjust to these structural forces while, at the same time, contending with an indigenous inflationary disease that had emerged through the sixties but had been gravely aggravated both by the structural shocks and by the coincident world boom of the early seventies as it lurched against capacity constraints. By the mid-seventies inadequate economic performance, continuing inflation, and the gradual movement of world monetary and fiscal forces towards restraint combined to breed stagflation. The sharp tightening of monetary policies in the early eighties in response to the inflationary impulse from the second energy shock converted stagflation to outright recession. Though most industrial, and many of the newly developing countries have recovered beyond their pre-recession peaks, the recession has left an apparently intractable legacy of high unemployment, fiscal deficits and world debt. The world appears "stranded on a frustrating plateau without adequate dynamic forces either in Canada or in the international economy to carry us to a satisfactory level of employment."[10]

The third set of forces comprises the varied reactions to government and the welfare state which have been bred by the first two. General dissatisfaction with the growth of government and disappointment with the policies of the welfare state are, of course, widespread. Reaction has flowed not only from the political and economic right, those who had never been disposed to accept the "neoclassical synthesis" of neoclassical microeconomics with Keynesian macroeconomics, but also from the old left who, with their traditional vulnerability to guilt, believe that interventionist policies and too avid a pursuit of full employment and income redistribution may, indeed, have winged the golden goose. The apparent productivity collapse circa 1974 in all industrial countries has been employed as evidence by those who believe that some measure of the blame for inadequate performance could be ascribed to the structure of policies in industrial countries themselves. Privatization, deregulation, a concern for efficiency rather than equity, and a reliance on private markets became the creed of a revived political and economic liberalism.

These three sets of forces have had a singular impact on Canada. The rentier benefits of a resource-rich nation have been eroded both by a steep decline in the terms of trade and by a steady erosion of monopoly advantages across the whole range of Canada's resource exports. The sudden reversal of the so-called energy revolution has, in turn, eroded advantages that were beginning to accrue to Canada, and particularly the western provinces, as a net energy exporter. Despite the recent sturdiness of manufacturing industry in central Canada, fears remain about Canada's capacity and disposition to remain competitive in a race driven by technological imperatives. For reasons that are beyond this essay fully to explore, Canada has displayed a rather more virulent form of the inflation disease than many of its competitors, and little apparent consensus appears in the country with respect to the directions Canadians would have their governments follow or themselves pursue.

It would be too much to claim that there has yet emerged a consensual interpretation of all these developments. Evidence that the productivity collapse is a statistical illusion brought about by the strong cyclical and structural forces at play contests with interpretations which doubt Canada's capacity to adapt easily to a world in which resource riches have less importance and in which technological inventiveness, innovation and dispersion make the ecological virtues of diversity, mobility and adaptability the determining elements in economic fortune.[11] Nor has there yet emerged in Canada a clearly dominant ideology between those who would rely on giving market forces full play and those who would rely on a more deliberately planned and contrived economic advance. The diversity of view which surrounds the U.S. free trade initiative reflects, at least in part, this irresolution.

Few, however, would contest the notion that the world has become a more competitive place in its trade in goods, raw materials and manufactures, and in the increasing importance of services. Whether one takes a more or less extreme view of Canada's prospects, there can be less tolerance for economic inefficiency. The huge distortions brought about by our present tax system must be major candidates for repair. Investment decisions and personal spending and saving decisions yield vastly different orderings when their rates of return are measured on a pre- or post-tax basis. There is scant evidence that the thirty to forty billion dollars of tax expenditure at the federal level in the personal, corporate and sales tax fields yield net economic benefits to the nation at all commensurate with their cost. In an anti-interventionist age with broad public distrust of governments' capacity to direct resources in the interest of economic growth, the hidden distortions brought about by the tax system must be as deserving of scrutiny as the more visible use of expenditure, law and regulation.

Nor can there be much doubt that the deeply entrenched fiscal deficits spawned by the past decade must find their repair through scrutiny of both sides of governments' budgets. The most focussed criticism of the Conservative government's address to this issue has been directed at the degree to which tax increases rather than absolute expenditure reductions have been employed. It is perhaps more critical that these increases have been structured on top (via surtaxes, etc.) of an unrationalized and unreformed system.[12]

While this structure of argument thus responds to the first two of our questions – the role of tax reform in addressing growth and deficit anxieties – the imperative for reform is only strengthened by the impending tax reform revolution in the U.S.. Aside from the need to respond to its likely impacts upon personal and corporate behaviour and competitiveness in Canada, what must command political attention is the degree to which the proposed reforms have a broad spectrum of public support, even among corporate communities which will bear heavier imposts as a result. It is as if the wide recognition of the complexities, non-neutralities and inequities of the U.S. systems has created a collective will for reform that invokes the better judgment even of those communities who will benefit little directly, or even experience some disadvantage. The prospect that less time, resources and innovative energy will be devoted to tax-motivated acts and to the tax planning and advising industries may turn out to be the seat of the most productivity enhancing impact of all.

These last considerations form a bridge from the conjunctural to what I have called the more systemic or philosophical reasons for believing that tax reform must ascend the Canadian agenda. Before attending to them, I will note only briefly, since the argument is developed more fully elsewhere, that the lack of palpable equity in the personal tax system (both horizontally and vertically – among those of equal capacity and between those of differing capacities to pay) may seriously exacerbate the restless quarrel over income shares which marks every industrial society[13] To the degree it does so, inequity becomes an important contributor to an endogenous inflationary momentum, or put the other way, an important element in the calculation of slack which must be maintained if inflationary forces are to be contained. If the disappointing performance of the last decade and one-half reflects the gradual turning, particularly of monetary authorities, to the fight against inflation rather than the management of structural change, then the contribution of the tax system to distributive imbalances and share quarrels becomes an important "conjunctural" reason for seeing important gains from reform.

The Philosophical

Modern public finance theory divides the responsibilities of government into the public household functions of efficiency, equity, stability and growth.[14] Concern for efficiency and growth lay emphasis upon the allocative benefits of greater neutrality in the tax system. The stress on the neutrality aspects of fairness also reflects a rightward swing in popular political temper and a greater disposition to lay faith in the allocative disciplines of the market. Excessive concern with the equity aspects of fairness on the part of governments is seen by many as at least a contributor to inadequate economic performance if not at the root of our present difficulties.

For the Royal Commission on Taxation (the Carter Commission), however, equity became the single most important criterion around which reform must be constructed.[15] "Unless the allocation of the burden is fair, the social and political fabric of a country is weakened and can be destroyed .... Should the burden be thought to be shared inequitably, taxpayers will seek means to evade their taxes .... When honesty is dismissed as stupidity, self-assessment by taxpayers would be impossible and the cost of enforcement high."[16]

The descent from Carter to the government's 1969 White Paper response, to the 1972 reform legislation, and the festooning of the tax system with expensive and complex incentives in virtually all succeeding budgets, has left Canadians with a tax system marked by vertical and horizontal inequity. With a nominal federal corporate tax rate of 36 per cent, the corporate system has for some time yielded less than 20 per cent of profits on average with vastly different rates among firms and industries. Within the personal system, the differential advantages offered to saving and to property forms of income have tilted the system against those who draw their income principally from wages and salaries, with again astonishing ranges of horizontal and vertical difference among reporting individuals.[17] The restless distemper with the system that has resulted, the explosive growth of the tax planning and avoidance industries, and the growth of the "cash" or underground economy are all evidence of a society with a diminishing sense of shared purpose in financing public purpose. Individual taxpayers increasingly march to the letter rather than the spirit of the law and few would respond easily to

Oliver Wendell Holmes who said "I do not mind paying taxes for we purchase civilization with our taxes." In short, inequity and complexity (and inadequacy of yield) may be as deep systemic crises as the efficiency and growth costs of non-neutrality.

No particular venality can be assigned to the citizenry or short-sightedness to governments. Economic theory has provided broad streams of rationalization for the use of the tax system as a prescriptive and proscriptive device. One stream arises from the recognition of economies and diseconomies external to the firm where social benefits not privately appropriable, or costs not born by their originator, lead to the under-supply or over-supply of goods and services. Much of the rationalization for government intervention in the modern micro economy has grown from the legitimation of the role of taxes and subsidies in correcting departures from a competitive optimum brought about by the workings of externalities.

Infant industry defences of government intervention together with a belief in internal economies of scale, together with a virulent international competition in subsidizing industrial location and trade, have led to a further range and sanction of tax-financed initiatives. This has become particularly so in recent years as nations, constrained in the explicit use of tariffs and quotas, nonetheless have sought to export unemployment through the internal use of a complex range of subsidy and tax incentive. Broad classes of industrial structure (such as "small business") or type of business (such as manufacturing) have become the permanent recipients of differential tax advantage. More recently, the high risks attached to fundamental research and development and the belief that fortune will attach to those who lead in technological innovation have become important sources of pressure on governments to lodge additional structures of incentive in the personal, corporate and sales tax fields. In Canada, the Scientific Research Tax Credit, introduced in the 1983 budget, has become important evidence of the vulnerability of a system used in this way.

In industries such as agriculture, programs born of the legitimate aim to stabilize inherently unstable flows of income have become embedded as complex layers of subsidy through price and expenditure supports and differential tax advantage.

Just as generalized and specific investment incentives have found justification in economic theory so too has persistent fear of undersaving. This, among other reasons, has led to the advocacy of expenditure-based rather than income-based taxation, a development that we shall examine in the next section. In the meantime the personal tax system has increasingly offered differential reward to saving and to forms of income derived from saving which, whatever their immediate justification, have been a major contributor to a reduction in progressivity and a perception of unfair burden-sharing.

Somewhat apart from the rationalizations of economic theory, the tax system has been employed as a device for supporting a range of socio-political ends. Support to cultural industries, charities and political parties are examples. But explicitly outside the positive structures of economics, the tax system has been used in an effort to redistribute income as part of the elaboration of the structures of the welfare state. Progressivity itself, old-age and child benefits, incentives to education, training and health and other exemptions and credits interact with expenditure programmes in influencing patterns of income and wealth distribution and access to public services.

Attention to the particular rationalizations for tax intervention have tended to dominate consideration of the case of extreme positive externalities. Such extreme externalities form the core of the defense of state activities since they define a category of goods whose provision must be financed collectively if full public benefits are to be realized. Older examples of public goods, as they are called, include defence, policing, and provision of public amenity. More recent examples would embrace fresh air, water and the general quality of physical and human environments. More for some means no less for others, but all must share in the costs of assuring their provision. Trust in the tax system, as in the rule of law, has the character of a public good. Sustaining that trust demands both public recognition of its social value and the collective will to act in ways that preserve it.

Whatever influence the proliferation of tax-sheltering devices has had upon repairing market failures, directing effort and resources, and altering distributional outcomes, it has done so at the cost of foregone revenues, enormous complexity and wide differences in tax burdens. The essential nexus between the provision and the financing of public goods and services has been obscured. Quite apart from inevitable disagreement over the bill of goods being financed, complexity and the lack of transparent equity threatens not only the self-assessment system but precisely the weakening of the socio-political fabric through the loss of trust which came to concern the Carter Commission.

In short, rationalizations for government expenditure and tax intervention which emanate from many streams of contemporary economics have sponsored the evolution of the present tax system. This system is in conflict with one which might have flowed from a stream laying greater emphasis upon the provision and financing of collective goods and of the public good character of the tax system itself. While giving support to the enormous expansion in the role and functions of government, the present system has both obscured and diminished

117

support for collective purposes, diminished respect for government itself, and eroded any individual or collective sense of responsibility for paying the bills. Indeed, licenced by the apparent support of authority and law, minimizing one's tax burden rather than any notion of community burden-sharing has become the contemporary ethic.

This view of matters is, of course, not uncontroversial. Collective definition of what are or what ought to be public goods and collective consensus on how they are to be provided and financed comes close to the heart of contemporary controversy in economics and public choice theory. In its support, Hirsch provides a profound analysis of the erosion of collective purpose and of the capacity to recognize and serve collective needs under the influence of excessive preoccupation with individual maximization and choice.[18] Boulding assails contemporary economics for its single-minded preoccupation with exchange and lack of attention to the role of grants.[19] Grants span the spectrum from voluntary to coerced but have no *quid pro quo*, or at least none that is explicit and direct. The more they are voluntary, the more they spring from motives which recognize collective purpose and need. The more they must be coerced, the more they take the form of tribute. Taxes are grants and the degree of their voluntariness is the measure of a society's capacity to agree on collective purposes and needs, and to concur in the collective means by which they will be served and provided.

On the other hand, however, contemporary economic theory, in its reversion to a formal neo-classicism, tends to underplay the importance, if not the existence, of extreme divergences between private and social costs and benefits, and hence the importance of public goods.[20] This lack of interest, together with the liberal drift in political disposition and the general public disesteem of government, has diverted attention from the problems surrounding the identification and provision of public goods. Not surprisingly, the public good character of the tax system itself has not dominated, indeed has been little recognized, as a characteristic likely to be eroded by the system's excessive use as an incentive and privileging device.

Furthermore, the emergence of public choice theory with its assumption of a narrow self-interest underlying the motives and actions of politicians and public servants, has cast further doubt on the capacity of the state to intermediate in the process of identifying and seeking to finance public goods and services[21] Again, not surprisingly, attention and a seeming legitimacy has been directed to the mechanisms of tax burden minimization rather than sharing.

Issues in Tax Reform

While the more philosophical argument for fundamental reform would, therefore, not go unchallenged, there would nonetheless seem to be rather powerful political, economic and social reasons for reform that is: base-broadening (that is, relatively free of tax expenditure and embracing as broad a definition as possible of the flows and stocks to be taxed); neutral in an efficiency sense; equitable in the sense of being perceived as fair by the community; and with as low average and marginal rates in both the personal and corporate systems as base-broadening can provide.

But should the government be persuaded of reform with such radical intent, Finance Minister Wilson will find himself confronted by a lengthy set of further issues about which reasonable persons may differ and upon which no science can throw definitive light. They concern such issues as the meaning to be attached to the notion of equity; the appropriate bases to be taxed; the appropriate distribution of burden between major components of the system – personal and corporate income taxes and consumption taxes; the role of wealth taxation; a host of more technical issues; and what attention to give to issues of transition, recognizing that any reform must disrupt tax planning, create winners and losers, and differentially benefit present or future asset owners. Only the principal among these issues can be surveyed here.[22]

For the Carter Commission, several principles were clear. The preferred and (in time) the only tax should be the personal income tax. Income should be subject to the widest possible definition including gifts and inheritances. Tax rates should be progressive based on ability to pay or "economic power". The corporate tax should be retained for only two purposes: to prevent undue deferral of personal tax; and to tax income accruing to foreign owners.

All of these principles are now the subject of some contention. The notion of consumption or expenditure has come to contend with income as the appropriate tax base. There has been a general retreat from the taxation of wealth and, presumably, from the acceptance of a definition of income which includes wealth transfers. The notion of the "flat tax" or proportional tax is advocated in opposition to highly progressive structures. And, at least in the U.S., the low prospective personal and corporate rates have been achieved by broadening both bases, the corporate even more than the personal.

The growing advocacy of a consumption or expenditure base rather than an income base rests principally on three considerations. The first is the acknowledged difficulty of measuring flows of income from capital adequately or appropriately in an income base. A consumption tax would, of course, make the effort unnecessary. Second, under the influence both of growing alarm about the sturdiness of the savings-investment process through the 1970s and a desire to promote private provision for future income needs, most income taxation systems in the industrial world moved to differentially advantage savings and hence to move in a consumption tax direction. Third, under the influence of neo-conservative and "supply-side" theorizing, there may be said to have been a growing political conviction that savers "ought" to enjoy relative advantage.

"Supply-side" influences relate as well to the advocacy of flat marginal rates over progressive systems. Most consumption tax advocates recognize that, since savings would be untaxed, more rather than less steeply graduated marginal rates would be required on expenditure both for revenue and equity reasons.[23] But this advocacy conflicts with those who, purportedly in the interests of economic growth, would see virtue in a combination of both flat marginal rates and untaxed savings.

Without either sharply progressive rates in an expenditure tax system or a progressive income tax, one could expect wealth disparities arising from accumulated savings to grow over time. This tendency to wealth disparity would be exacerbated if inheritances remain excluded from the base, if the current lifetime exemption of $250,000 of taxable capital gains remains in force, and if the federal government and the provinces continue to eschew estate and succession duties. While there has been a general drift away from wealth taxation around the world, Canada is one of the leaders among OECD nations in levying the lowest imposts against stocks of wealth.[24] Particularly with the U.S. reverting to a proposed full taxation of long-term capital gains, it is doubtful if a perception of fairness could be sustained if the entire matter of wealth taxation were not addressed in a reform package.

Perhaps next in importance is the intended reform of the manufacturer's sales tax. While Mr. Wilson's intention to reform what has become a very bad tax has received wide support, the structure, role and philosophy underlying the proposed business transfer tax is still unknown. Presumably it is to be a broad-based tax extending to all value-added in the economy and not just manufacturing activity. If extended to retail activity it will compete, though perhaps not visibly, with provincial sales tax regimes. This possibility will be examined further when we come to examine the federalism aspects of tax reform. Such a value-added or business transfer tax is in most respects an alternate version of an expenditure tax and as such raises important questions about its relative role in the Canadian tax system. As with all sales taxes, it will be flat-rated and proportional to expenditure, but regressive with respect to income. Mr. Wilson took the first step in his 1986 budget to seek to alter this regressivity by the introduction of a refundable tax credit which would offset the sales tax obligations of those with low incomes. But sales taxes remain regressive through the middle income range and a refundable credit with the reach to alter this outcome would become increasingly expensive in terms of foregone income. This in turn raises the question of what revenue reliance is to be put upon the remodeled business transfer tax. It is potentially, because of its reach, a major revenue raiser. Fears have been expressed that it could come to rival the personal income tax in the government's arsenal and lessen the imperative of personal tax reform. But it is presumably because so many of the issues which surround the business transfer tax impinge on the larger questions of reform that Mr. Wilson has, for the moment, held back the promised white paper while these interrelationships are more carefully addressed.

A number of issues, critical to any reform agenda, can only be touched upon here. Distortions and unfairness arise from the expensing for tax purposes of interest on borrowings to finance tax-preferred flows of income or assets, personal or corporate, all made more advantageous when inflation rates are high. This practice has come to be called tax arbitrage and as such "the most critical issue of tax reform facing us today."[25] The relative burden to be put on the personal and corporate systems and the relationships between the reform of each will be critical. The relatively low personal rates which have emerged in the proposed U.S. reform have been made possible by the revenue gained from the elimination of important tax expenditures in the corporate system, in particular the investment tax credit. The treatment of inflation and the degree to which proposed reforms are inflation-proof will be an important element in determining the sturdiness of a reformed system. Many more technical issues, with interests committed in favour and against reform, must be confronted.

Should the federal government opt for radical rather than incremental reform, perhaps the most critical factor in the outcome will be the manner in which transitional issues are handled. Quite apart from the relative favours it dispenses, a system laden with tax expenditures creates a history and a set of plans and expectations all licensed by apparent legal inducement and entitlement. Radical reform would make major changes in the rules of the game. Not only would there be winners and losers, and quite disparate judgments on the efficacy of any reform proposed, but it would be almost impossible to escape the charge of retrospective and prospective change that offends against vested right. This sense of offense can be mollified by careful attention to issues of grandfathering and transition that extinguishes right and entitlement over a reasonable period.

But in the end radical reform must have its appeal against the status quo, or any more incremental transition from the status quo, by the imminence of its regime of transparent neutrality and equity, and by the assurance that its horizontal and vertical structuring can resist future incursion or erosion. Too prolonged a transition can cloud that perception and weaken the economic and ethical appeal of the reform itself. It is clear that the American reform process has arrived at its present juncture through the recognition that radical reform is an elaborately constructed house of cards, a house that can transform itself to brick if allowed to stand, but which is entirely vulnerable to the careless tampering with any card that violates its structure.

Tax Reform and the Federation

While the formal process of U.S. reform has proceeded independently of the States, it is inconceivable that comprehensive reform could proceed in Canada without intensive consultation with, and indeed the substantial agreement of, the provinces. There are at least three reasons for this. First, despite occasional worries about tax disharmony in the context of debates on the quality of the economic union, the existing degree of integration between federal and provincial tax systems is, perhaps, more remarkable than its absence.[26] Second, the degree to which this "harmonization" ought to be preserved or even enhanced must be a central reform issue in its own right. Third, while these considerations apply equally to the personal and corporate systems, the potential arrival of the business transfer tax raises particular issues of the degree of integration to be sought with provincial sales tax regimes.

Under the Federal-Provincial Fiscal Arrangements Act, the federal government administers and collects income taxes for any province which agrees to accept the federal definition of the relevant tax base. In all but three provinces, Quebec, Ontario and Alberta, this is the case for the corporate income tax. Only Quebec has opted out of the federal personal tax system. In all cases the provinces have generally moved to follow federal changes and maintain their definitions of the tax bases in conformity with the federal definition. The system of allocating corporate profits to province of origin has not been a source of contention nor have there been threats of double-taxation as in the use of unitized tax systems which have recently vexed the U.S..[27] All provinces who subscribe to the tax collection agreements have the right to make requests of the federal Minister of Finance that the federal government collect (or forego), on their behalf, specific taxes or incentive arrangements. While refusal by the federal Minister on the grounds of violence to principle or too great violence to base definition has, at times, been a source of some contention, enough requests have been accepted to provide the system with some flexibility. Though there has been some tendency for requests to grow, and periodic consideration by some provinces of the virtue of opting out, the remarkable thing has been the degree to which both systems have remained substantially integrated.

It is for this reason that even modest initiatives by the federal government require careful examination for their consequence for provincial revenues and the distribution of their effects among provinces. Any budgetary measure which alters the definition of the base will have these effects. This is why the federal government has had so frequent recourse to revenue measures in the form of surtaxes on, or reductions of, federal tax. These measures leave the base definition undisturbed and hence have no impact upon provincial revenues. Comprehensive reform of either the personal or corporate systems, or reform of both in a manner, say, that resulted in revenue neutrality for the federal government overall would be likely to have at least important distributional implications among provinces. If such a reform were also to include a greater reliance on revenues generated by a radically reshaped manufacturer's sales tax, the absolute consequence for the revenues of all provinces would be equally serious. Clearly any reform which was directed to significant base-broadening and rate reshaping would require the full participation of the provinces, if not their full consent.

Such a process would inevitably lead to a reexamination of the virtues and disadvantages of the present substantial degree of harmonization. Indeed, if the process of federal-provincial consultation were to go badly or not be fully engaged, one could expect a substantial goad to disintegration. It has been a contention of this paper that fairness and simplicity are at least as important reasons for contemplating radical reform as any of the reasons arising from conjunctural or U.S competitive reasons. It might therefore be argued that any breakdown in federal-provincial process or any result that set independent provincial systems against a reformed federal system would lose a good deal, through new complexities, that might otherwise be gained from reform. By the same token this is to argue that Canada, on balance, has been well served by the high degree of integration of its taxing systems. Arguments which see merit in a more decentralized, diverse and provincially-independent economic union must contend with the substantial costs in loss of public perception of national goods, services and public purposes and the agreed means of sharing their financing which might be entailed.

Harmonization in the sales tax field has meant the avoidance of co-occupancy. The provinces have come to occupy the retail sales tax while the federal government has employed the relatively invisible manufacturer's sales tax. The proposed federal business transfer tax, if it is to be a comprehensive value-added tax, would disturb this implicit allocation of the field in two major ways. If extended to the retail level, even if relatively invisibly, it would compete with a major source of provincial revenues in a field that the provinces have come to believe, in practice if not in law, is their exclusive preserve. The business transfer tax would also become a powerfully elastic source of federal revenue, so powerful that it might greatly reduce the relative importance of the personal income tax and, for this reason, even displace the will to reform. The provinces, therefore, would seem bound to see a business transfer tax as having major implications for the adequacy and elasticity of their traditional revenue sources. If peace is to be maintained and the larger purposes of reform to be served, the possibility of moving to value-added as well as income tax collection agreements with a harmonized base must be examined. Provincial diversity and need could be served by permitting, as with the income tax, marginal differences in provincial rates once the broad division of the pie had been agreed. In addition, provincial variation in tax credit mechanisms to relieve the regressivity of the business transfer tax could easily be permitted.

While these may seem heady heights to scale in engineering comprehensive reform, it is difficult to see how the large possibilities that lurk in reform can be achieved without provincial agreement and collaboration. The advent of the business transfer tax can act as the goad to such comprehensive reform, or it can become a major force in provoking disintegration and a constitutional struggle to protect provincial revenue sources.

Tax Reform and Reform of the Social Security System

Finally, just a few notes on the relationship of tax reform to the other impending Finance white paper on the reform of the social security system. Many of the same ills afflict the income-support system as afflict the tax system. The system is overly costly and inefficient in directing resources to those it is intended to serve. Its distorting effects upon the allocation of human resources and effort are almost unknowable. Though more obviously progressive in the sense of extending larger benefits to those with lower incomes, its complex patchwork of federal, provincial and municipal expenditure and tax benefits disguises its equitability and lessens public commitment.

124

Reform, driven primarily by the perceived need to conserve resources, confronts at least three major imperatives. Entirely aside from questions about the overall adequacy of Canadian welfare and social security structures, it has become apparent that there are glaring inadequacies in their coverage. Single parent families headed by women, and single or widowed middle-aged women are two rapidly growing groups in distress which present systems serve inadequately, if at all. Simply layering a new programme of benefits on top of present tax and expenditure programmes does not seem a viable alternative. It has long been evident that marginal tax-back rates which approach one-hundred per cent in provincial welfare programmes (principally those jointly funded by Ottawa under the Canada Assistance Plan) actively discourage transitions from welfare to work. Any reformed system must seek to ameliorate this dollar-for-dollar loss of assistance payments for those in transition through training, retraining or part-time work. Finally, the welfare system has fallen into disrepute as much among those who are its recipients as among those who pay taxes in its support. Reform must seek to construct a system which is less dependency-creating, less visible and demeaning in its income-testing mechanisms, and more transparent in its design and purposes.

Arguments such as these, together with the recognition that reform must make better use of the existing and not an expanded pool of resources, have revived interest in guaranteed annual income designs. There is not the space here fully to review these developments. But by integrating the social security system with the tax system by the use of refundable tax credits, such designs assure universality of coverage, progressivity of treatment, and marginal tax-back rates that permit social benefits to flow into low middle-income ranges before they are totally taxed back. One such design has been described by Wolfson.[28] As Wolfson points out, the failure of the Macdonald Commission to adequately take account of the virtues of total tax system integration weakens their proposal for a Universal Income Security Payment.[29]

It should be apparent that there is good argument for considering tax and welfare reform in a single integrated package. Indeed, as has been argued in this paper, issues of public understanding, acceptance and commitment should make such an integration central to both the processes and purposes of reform.

Some Concluding Thoughts

It must be acknowledged that comprehensive reform of the tax and social security systems inevitably raises further reform issues. Aside from the structuring of income guarantees within the tax system, reform which made the sparest possible use of exemptions, deductions and specialized tax credits would compel the more explicit use of the expenditure system to further the particular designs of government. While this implication has always met strong resistance within the business community, it can, of course, be argued that such a reform, in itself, would lead to a more accountable and efficient use of public funds.

Similarly the whole role and structuring of assisted retirement saving plans would need to be examined in the larger context of the long delayed reform of the country's public and private pension arrangements.

The determination to carry out the reform of the U.S. system within the constraint of overall revenue neutrality has probably assisted the reform process. Together with the broadening of tax bases, and despite the shift of relative burden to the corporate tax, it is the primary reason why that reform has been able to cast up striking reductions in corporate as well as personal tax rates. Nonetheless, given the dimension of the U.S. deficit problem and despite the President's resistance, it seems likely that increases in these rates cannot long be postponed. There is a risk that these increases when they come may cast some cloud upon the reform process itself. In the knowledge that U.S. rates must ultimately rise, it is to be hoped that too avid a pursuit of apparent competitiveness with the U.S. system will not lead Canadian authorities to neglect the opportunity for deficit reduction that resides within base-broadening reform.

Critics will argue that reform on the scale suggested in this paper is beyond the capacity or the will of the political process. It can be argued in turn, however, that only radical reform has any chance of being brought to a successful political conclusion. For only if a strong majority of taxpayers can come to recognize that they have a personal stake in the success of the reform process, can it withstand the pressures for retreat which ultimately stampeded the federal government into rejecting the principles and proposals of the Carter Commission. And only radical reform can restore a public commitment to the provision of public services and their financing. Equity, neutrality and ease of understanding may be principles of reform more capable of withstanding the assaults of special interest than any more incremental process. And at the end of the day major reform may offer more dramatic benefits. The "irresistible logic of tax reform" might just create, as it has in the United States, the broad coalition required to see it through.

Notes

1. Royal Commission on the Economic Union and Development Prospects for Canada, Ottawa, 1985.

2. *Ibid.*, Vol. II. pp. 207-209.
3. Anthony F. Sheppard, *Taxation Policy and the Canadian Economic Union*, Research Volume 65 of the Macdonald Commission Studies. Robin W. Boadway and Neil Bruce, *Theoretical Issue in Tax Reform*, Research Volume 26 of the Macdonald Commission Studies. France St-Hilaire and John Whalley, *Reforming Taxes: Some Problems of Implementation*, Research Volume 26 of the Macdonald Commission Studies.
4. Hirschman, Alberta, *Shifting Involvements* (Princeton University Press, 1982).
5. Lead Editorial, *The Globe and Mail*, 25 June 1986.
6. *Canada: The State of the Federation 1985*, Peter M. Leslie, (ed.), (Kingston, Ont: Institute of Intergovernmental Relations, 1985), Preface p. iii.
7. See, for instance:
   Courchene, Thomas J., *Equalization Payments: Past, Present and Future*, (Toronto: Ontario Economic Council 1985).
   Courchene, T.J., Conklin, D.W. and Cook, G.C.A., *Ottawa and the Provinces: The Distribution of Money and Power*, (Toronto: Ontario Economic Council, 1984).
   Mark Krasnick, Editor *Fiscal Federalism*, Research Volume 65, Royal Commission on the Economic Union and Development Prospects for Canada, Ottawa, 1985.
   Royal Commission on the Economic Union and Development Prospects for Canada, Volume III, Ch. 22, Ottawa, 1985.
8. Galper, Harvey and Pechman, Joseph, Forum, Realizing a Decades-Old Dream, The Irresistible Logic of Tax Reform, *The New York Times*, Sunday 11 May 1986.
9. For a more detailed account of this structure of interpretation see my, "Consensus, Flexibility and Equity", in *Canadian Public Policy*, Vol. XII, No. 3, 1986.
10. Bryce, Robert B., *Maturing in Hard Time* (Kingston and Montreal: McGill-Queen's University Press, 1986), Preface p. x.
11. Helliwell, John F., MacGregor, Mary E., and Padmore, Tim, *Economic Growth and Productivity in Canada, 1955-1990*, in Research Volume 22, Royal Commission on the Economic Union and Development Prospects for Canada, Ottawa, 1985.
12. Auld, D.A.L., "Fiscal Philosophy or Political Expediency: The Federal Budget Plan", *Policy Forum on the February 1986 Budget*, (Kingston: John Deutsch Institute for the Study of Economic Policy, 1986).
13. Stewart, *Supra*.

14. See, for instance, Musgrave, Richard A., *Public Finance in Theory and Practice*, (New York: McGraw-Hill, 1984).
15. Royal Commission on Taxation, Ottawa, 1968, Vol. I, Ch. 1.
16. *Ibid.*, Ch. 1, various passages.
17. *Analysis of Federal Tax Expenditure for Individuals*, (Ottawa: Department of Finance, November, 1981).
18. Hirsch, Fred, *The Social Limits to Growth* (Harvard University Press, 1976).
19. Boulding, Kenneth E., *A Preface to Grants Economics* (Praeger Publishers, 1981).
20. Reder, M., "Chicago Economics", *The Journal of Economic Literature*, Vol. XX #1, 1982.
21. For an interesting example of a conclusion which might have been drawn from public choice theorizing see the concluding paragraphs of: Drummond, Ian M., "On Disbelieving the Commissioner's Free-Trade Case", *Canadian Public Policy*, XII Supplement, February, 1986.
22. I am grateful for an unpublished paper by Gordon Bale, "Comparative Reflections on Tax Reform", delivered to a Conference Board conference, June, 1986 for a comprehensive survey of reform issues from which much of the following section is drawn.
23. Boadway, R.W., "Phasing in Tax Reforms", *Policy Forum on the February 1986 Budget* (Kingston: John Deutsch Institute for the Study of Economic Policy, 1986).
24. *A Review of the Taxation of Capital Gains in Canada*, (Ottawa: Department of Finance, 1980).
25. Steuerle, E. "Tax Arbitrage, Inflation, and the Taxation of Interest Payments and Receipts" (1984), *30 Wayne Law Review 991*, p. 1009.
26. The Hon. Allan J. MacEachen, *Federal-Provincial Fiscal Arrangements in the Eighties*, (Ottawa: The Department of Finance, 1981).
27. For a discussion of the concept of unitary income and taxation see Break, George F., *Financing Government in a Federal System*, (Studies of Government Finance, The Brookings Institution, Washington, D.C., 1980).
28. Wolfson, Michael, "Guaranteed Annual Incomes for Canadians", *Policy Options*, Jan/Feb. 1986.
29. Royal Commission on the Economic Union and Development Prospects for Canada, Ottawa, 1985, Vol. II, Part V, Ch. 19.

6 ALL TALK, NO ACTION:
THE TELECOMMUNICATIONS DOSSIER

Richard J. Schultz

Fifteen years ago, a major federal review of the telecommunications sector concluded that "... federal and provincial interests in telecommunications are complementary rather than conflicting, and afford ample opportunity for constrictive cooperation by all governments in Canada."[1] While it does not rank with "peace in our time" or the election of Dewey as President as one of history's major foolish predictions, in Canadian terms it may be close. In the last 15 years, there has been little cooperation, constructive or otherwise; far from being complementary, federal and provincial interests have been sharply divergent and their relations in this sector characterized by uninterrupted conflict. While there has been little progress in resolving disputes there certainly has been a great deal of talk. Seven ministerial conferences, innumerable bilateral meetings, scores of intergovernmental task forces: all this activity with nothing to show for it other than a demonstrable "failure to communicate".

The time for talk, however, has ended although the decision was not taken by ministers and their officials. To the contrary, it has been imposed on them largely because the courts have emerged as a primary player in the intergovernmental system. The politicians have been put on notice that, if they do not act quickly to resolve their differences, the judiciary will impose, if not a final settlement, a radically reduced set of options. This paper reviews the events that have produced this situation and analyzes some of the major alternatives that now confront the intergovernmental negotiators.

Part One: The Industry

Before undertaking such a review and analysis, those characteristics of the telecommunications industry that are politically salient need to be sketched. For our purposes, they are three-fold. The telecommunications industry is diversified, decentralized and integrated.

There are several dimensions to the diversity of the Canadian telecommunications sector. The first is the ownership structure which, as Table 6.1 demonstrates, is highly complex. We have privately-owned, publicly-owned, foreign-owned and joint public-private enterprises. Although Janisch has argued that ownership per se may be "relatively unimportant because of the overriding nature of common telecommunications objectives", this is probably valid only for corporate management.[2] In terms of intergovernmental relations, it is clear that while all provinces have a great deal at stake, those provinces most strenuously opposed to any change in the status quo, particularly change that dilutes their control, are the three prairie provinces that own their own telephone companies. This position has been most clearly articulated by the Saskatchewan Minister of Communications who stated that Sasktel, "... not only has been the engine through which telecommunications services have been made universally available and accessible, but it also has become a prime factor in the economic life of our province as a major employer of our citizens and as a major purchaser of goods and supplies."[3]

Table 6.1
Ownership of Canadian Telecommunications Carriers

Company	Type of Ownership – Principal Shareholder
AGT	Province of Alberta (100%)
Bell Canada	Investor owned (Bell Canada Enterprises - 100%)
B.C. Tel	Foreign investor owned (through subsidiary of GTE of United States – 51%)
CNCP Telecommunications	Joint Venture (Government of Canada through CNR and Canadian Pacific – each party 50%)
"edmonton telephones"	City of Edmonton (100%)
Island Tel	Investor owned (Maritime Tel & Tel – 36%)
MTS	Province of Manitoba (100%)
Maritime Tel & Tel	Investor owned (Bell Canada Enterprises – 36%)
NBTel	Investor owned (Bell Canada Enterprises – 35%)
Newfoundland Telephone	Investor owned (Bell Canada Enterprises – 61%)
Northern Tel	Investor owned (Bell Canada Enterprises – 98%)
NorthwesTel	Government of Canada (through Canadian National Railways – 100%)
Québec Téléphone	Foreign investor owned (through subsidiary of GTE – 55%)
SASK TEL	Province of Saskatchewan (100%)
Télébec Ltée	Investor owned (Bell Canada Enterprises - 100%)
Teleglobe Canada	Government of Canada (100%)
Telesat Canada	Joint Venture (Government of Canada – 50%; approved telecommunications common carriers listed in Schedule 1 of *Telesat Canada Act* – 50%)
Terra Nova Tel	Government of Canada (through Canadian National Railways – 100%)
Thunder Bay Telephone	City of Thunder Bay (100%)

Source: Richard Schultz and Alan Alexandroff, *Economic Regulation and the Federal System*, Royal Commission on the Economic Union and Development Prospects for Canada, Vol. 42, Toronto, University of Toronto Press, 1985, (63-101) Table 3-2, p. 67.

The second dimension of the diversity of the telecommunications industry pertains to the relative size of the individual components. Although there are more than 300 telephone companies and other telecommunications carriers in Canada, 19 companies dominate the industry in that they provide approximately 99 per cent of the services. The details are found in Table 6.2. As can be seen from this table, there are considerable variations. The significance of the size dimensions is that some of the provincial governments perceive the telephone companies operating within their jurisdiction to be highly vulnerable notwithstanding their existing monopoly status.

Table 6.2
1982 Telecommunications Carriage Market by Company

	Total Operating Revenues	Share
	($ millions)	(%)
Bell Canada[a,b]	4.359.3	51.9
B.C. Tel[b]	1.009.4	12.0
AGT[b]	825.3	9.8
CNCP Telecommunications	302.2	3.6
SASK TEL[b]	295.7	3.5
MTS[b]	244.6	2.9
Maritime Tel & Tel[b]	235.9	2.8
NBTel[b]	191.5	2.3
Teleglobe Canada	170.2	2.0
"edmonton telephones"	151.1	1.8
Québec Téléphone	139.6	1.7
Newfoundland Telephone[b]	109.6	1.3
Télébec Ltée	80.9	1.0
Telesat Canada[b]	59.0	0.7
NorthwesTel	48.9	0.6
Terra Nova Tel	33.2	0.4
Island Tel[b]	26.5	0.3
Northern Tel	21.1	0.3
Thunder Bay Telephone	16.0	0.2
Total	8.320.0	99.1

Source: *Ibid.*, Table 3-1, p. 65.
Note: Because of rounding, columns may not add up to the total indicated.
a. Telecommunications operations only.
b. Members of Telecom Canada.

An aspect of this vulnerability involves the third dimension, which can be labelled toll dependency. Although this takes us ahead of our story somewhat, it is no secret that the central political conflict in telecommunications involves the extent to which competition in the provision of long distance telecommunications services is to be permitted in Canada. Such competition threatens the current system of cross-subsidies or "contributions" that long distance services make to local service. Although all telephone companies will feel the impact of such competition, each will not be affected to the same extent. Some of them appear to be more dependent on long distance revenues than others. In 1982, for example, 53 per cent of total operating revenues of all members of Telecom Canada came from long distance rates. Bell Canada was below average (49.5 per cent); for Saskatchewan it was 65 per cent, for Alberta 64 per cent and for Manitoba 59 per cent. Moreover, although no published figures are available, it appears that for some companies, interprovincial toll revenues, the most vulnerable source of revenue, may contribute a very large proportion of the overall toll revenues.[4]

The second central characteristic of the telecommunications sector is its decentralized nature. Indeed, telecommunications may be the most decentralized policy sector in Canada. Each government is exclusively responsible for regulating the telephone companies within its jurisdiction. This means that each government has regulatory authority over the intraprovincial, interprovincial and international rates and services of the companies over which it has jurisdiction. Table 6.3 lists the regulators of the 19 largest companies. It is worth noting that the federal government's jurisdiction extends to 70 per cent of the total telecommunications business in Canada while provincial jurisdiction represents the remaining 30 per cent. It is important to underline, however, the wide variations in provincial jurisdictions. The three prairie provinces and three of the maritime provinces have jurisdiction over 100 per cent of telephone companies operating in their provinces. Newfoundland has jurisdiction over 72 per cent, Quebec over 12 per cent, Ontario over 4 per cent and finally British Columbia over .5 per cent.

Table 6.3
Canadian Telecommunications Carriers and Their Regulators

AGT	Public Utilities Board of Alberta
Bell Canada	Canadian Radio-television and Telecommunications Commission (CRTC)
B.C. Tel	CRTC
CNCP Telecommunications	CRTC
"edmonton telephones"	City of Edmonton
Island Tel	Public Utilities Commission of Prince Edward Island
MTS	Manitoba Public Utilities Board
Maritime Tel & Tel	Nova Scotia Board of Public Commissioners
NBTel	New Brunswick Board of Public Utilities Commissioners
Newfoundland Telephone	Newfoundland Board of Public Utilities Commissioners
Northern Tel	Ontario Telephone Services Commission
NorthwesTel	CRTC
Québec Téléphone	Régie des services publics du Québec
SASK TEL	Saskatchewan Public Utilities Review Commission
Télébec Ltée	Régie des services publics du Québec
Teleglobe Canada	Not regulated
Telesat Canada	CRTC
Terra Nova Tel	CRTC
Thunder Bay Telephone	Ontario Telephone Service Commission

Source: *Ibid.*, Table 3-3, p. 68.

The decentralized nature of regulatory responsibility is significant for several reasons. In the first place, the federal government, notwithstanding the extent of its jurisdiction, is in effect largely a regional, not a national, regulator. It is only a national regulator with respect to CNCP and Telesat which together account for approximately only 4 per cent of the telecommunications market in Canada. Secondly, those provinces with exclusive jurisdiction do not want their authority diluted. Finally, the three provinces with very limited jurisdiction are interested in expanding their influence at least over telecommunications companies within their territories, particularly as telecommunications assumes an enhanced social and economic role.

Given the diversity of ownership and decentralized regulatory systems, the third characteristic of the Canadian telecommunications system may appear to be paradoxical: the almost total integration of the system. This integration occurs at two levels. The most basic is at the level of the subscribers of the public telephone system who are linked to one another wherever they live in Canada. Justice Reed had described this as "pervasive integration" inasmuch as "the same telephone sets, lines, exchanges and microwave networks are used for the provision of local and interprovincial services as well as international ones."[5] The far more important level of integration is systemic. Integration does not occur simply as a consequence of minimal functional collaboration between individual telephone companies. The dominant carriers have, since 1931, recognized their interdependence and made a commitment to develop a shared, collectively managed, national network. Their organization, Telecom Canada (formerly the TransCanada Telephone System), "engages in planning for the construction and operation of the overall network which is comprised of each member's facilities; sets technical standards; establishes terms and conditions under which telecommunications services will be provided by the members; performs a joint marketing function; determines rates; acts as the pivotal entity for negotiating and implementing agreements for the provision of international services; operates a system of revenue sharing...."[6] In short, the Canadian system is a complete national system with a degree of integration comparable to that found in countries served by only one company.

The integration of the Canadian telecommunications system is politically significant because, notwithstanding its pervasiveness, it may be more fragile than is conventionally assumed. It is almost exclusively the work of a very restricted set of actors who shared common premises and objectives. These actors were overwhelmingly corporate, non-political and non-governmental, notwithstanding the participation of the prairie crown corporations. The erosion of shared objectives and/or the emergence of additional actors who demand a role in the system either as service providers or as system decision-makers could easily undermine the system's integration and result in fragmentation.

Part Two: Pressures for Change

Only five years ago, the *Economist* wrote that "once upon a time the world of telecommunications was cosy and boring. Few national leaders paid much attention to it and no political hostess felt her dining table

adorned by the presence of a minister for post and telephones."[7]
Although the impact on dinner parties remains unknown, as the
Economist went on to note, the telecommunications sector is now
anything but cosy and boring. The most constant feature for the past
decade has been change, change that has touched almost every
participant from the largest corporations to the individual residential
subscriber. Stability, continuity and predictability have been replaced by
turbulence, discontinuity and a palpable sense of the unknown. The
result has not only been turmoil for the industry but trauma for political
decision-makers.

It is not necessary, for our purposes, to account at length for this
upheaval.[8] Mention should be made, however, of the single most
important contributing factor, technological change. As a result of
phenomenal advances in microelectronics and the convergence of
communications and computers there are few areas of
telecommunications that have not experienced the impact of the force
of technological change. Switching, transmission and signalling systems
as well as customer premises equipment have all been transformed. The
primary consequences of these changes has been to change radically the
character of the telecommunications market. As a recent American
report noted, technological change has "created alternative ways to
deliver traditional services, expanded the range of new services, and
enabled more firms to enter both the equipment and service
markets...."[9]

While care must be taken to avoid the too easy assumption of
technological determinism, it is undeniable that the "innovation-driven
chaos" now characteristic of the telecommunications sector has brought
into question many of the economic and political choices that have been
the cornerstones of public policy. Most importantly, technological change
has posed a challenge to the traditional premises or principles underlying
the telecommunications system. These have included the concepts of
territorial monopoly and end-to-end-service control for carriers. In
addition, the telephone pricing system which has been based on both
value of service rather than cost of service principles and system-wide
rate averaging has been challenged. It is this pricing system which has
been the cornerstone of the extensive cross-subsidization, or "hidden
welfare system" as I have described it, in telecommunications prices.[10]

The reappraisal of central premises and principles is not a mere
philosophical exercise. The results can be expected to have profound
economic and political implications for federal and provincial
governments as regulators, owners of telecommunications carriers and
as policy-makers. The most predictable outcome will be the unravelling
and replacing of historic relationships between telephone companies and

their subscribers as well as among the constituent members of the telecommunications industry and associated sectors. Such a result can only lead to intense political turmoil at many levels: carrier-subscriber, carrier-carrier, interregional and indeed international.

The reason for such turmoil is that the system of cross-subsidization now central to telephone pricing is gravely threatened. Reducing the cross-subsidization now extant would involve a fundamental redistribution of income. One measure of the amounts involved is suggested by Bell Canada which contends that in 1982 non-competitive long distance services subsidized its local services by approximately $1.2 billion. In terms of the impact on residential customers, it is maintained by several sources, including the CRTC, that local rates could easily double, if there was a move to recover fully their economic costs.[11]

The substantive issues involved are essentially two-fold and can be loosely categorized under the headings of social and economic policy. With respect to the former, there is serious concern about the implications of any major change in the pricing system on the availability of basic telephone service. Canada has perhaps the most universally available service with 98 per cent of Canadians having access to a telephone. The comparable American figure is 92 per cent. The fear is that increasing basic rates to reflect their costs may place an undue burden on the poor, the elderly and the unemployed. For governments generally, the concern is that in a period of great financial restraint, they may be called upon to undertake a major new subsidy program. For some provincial governments, most notably those in the prairies, the fear is intensified because of their deliberate policy of keeping local rates at the lowest levels in the country. Consequently their subscribers may face the largest increases. What particularly exacerbates their concerns is that there is a significant degree of inter-regional cross-subsidization in the present pricing system which is threatened.

There are major economic policy implications in any significant revision to the pricing system. In particular, our proximity to the United States where the most profound changes have already occurred is already having serious repercussions. Telecommunications costs for corporate users in the United States have been significantly lowered in the past few years. According to a recent federal-provincial study, the magnitude of the Canadian-American differential is of an order of 37 per cent for message toll services, 49 per cent for private line voice rates and 52 per cent for private line data rates[12] This study went on to conclude that the Canadian adaption of U.S. rates "would result in annual telecommunications expenditure reductions for Canadian industry of the order of $675 to $879 million over the 1986-1990 period."[13]

Canadian governments must be concerned about such price differentials for several reasons. The most immediate is that they can create incentives for Canadian users to attempt to bypass the Canadian network and to route their traffic through the United States. Of longer term significance is the effect of inflated telecommunications prices on Canada's overall international competitiveness. Increasingly, economic activities of a wide variety are dependent on telecommunications systems and services. Inflated prices, particularly if they are combined with restricted choice and flexibility for users, will undoubtedly have a negative impact on our competitive performance.

Not surprisingly, as with the social policy concerns, there are significant regional variations, and consequently intergovernmental dimensions, to the economic policy issues. Reducing corporate telecommunications costs can be expected primarily to benefit Ontario and Quebec corporate users. The fear of some provincial governments is that this will further slow economic activity in favour of central Canada to the detriment of the rest. An additional concern arises from the fact that provincial telecommunications companies play a major economic role within their jurisdictions in terms of employment and procurement. As the quotation above from the Saskatchewan Minister of Communications illustrates, these companies are perceived to be pivotal economic actors. As owners or simply as policy-makers, provincial governments fear that this role can be seriously reduced or impaired.

Part Three: The Catalysts

Canadian governments have not been oblivious to the trends in telecommunications and their implications for public policy. In fact the federal government has been internationally acknowledged because as early as 1968 it was the first to "recognize the full range of connections among the various communications and information resources ..." and has been praised for having moved more than any other country "toward a comprehensive communications and information resources policy...."[14] For their part, many of the provinces also demonstrated an early appreciation of the alternative directions the telecommunications sector could follow and how unsettling this could be for their traditional public policies. Yet despite their prescience, neither federal nor provincial governments has been able, over the last two decades to put in place their preferred policy options, although perhaps it could be said that the majority of provincial governments have been somewhat more successful if only because they have been able to slow the rate of change.

Once individual governments began to appreciate the dangers posed by the impending change in telecommunications, the intergovernmental dimension took on a highly enhanced status. Both levels of government recognized that neither could significantly advance its interests without the agreement of the other. Despite their best efforts over 15 years, such an agreement was not forthcoming. Notwithstanding the initial expectations, federal and provincial interests proved to be far more conflicting than complementary. Intergovernmental cooperation was not forthcoming.

An extensive discussion of the intergovernmental conflicts is not necessary for our purposes[15] We will limit ourselves to a statement of the basic positions and an analysis of why agreement was not possible. From the outset, the federal government stressed that the decentralized nature of the telecommunications system was a cause for concern because it did not allow for sufficient recognition of a "national dimension" in telecommunications and impeded the achievements of national objectives. In one of its earliest statements the federal government complained that "there has been little opportunity for expression of the public interest, in a national sense, in the orderly development of telephone systems in Canada."[16] Moreover, the federal government indicated not only that it wanted a much greater say over telecommunications but also the thrust of the public policies it favoured. It suggested that it was predisposed both to the introduction of competition and to lowering the cost of long-distance services. For their part, provincial governments categorically and emphatically rejected the federal government's proposals. Although there was less agreement on the substance of telecommunications policy, the provinces were unanimous in their demand that not only should the federal role not be extended, it should be reduced by the transfer of significant federal powers to provincial governments.

Given these diametrically opposed positions and the lack of willingness of either side to move, the failure of the negotiations over the last 15 years is hardly surprising. Despite all the attempts that were made in that period, it was only in the early months of 1986 that the first signs of possible progress emerged. It is important, however, to realize that if an intergovernmental agreement is forthcoming, it is primarily because external forces have acted as catalysts to produce such an agreement. Without such catalysts, it is entirely possible that the 15 year intergovernmental stalemate would continue.

The first catalyst has been the Canadian Radio-television and Telecommunications Commission (CRTC) which was given jurisdiction for telecommunications in 1976. Immediately upon receipt of its new mandate, the CRTC assumed a very aggressive posture towards telecommunications. It reassessed on its own initiative the premises of traditional regulation and in a series of decisions, without any legislation change to support it, radically revised the interpretation and consequently the substance of federal telecommunications regulation.

Four decisions, in particular, stand out. One was the decision to allow customers in federally-regulated jurisdictions to attach their own equipment to the telephone system.[17] This decision, which effectively adopted the approach followed in the United States by the Federal Communications Commission, in effect signalled the end of the principle that carriers are responsible for end-to-end service. Most provincial governments were opposed to the CRTC's decision because of the fear that it would lead to similar demands within their jurisdiction. This did occur but they have been able, thus far, to resist the pressure in that they have restricted customer attachment essentially to residential extension equipment. They have not extended liberalization to business customers to permit them to attach, as they can in federal jurisdiction, their own private exchange equipment.

The second CRTC decision to importance subjected Bell Canada and B.C. Tel's TransCanada Telephone System rates and practices to regulatory scrutiny.[18] Although initially the CRTC proposed to review a number of issues involving the prices and practices of TCTS members, it backed away from such a comprehensive review when its jurisdiction was challenged and opted to confine itself to those matters pertaining only to Bell Canada and B.C. Tel. Even thus restricted, this was the first time any regulator had entered the regulatory void in which TCTS had existed since its creation in 1931. This initiative caused concern for a number of provincial governments especially when, in its decision, the CRTC ruled that it was unfair to the customers of the two companies to include revenues in the TCTS settlement plan for services which did not employ facilities of other member companies. Consequently, the Commission ordered both companies to renegotiate with the other members of TCTS to exclude revenues generated from services using the facilities of less than two members. This involved traffic both within Canada and between Canada and the United States and Canada and overseas. The rationale underlying the CRTC's decision was that Bell and B.C. Tel were unfairly cross-subsidizing the other members of TCTS.

The two decisions causing the greatest concern for provincial governments were those arising from applications by CNCP to extend competition with Bell Canada and B.C. Tel. The first successful application was for the right to compete in data communications and private voice services.[19] This application was opposed by all three prairie provinces and the four Maritime governments. Their common concern was that, unlike the first two decisions referred to, approval of CNCP's application could have a significant, albeit indirect, impact on the revenues of non-federally regulated telephone companies. They objected as well to the fact that such a major change in the structure of telecommunications was to be made not by elected policy-makers but by an independent regulatory agency.

Provincial opposition was only intensified by the 1983 application by CNCP to provide long distance public voice service. If granted this would lead to full interexchange competition similar to that found in the United States. The first CNCP decision had not had the impact on their revenues that had been feared, in part because CNCP was not as aggressive a competitor as presumed, in part because it was hobbled in its ability to compete by the unwillingness of non-federally regulated companies to grant access equivalent to that obtained from the CRTC. Nevertheless, the provincial governments opposed the 1983 application on the grounds that, if granted, it would lead to a significant erosion of the revenues from the two federally-regulated territories that went into the Telecom Canada Revenue Settlement Plan. Altough the estimates varied, it was suggested that granting the application would lead to an increase in local rates ranging from 4 per cent to 10 per cent in other jurisdictions.[20]

Although the CRTC ruled that granting the CNCP the right to provide an alternative public long distance service in competition with that provided by Bell and B.C. Tel, most provincial governments were not relieved by the decision. CNCP's application was rejected on fairly narrow grounds based primarily on the inadequacy of CNCP's financial plan and the fears that CNCP would not be sustainable if competition was permitted. What troubled provincial governments was that the CRTC endorsed the principle of competition in public long distance service, an endorsement that the Saskatchewan Minister of Communications has described as a "a ticking bomb".[21] Adding to provincial concerns, the CRTC ruled that long distance rates were too high in Canada and ordered a freeze on the contribution that long distance services now make pending a further review of such rates.[22]

Although for more than a decade, provincial governments had considered the CRTC as the greatest threat to their interests, in 1984, a new threat emerged, one that in combination with the CRTC raised the spectre not only of a competitive telecommunications system but one under exclusive federal jurisdiction. The new threat came from the judicial system which hitherto had been an insignificant actor with respect to telecommunications. In the end it was the combination of CRTC and judicial decisions that brought federal and provincial governments back to the bargaining table.

One of the more perplexing aspects of the Canadian telecommunications system is that its decentralized nature does not correspond to the constitutional allocation of jurisdiction for telecommunications. Under section 92(10)(a) the Constitution Act 1867, exclusive provincial jurisdiction over "local works and undertakings" does not extend to "lines of Steam or Other Ships, Railways, Canals, Telegraphs, and other or others of the Provinces, or extending beyond the Limits of the Province. . . ." The one and only major case interpreting this section as it pertains to telecommunications was decided in 1905 when it was held that the federal government had exclusive jurisdiction over Bell Canada because its local and long distance functions did not constitute separate and distinct undertakings for regulatory purposes.

Although the logic of this decision would appear to support a claim by the federal government for exclusive jurisdiction over telecommunications companies, given their integrated nature, no such claim was ever made. For their part the provinces came to assume that they possessed exclusive jurisdiction over the non-federally regulated companies although no attempt was ever made by them to have their jurisdiction confirmed by the courts. In 1980, for example, when Alberta Government Telephones challenged in the courts a CRTC ruling in the TCTS rates and practices hearing, it did not do so on jurisdictional grounds.

It is highly likely that if it had been left to the governments alone, the constitutional "sleeping dogs" would have been let lie. In 1982, the dogs were forcibly awakened, however, as a result of an application to the CRTC by CNCP for an order requiring AGT to interconnect with it on terms similar to those granted with Bell and B.C. Tel. CNCP had not been able to negotiate acceptable interconnection rights with any of the non-federally regulated carriers and decided that individual negotiations with seven jurisdictions "would obviously incur repeated resource expenses, and force a variety of incompatible results." The CRTC application was "to bring this chaos to a head."[23]

When Alberta Government Telephones applied to the Federal Court for a writ of prohibition to prevent the CRTC from proceeding with the application, the constitutional issue was finally before the courts. AGT argued that the CRTC had no jurisdiction because AGT was both a local work and undertaking and, as a provincial crown agent, immune to federal jurisdiction. In her October 1984 decision referred to above, Justice Barbara Reed found that, because of AGT's physical facilities, the range of services it offered and most importantly the nature and quality of its relations with Telecom Canada, "the evidence seems to leave little scope for anything but a conclusion that AGT engages in a significant degree of continuous and regular interprovincial activity, and therefore must be classified as the latter."[24] On the second issue, however, Justice Reed ruled in favour of Alberta, namely that, as a crown agent, AGT was not within federal jurisdiction.

Under the Federal Court decision, all members of Telecom Canada, except AGT, SASK Tel and Manitoba Telephone Systems(MTS), were made subject to CRTC jurisdiction with respect to all their telecommunications services whether intraprovincial, interprovincial or international. Both parties appealed the decision to the Federal Court of Appeal, CNCP on the crown immunity issue and AGT on the jurisdictional question. In December 1985, the Court of Appeal unanimously upheld the decision that AGT was not a local work and undertaking. Furthermore, it also ruled that AGT was not immune from federal jurisdiction because it had stepped outside of its statutory mandate by operating a federal undertaking.[25] This meant that AGT, Sask Tel and MTS joined the other telephone companies subject to CRTC jurisdiction.

Leave to appeal the decision to the Supreme Court of Canada has been granted and the appeal is expected to be heard within the next year. Assuming that the Court of Appeal's decision is upheld and few expect otherwise, the result of the long-delayed and avoided judicial determination of jurisdiction is that the telecommunications system will be radically altered. It will cease to be the highly decentralized system it has been and will be replaced by a tightly centralized system. The CRTC alone will have jurisdiction; its policies on competition, terminal attachment and pricing will apply to all telecommunications companies in Canada.

Part Four: Back to Bargaining

By the fall of 1985, the combined spectres of competition and CRTC regulation were enough to spur federal and provincial ministers to attempt to restart the negotiations. The backdrop to the negotiations had been dramatically changed since the last conference held in 1982. On the one hand, the CRTC appeared to be prepared to permit full competition, if a satisfactory application could be developed, a decision which provincial governments feared would have profound repercussions for the revenues of their telephone companies and consequently subscribers. On the other hand, even if the CRTC did nothing, the provinces were faced with the probability that federal jurisdiction i.e., CRTC policies, could be imposed on the provinces by judicial decision.

For his part, the situation facing the federal Minister of Communications, Marcel Masse, was hardly more satisfying. It is true that he appeared to have all the trump cards in his hand but in fact they were cards he neither wanted nor ones he thought he realistically could play. Moreover, he faced the danger that he might be forced to play them against his own wishes. The new government, after all, had been elected on the pledge of national reconciliation, and it would not help the cause if he imposed a national policy from above. Masse had in fact been warned by his officials in 1985 to avoid any discussion of jurisdiction because it would be "disastrous" – it would permit the provinces to make a common front against the federal government.[26] On the other hand as Cabinet had not yet secured the power to issue policy directives to the CRTC, the danger was that the Commission would take the initiative away from the government. This fear was greatest with respect to telephone pricing issues where the concern was that CRTC actions would trigger another common front against the government, this one joining consumers and provincial governments.

If these problems were not enough to befuddle ministers and their officials in their preparations there were two other matters to add to their burden. In the first place, while the federal minister knew what he wanted to avoid, he had no definite ideas as to the contents of the national policy that he wanted to introduce. It is true that he had articulated a set of four principles to guide the development of policy but work had not gone beyond those very vague and potentially contradictory guidelines.[27] For their part, provinces were not in a much better position. Before the courts had become involved, provincial governments opposed to federal initiatives could insist that they would not agree to any change in their jurisdiction. Now it appeared that change was coming, and provincial agreement or not, the provinces faced a quandary. Some wanted to fight to the end, others wanted to make the best deal they could while others, most notably those with little jurisdiction to lose, were concerned about finally getting a share of the action. In short, given both the judicial decisions and the uneven distributional consequences of CRTC actions and policies, there was no longer any basis for the provincial common front which had characterized telecommunications negotiations since 1972.

It is not surprising, therefore, that at the February 1986 meeting all of the participants adopted a minimalist strategy. No one sought to force any other party into a corner and no one expected the meeting to arrive at any decisions. No participant was disappointed. The impending court decision was almost completely ignored although the Saskatchewan minister insisted that come what may Saskatchewan expected to continue to exercise its jurisdiction. How this was to be done was not explained.[28] If governments could not control the courts, they claimed that they could control the CRTC. Consequently, a great deal of the discussion concentrated on the theme that governments, not regulators, should make policy. Unlike the situation with the courts, participants thought they knew how the CRTC could be brought to heel, namely by policy directive from the government. However, while the principle was endorsed, there was no attempt to be specific about the substantive contents of any possible directive.

The conference participants made little advance on the substantive problems facing them. The only step they made was to accept the four principles advanced by the federal minister but even this was conditional upon adding two more, namely that regional economic development must be a priority and that responsibility for policy development must rest with governments. Aside from this, the primary results were to establish a Committee of Ministers "to maintain progress in developing" telecommunications policy and to proceed with three studies, one on pricing and universality of service, a second on the impact of international competition on the industry and its users and a third on the impact of telecommunications on regional economic development.

By far the most important work to be done is that by the ministerial committee. Its mandate is to focus on "roles and responsibilities", a euphemism for jurisdiction, of the respective governments. This committee met in Vancouver in June of 1986 to consider a report from a task force of officials who had been asked to define the status quo, to describe the basic issues and present the objectives of the governments as well as the options to achieve them. Not surprisingly, the task force focussed primarily on the inter-related issues of telecommunication rates and the introduction of extension of competition. Perhaps the most significant part of the task force's work was its survey of the basic options available to governments. At the June meeting, the ministers, not unexpectedly, rejected three of the four options discussed, the status quo and either exclusive federal or provincial jurisdiction, and ordered the officials to undertake further analysis of the fourth which was labelled "shared jurisdiction". A report from officials is to be the basis for the next intergovernmental ministerial meeting to be held in November 1986.

The fact that ministers will be meeting for the third time in less than eight months suggests that they recognize that if they do not resolve their disagreements, a solution satisfying no one may be imposed on all of them. An additional positive sign is that they are concentrating on the "shared jurisdiction" option. This may be the first significant breakthrough in the lengthy negotiations if it means that the hard-line provinces, namely the three provinces, have conceded that their decade-long intransigence is no longer tenable. By agreeing to focus on the shared jurisdiction option, the prairie governments appear to have accepted that they must move off their insistence on the maintenance of exclusive jurisdiction

However promising these first tentative steps may be, difficult negotiations remain before a satisfactory resolution of this conflict can be achieved. For its part, the federal government can be expected to insist that it must have some authority over those aspects that pertain to the "national dimension" of telecommunications. These include primarily interprovincial and international carrier arrangements, rates and services as well as policies governing competitive services. There is no evidence suggesting any federal desire to regulate intraprovincial rates and services. On their side, provincial demands fall into two categories. Those provinces now with exclusive authority over telecommunications wish to ensure that they do not lose all influence over the most lucrative parts of the industry wich are – the interprovincial toll services. They want to be in a position to protect, as much as they can, the revenue base of their carriers so that they can continue to employ those carriers as instruments for pursuing economic and social policy objectives. For these provinces their greatest fear is that they will be left with responsibility for the high cost area of telecommunications – local telephone service – where the greatest economic and political problems are expected. Although this is undoubtedly a bargaining ploy, those provinces which only regulate but do not own their own carriers have maintained that, rather than be responsible only for intraprovincial services, they would prefer to see the federal government assume complete jurisdiction. The second category of provinces that need to be satisfied consists of those three provinces with no authority over the major carriers within their jurisdiction. They want this changed but share their counterparts' concern about being assigned the high economic and political cost areas.

Although the preceding is admittedly an oversimplification of the positions of the parties in conflict, it is accurate and precise enough for us to advance a major conclusion. A "shared" division of jurisdiction predicated on what Prime Minister Trudeau called the "clear and simple" federal principle will not be acceptable to provincial governments. Such a jurisdictional sharing would assign exclusive responsibility for interprovincial and international activities to the federal government and intraprovincial activities to provincial governments. Any attempt to assign exclusive responsibilities is bound to fail and no doubt should, given the development of the industry. Consequently, it is necessary to develop a system for truly sharing jurisdictions in the broadest sense of that concept.

It would appear, to this observer, that the only way out of the conundrum now facing federal and provincial governments in telecommunications is to develop novel methods which will not divide jurisdiction but bring together, where necessary and appropriate, decision-makers, both political and regulatory. It is thus inevitable that there will be no neat solutions to the problem. Overlapping lines of authority are unavoidable. This will, no doubt, cause some confusion for governments, carriers and users but rather than wasting efforts developing tidy but unworkable solutions, attention must be paid to devising structured systems for managing inevitable confusion and conflicts.

The principal solution to the intergovernmental conflict would appear to be the development of a system of joint boards. Such boards could have jurisdiction for both interprovincial and intraprovincial activities. In fact, the concept of a joint board shared by Quebec and Ontario for the regulation of the intraprovincial aspects of Bell Canada could conceivably satisfy those provinces' demands for a significant role without requiring a breakup of Bell into two companies, Bell Quebec and Bell Ontario. To develop an effective decision-making system centred on joint boards will require both a great deal of original thinking and a willingness to eschew traditional stereotypes. To be successful both in winning intergovernmental support and in regulating a complex industry fraught with political turmoil, intergovernmental negotiators will have to resolve a number of complex issues. These involve the mandates, membership, appointment procedures, and methods of policy direction and appeals.

Conclusion

The coming year will witness major changes in the telecommunications industry in Canada, changes that will both be shaped by and influence the intergovernmental system. For almost two decades governments have not been able to resolve their disputes over either policy or regulatory structures governing the telecommunications sector. Yet the industry has not been as immobilized as the governments. It has gone through dramatic and profound changes which have brought into question traditional relationships and long-standing industry principles and supporting public policies.

In the face of governmental immobility and technological change, other actors have entered the fray. These actors, most notably the courts and the CRTC, threaten to push aside those who claim the authority of political decision-makers and to impose fundamental policy choices on both the industry and the governments. In the past year, ministers appear to have recognized the precariousness of their position and how easily they may be preempted. To regain both the initiative and to reassert their primacy as policy-makers, ministers are now committed to developing a system of sharing jurisdiction amongst governments for telecommunications. To go beyond such a commitment in principle will require both flexibility and ingenuity. Canadian governments are now united in insisting that in telecommunications we must have Canadian solutions to Canadian problems. If governments fail to meet the tests of flexibility and ingenuity, regulators and courts will make the choices for them. This has been the recent American experience.

Notes

1. Department of Communications, *Instant World: A Report on Telecommunications in Canada* (Ottawa: Information Canada, 1971), p. 211.
2. H.N. Janisch, "Telecommunications Ownership and Regulation in Canada: Compatability or Confusion", paper prepared for the 12th Annual Telecommunications Policy Research Conference, Airlie, Virginia, April 1984, p. 13.
3. Gary Lane, Minister of Finance and Communications, "Opening Statement", Federal-Provincial Territorial Conference of Ministers Responsible for Communications, Montreal, 27-28 February 1986, Document 830-216-013, p. 7.
4. Telecom Canada, Statistics 1982.
5. *Re Alberta Government Telephones and Canadian Radio-television and Telecommunications Commission* (1984) 15 D.L.R. (4th), p. 530.
6. *Ibid.*, pp. 530-31.
7. *The Economist*, "The Born Again Technology", 21 August 1981.
8. For a useful overview see W.S. Baer, "Telecommunications Technology in the 1980's" in G.O. Robinson (ed.) *Communications for Tomorrow: Policy Perspectives for the 1980's* (New York: Praeger, 1978).
9. National Telecommunications and Information Administration, "Competition and Benefits Report", November 1985, p. 6.
10. For useful overviews of traditional telecommunications pricing see John R. Meyer *et. al., The Economics of Competition in the Telecommunications Industry* (Cambridge: Oelgeschlager, Gunn & Hain, 1980) esp. chap. 3 and Leland L. Johnson, "Why Local Rates are Rising", *Regulation* July-August 1983. A report to ministers by a Canadian regulatory task force on an "Examination of Telecommunications Pricing and Universality" is to be released in the near future.
11. *Interexchange Competition and Related Issues*, Telecom Decision CRTC 85-19, 29 August 1985, p. 55.
12. D.A. Ford and Associates, "The Impact of International Competition on the Canadian Telecommunications Industry and its Users", September 1986, p. 3.
13. *Ibid.*

14. O.J. Ganley and G.D. Ganley, *To Inform or Control: The New Communications Networks* (New York: McGraw Hill Book Co., 1982) pp. 151-152.

15. For a review see Richard J. Schultz, "Partners in a Game without Masters: Reconstructing the Telecommunications Regulatory System", Robert J. Buchan, *et. al., Telecommunications Regulation and the Constitution* (Montreal: Institute for Research on Public Policy, 1982).

16. Minister of Communications, *Proposals for a Communications Policy for Canada* (Ottawa: Information Canada, 1973), p. 7.

17. *Attachment of Subscriber-Provided Equipment*, Telecom Decision CRTC 82-14, 1982.

18. *Bell Canada, British Columbia Telephone Company and Telesat Canada: Increases and Decreases in Rates for Services and Facilities furnished on a Canada-wide Basis by Members of the Trans-Canada Telephone System, and Related Matters*, Telecom Decision CRTC 81-13, 7 July 1981.

19. *CNCP Telecommunications: Interconnection with Bell Canada*, Telecom Decision CRTC 79-11, 17 May 1979.

20. *Interexchange Competition and Related Issues*, Telecom Decision CRTC 85-19, 29 August 1985 at pp. 14-15.

21. Gary Lane, *op. cit.*, p. 14.

22. CRTC, *ibid.*, p. 68.

23. Joseph S. Schmidt and Ruth M. Corbin, *Telecommunications in Canada: The Regulatory Crisis*, September 1983, p. 220.

24. *Re Alberta Government Telephones ...*, p. 533.

25. *CNCP Telecommunications v. Alberta Government Telephones and the Canadian Radio-television and Telecommunications Commission*, Federal Court of Appeal, 4 December 1985.

26. Department of Communications, "May 1985 Cabinet Document (Draft)", p. 6.

27. Honourable Marcel Masse, "Looking at Telecommunications: The Need for Review". Address to the Electrical and Electronic Manufacturers' Association of Canada, Montebello, Quebec, 20 June 1985. The four principles were "universal access at affordable rates", "technological progress to benefit all Canadians", "maintain international competitiveness" and "a uniquely Canadian approach".

28. Gary Lane, *op. cit.*, p. 8 and p. 12.

7 THE EVOLUTION OF CANADA'S NEW ENERGY POLICY

David C. Hawkes and
Bruce G. Pollard

Introduction

In 1985, the federal government reached two important intergovernmental agreements with the western oil and gas producing provinces and introduced a comprehensive program for frontier exploration and development. Together, these three initiatives erased virtually all remnants of the Trudeau government's much-criticized National Energy Program (NEP), and replaced it with what amounted to a new energy policy. In eastern Canada, the Mulroney government also reached an agreement with the Newfoundland government over offshore resources (the Atlantic Accord).[1]

In this chapter, we trace the replacement of the NEP by the Western Accord, the Natural Gas agreement and the new Frontier Energy policy. In doing so, we examine whether the new energy policy evolved as a response to the changed international economic environment, or whether it was driven by the ideological considerations and policy prescriptions of the new government. We then explore the new-found harmony in energy policy, and how enduring it might be. Is it solely attributable to political will, or the federal government's announced commitment to national reconciliation, or have changed world economic conditions enabled the federal government to achieve its energy policy objectives without provoking regional conflict? We conclude with an examination of the current crisis in the world oil market, and how this affects the role of the federal government in the energy sector.

Although intergovernmental relations are often shaped by the domestic milieu, at other times they are shaped by the international environment. For example, often the best predictor for disruptive – or smooth – federal-provincial relations in the energy sector is the world price of oil. Sharp increases or decreases in the world price – "price shocks" – tend to be disruptive, while price stability often has the opposite effect. During the period of federal-provincial energy negotiations under scrutiny, 1984-1985, stasis existed in energy pricing. We shall argue that this provided the new federal government with a "window of opportunity" to strike a new deal with the producing provinces. In times of stable – and relatively low – petroleum prices, federal and provincial governments do not argue about increasing their respective shares of the economic rents. Instead, they attempt to cooperate and make the necessary adjustments in order to keep the industry healthy. The ideology and policy prescriptions of the Mulroney government, including the deregulation of oil and gas pricing and the "denationalization" of private investment (in response to the Trudeau government's policy of Canadian public ownership), meshed well with the response demanded by the changed international economic situation.

The new energy policy, in particular the Atlantic and Western Accords, has been heralded by the federal government as indicative of a new era in federal-provincial relations. However, the new energy policy may not be the precursor of things to come in Canadian federalism. More likely indicators, in our view, are negotiations on such fronts as fiscal arrangements and regional economic development policy, which are more sensitive to the domestic political and economic environment.

The domestic economic setting in western Canada is bleak, with low commodity prices for oil, gas, wheat, lumber, cattle, and minerals. All of this points to the need for price stability, particularly in the resource sector. Already calls have been heard from segments of the petroleum industry for the re-introduction of government intervention, in the form of a Canadian floor price for oil. The recent and dramatic drop in world petroleum prices does not augur well for harmonious federal-provincial relations in the energy sector.

Background

When the Mulroney government removed federal controls on the domestic price of petroleum in 1985, it was not merely reversing a policy of the Trudeau Liberals. Administered prices had been introduced a quarter of a century earlier, when the Diefenbaker government initiated a National Oil Policy (NOP) in 1961. This policy provided for the division of the Canadian oil market and the establishment of regionally differentiated prices. The market east of the Ottawa Valley received less expensive imported oil, while the more expensive Alberta crude oil went to Ontario and the West. Unlike the period from 1973-1985, the NOP favoured the producing provinces over Ontario. Denied access to lower-priced imported oil, most Ontario consumers had to pay more than the world price.

All this changed in 1973, when action by OPEC (the Organization of Petroleum Exporting Countries, the international oil cartel) led to a dramatic increase in the world price of oil. The price of oil at the refinery gate in Edmonton, which at just $3.00 per barrel in 1972 had been higher than the international oil price, now began to fall below it; average prices of Middle East crude began to rise sharply in 1973. In order to protect Canadian consumers from the large rise in the world oil prices, the federal government moved in the fall of 1973 to freeze the price of domestic oil. Later that year, it announced the end of the regionally differentiated price in favour of a single, "blended" oil price for all Canadians, adjusted only for transportation costs. In effect, a two-price system was maintained for oil, with a domestic price lower than the world price. For more than a decade thereafter this situation persisted, sparking what have been termed the federal-provincial "energy wars".

The situation with respect to natural gas was more complex. Prior to 1975, the price for natural gas in interprovincial trade was determined by negotiation between producers and TransCanada Pipelines, the sole purchaser and carrier of gas into markets east of Alberta. After 1975, the price of Alberta natural gas sold in interprovincial trade was administered under agreements between Alberta and the federal government. Natural gas prices were linked to crude oil prices, in that the price of gas was set at a certain percentage of the price of oil. Until 1980, prices were maintained at approximately 85 per cent of the price of oil, in terms of energy equivalence.

The National Energy Program

The most comprehensive and controversial policy on oil and gas resources was the Trudeau government's National Energy Program (NEP) introduced in 1980. The NEP had three basic objectives:

1. to make Canada self-sufficient in oil by 1990, thus ensuring security of supply;

2. to allow Canadians to participate in the energy industry and to share in the benefits of its expected expansion; and

3. to establish a petroleum pricing and revenue-sharing regime that was fair to all Canadians.[2]

A battery of initiatives was introduced to meet these goals. In order to meet the first, the Petroleum Incentive Program (PIP) was introduced, providing grants to encourage exploration and development by Canadian firms, especially in the frontier and offshore areas (known as the "Canada Lands", since they are owned and controlled by the federal government). Energy conservation and alternative energy measures, such as the "off oil" program, were implemented. To meet the second objective, the government announced a plan for "Canadianizing" up to 50 per cent of oil and gas production by 1990. Firms involved in frontier production had to be 50 per cent Canadian-owned, and the federal government reserved for itself a 25 per cent interest in all existing and future petroleum rights on the Canada Lands (known as the "back-in").

Measures designed to achieve the third objective, "fairness", had the greatest impact on federal-provincial relations. First, the NEP unilaterally imposed a new pricing regime under the Petroleum Administration Act (1975) for oil and gas, which restrained the pace and level of price increases to consumers. A "blended price" (of domestic and imported) oil would never be allowed to exceed 75 per cent of the world price, in order to maintain a competitive advantage for Canadian industry. Second, the federal share of oil and gas revenues was increased through the levying of a number of new taxes. From 1980 to 1983, the federal government would collect $24 billion, approximately 24 per cent of all revenues from oil and gas. Revenue shares were less favourable to the producing provinces. Of the total price of a gallon of gasoline coming from Alberta and sold in Toronto, 22 cents went to the federal government, 22 cents to the Ontario Government, 32 cents to the industry, and 19 cents to the Alberta Government.[3] As an "offset" to the producing provinces, a $4 billion Western Development Fund was announced, although it never came into existence.

Natural gas pricing was also affected by the NEP. In order to encourage the substitution of gas for oil, in keeping with the "off oil" program, the federal government abandoned the practice of setting the price of natural gas at 85 per cent of the price of oil. As a result, the price of gas fell to about 67 per cent of its oil equivalent.

Reaction to the NEP

The reaction of western provincial governments to the NEP was strong and negative. The Government of Alberta charged that one of the taxes introduced in the NEP, the Petroleum and Gas Revenue Tax (PGRT), was a wellhead tax and a "veritable royalty" – a sacrosanct provincial right.[4] Some segments of former Alberta Premier Peter Lougheed's televised address of 30 October 1980 are useful in describing the depth of western reaction to the National Energy Program.

> The federal budget and energy measures...are an outright attempt to take over the resources of this province...more and more decision-making and more and more control will be in the hands of the decision-makers in Ottawa....

> I can only surmise that Mr. Trudeau wants to see control of Alberta's resources essentially in the hands of Ottawa....

> ...they are trying to change the rules because we are winning for a short period of time....[5]

Almost immediately after the introduction of the NEP, the level of industry activity diminished in Alberta and Saskatchewan. Alberta's response was swift and forceful – a series of staged reductions in oil production, and the delay of the Cold Lake and Alsands oil megaprojects.

Pressure from both industry and the public, as well as an increase in the petroleum supply on the world market, forced the federal and Alberta governments back to the bargaining table. In September 1981 a new agreement was reached, although the key principles of the NEP remained intact. In terms of revenue-sharing, the federal government would receive 25.5 per cent, the Alberta government 30.2 per cent, and the industry the balance.[6]

The pricing schedule of both the NEP and the 1981 agreement assumed that oil prices would continue to rise. However, in 1983 the international price began to drop, and since the agreement made no allowance for this possibility, negotiations began anew. An accommodation not to increase the price of oil, as provided under the terms set out in 1981, was reached for the ensuing 18 months, unless there were major fluctuations in the world price. Moreover, the Canadian price would no longer be capped at 75 per cent of the world price unless there was a sharp increase in the latter.

The Western Accord

When the Mulroney government assumed office in 1984, it took three major policy steps to completely dismantle the National Energy Program. Two were in the form of agreements with the provincial governments of Alberta, British Columbia and Saskatchewan. The first, the Western Accord, addressed revenue-sharing and taxing powers with respect to oil in western Canada. The second, the Natural Gas Agreement, dealt with natural gas pricing. The third step was a package of measures with respect to exploration and development in the frontier and offshore regions.

The Western Accord, signed on 28 March 1985, had two prime objectives: to stimulate investment and job creation in the energy sector (through modifying the existing taxation and pricing regime), and to increase the degree of energy security for all Canadians. Free enterprise principles pervaded the Accord.

First and foremost, the Accord provided for the total deregulation of Canadian crude oil pricing and marketing. Its intent, and that of the subsequent natural gas agreement, was to replace prices set by government with prices set by the market. However, federal and provincial governments committed themselves to taking "appropriate measures" if prices escalated rapidly, or if security of supply was threatened.

With respect to revenues, the governments accepted the principle of taxing the industry on the basis of profits rather than gross revenues. A host of federal government oil and gas taxes introduced with the NEP were eliminated or phased out. This included the controversial Petroleum and Gas Revenue Tax (PGRT), which was removed immediately from applying to new production and would be completely phased out by 1989. Other taxes eliminated included: the Petroleum Compensation Charge (PCC), the Incremental Oil Revenue Tax (IORT), the export tax on oil (the Crude Oil Export Charge), and the Canadian Ownership Special Charge (COSC, first levied to help pay for Petro-Canada's acquisition of Petrofina in 1981). In addition, the Natural Gas and Gas Liquids Tax (NGGLT), which had been reset at zero per cent in 1981, was eliminated.

The Petroleum Incentive Program (PIP) was to be phased out as well, although outstanding commitments would be honoured through "grandfathering" provisions. Tax-based incentives, designed to stimulate investment, were to be of general application to the industry, rather than targeted at Canadian firms. The federal government's Canada Lands exploration and development bias was dropped.

The benefits from the changes to the federal tax regime were to flow to the oil and gas industry, and not to provincial government treasuries. The industry was to reinvest the savings in exploration and development, creating more employment. The federal government would monitor industry activity carefully in this regard.

One of the major points of discussion in the negotiations leading toward the Western Accord concerned the timing of the end of the PGRT. As then federal Energy Minister Pat Carney put it, "The big, big question in the negotiations was to ensure that we did not back out of the

156

tax too quickly in the first two years."[7] Provincial governments, spurred on by petroleum industrial interests, wanted the PGRT to be removed immediately. The federal government was not prepared to remove such a large source of revenue at one time. This was especially true given that the federal government was committed to making Petroleum Incentive Payment (PIP) grants until the end of 1987. Roughly half of these are paid for activity in the Scotian Shelf, and the other half for activity in Newfoundland and the Beaufort,[8] so in a sense the revenue from western Canadian production would continue to finance exploration and development outside the region. With the demise of the PGRT and the Canadian Ownership Special Charge, it was estimated that as much as nine billion dollars would be lost in federal revenues during the next four years, although reduced commitments under the PIP program would mean that the net cost of the new policy was substantially less.

The stipulation in the Accord that the provinces were forbidden to increase their revenues (that is, from filling in the "tax room" created by either deregulation or lower federal taxes) meant that the producing provinces had no choice but to lower their royalties. It was the unspoken provincial *quid pro quo* for the elimination of federal taxes. As then federal Energy Minister Pat Carney put it: "We were polite enough not to say that in the agreement, but that's what it means."[9]

The Natural Gas Agreement

In addition to its provisions concerning oil, the Western Accord endorsed the principle of a more flexible and market-oriented pricing mechanism for domestic natural gas. Negotiations for such a pricing regime began almost immediately following the signing of the Western Accord. On 1 November 1985, the energy ministers of the federal and provincial governments of Alberta, Saskatchewan, and British Columbia unveiled an agreement that would facilitate an orderly transition to market pricing for natural gas. It was to commence immediately and would be fully implemented within one year. The price of natural gas would no longer be related to the price of oil.

Under the new agreement, after 1 November 1985, natural gas customers were able to enter into new contracts with gas producers at negotiated prices. Moreover, distributors could enter into direct purchase arrangements at negotiated prices for gas that were incremental to those already committed under existing contracts.

The fear of the Ontario government that Alberta gas could be sold to American buyers at a lower price than to consumers in eastern Canada was also addressed in the agreement. The "Toronto Wholesale Price" floor for all exports was to be replaced with a regional reference price, ensuring "that any Canadian gas sold to the United States will not be priced lower than gas sold to Canadians for similar types of service in the area nearest the export point."[10]

Frontier Energy Policy

The third element of the Mulroney government's new policy on energy was "a new frontier energy policy to provide new petroleum exploration incentives, streamline the regulatory burden, and improve the federal royalty regime for oil and gas companies operating in Canada."[11] The package contained a variety of measures, including legislative changes to ensure that Petro-Canada would henceforth receive no preferential treatment, and a proposed Canada Petroleum Resources Act to replace the more arbitrary powers of the Canada Oil and Gas Act.

Fiscal initiatives involved a new Frontier Royalty Structure, limiting the royalty burden during the early stages of production, and a 25 per cent Investment Royalty Credit, to be applied to eligible frontier exploration costs equal to, or below, $5 million for new exploration wells. The credit is to be applied against royalties otherwise payable within the region. In addition, tax incentives were to replace the cash payments lost with the cancellation of the PIP program. A 25 per cent Exploration Tax Credit is to apply to qualifying expenses in excess of $5 million per well, for wells drilled anywhere in Canada.

Most newsworthy, however, was the elimination of the 25 per cent Crown share, one of the most controversial aspects of the NEP. It had given the Canadian government the right to "back in" to an oil or gas project once development had begun, and to claim 25 per cent ownership.

Canada's New Energy Policy

The Western Accord and the Natural Gas Agreement, together with the new Frontier Energy legislation, form a new energy policy framework for western Canada. However, despite the deliberate effort to dismantle the NEP, then federal Energy Minister Pat Carney maintained: "The Progressive Conservative party has always supported the goals of the NEP – the goals of Opportunity, Fairness and Energy Security."[12] The same apparent objectives, yet very different policies.

Two major differences between the energy policies of the Trudeau and Mulroney governments relate to the role of government in the energy sector, and the priority of "Canadianization" policies. With respect to the first, the Mulroney government accepted that the market-place should set prices for both oil and gas, and that private enterprise should be

158

encouraged to invest in this sector of the Canadian economy. Second, the Mulroney government believed that all private investment should be welcomed, regardless of nationality. Although the frontier development legislation has a 50 per cent Canadian ownership requirement (as did the NEP) for projects that have reached the development (as opposed to exploration) stage, Canadianization goals are a lower priority for the Mulroney government than they had been during the Trudeau years.

How can these different approaches be explained? Part of the answer lies in the different ideological persuasions and attendant policy prescriptions of the Trudeau and Mulroney governments. However, the new energy policy was also a response to dramatic changes in the international economic environment.

Explaining the Policy Change

Energy policy has been the showcase for the government of Brian Mulroney, elected in September 1984, to demonstrate its conciliatory approach to federal-provincial relations. As the Prime Minister reported to the First Ministers' Conference on the Economy, held in Halifax in November 1985:

> More than any other initiative of the federal government, perhaps the new national policy on energy marks the advent of reconciliation among Canadians and our progress toward renewed federalism.[13]

The ability of the Mulroney government to reach agreements with the western producing provinces, without strongly offending other regions in the country, reflects more than the new government's negotiating capabilities and conciliatory approach. The demand and supply of oil and gas in the international market – and the world price – have had important implications for the levels of interregional tension and federal-provincial conflict.

The impact of the international price on intergovernmental relations can be felt in two general ways. First, producing provinces, such as Alberta, favour a high price for their non-renewable resources, whereas consuming provinces, such as Ontario, favour a low price. Least conflictual would be a situation where the world and Canadian prices are fairly stable in a medium range, since falling prices produce a demand for federal price guarantees, while rising prices produce a demand for "protecting the consumer", setting Canadian prices below world levels.

Prior to 1973, domestic oil prices were about $0.50 to $1.00 above world prices. From 1973 to 1981, Canadian prices ranged from $4.00 to

$18.00 below world prices. By 1985, the Canadian and world prices were near par.[14] Throughout most of the 1970s and the early 1980s, the producing provinces argued that the Canadian price, which after 1973 was lower than the world price, should be raised toward the international standard as quickly as possible. In a rather compelling economic argument, they asserted that in an era of oil shortages they could sell all they wanted abroad at the world price. By selling to consumers in Canada at less than world price, the producing provinces were not obtaining full value for their resources, which were non-renewable.

After 1973, the price of oil in Canada increased steadily albeit gradually until 1986. After 1983, domestic increases were accompanied by a decrease in the international price of oil. As a result, the gap between the price in Canada and the world price was greatly diminished. When the federal government agreed with the producing provinces to deregulate the price of oil in 1985 – that is, to move to the world price – it did not result in a significant increase in the Canadian price. There was less objection from (and less impact on) the consuming provinces than there had been when a pricing schedule was developed in the early 1980s.

A second impact of the international situation relates to the absolute level and stability of the world price. If it is high relative to the recent past, and especially if it is expected to escalate further in the future, as it was during the late 1970s, then the value of oil and gas resources increases. The potential benefit of this for both the provincial and the Canadian economies is great, both in terms of increased resource rents and the employment generated by increased exploration activity. Conversely, when the world price of oil falls, the value of the resource decreases, often accompanied by a drop in royalty rates and government revenues. Given the high cost of exploration and development, a decline in these activities is also likely to follow.

Federal-provincial tensions peaked in 1980 at a time when the price of oil was high, and was expected to increase. The biggest issue related to the division of the spoils. The federal government imposed the NEP in order to ensure, in the "national interest", that all regions would share the benefit from the windfall. Tensions largely subsided when the price of oil dropped somewhat and stabilized at mid-range. The decline in exploration and development activity by 1983 was a concern to both federal and provincial governments. Dividing the resource rents was no longer the major issue. As a result, the 1983 talks between the federal and Alberta governments were mostly free from the acrimony that had dominated negotiations three years previously.

In addition, it appeared more urgent to offer incentives to increase the "Canadian" share of the industry when the value of the resources was high, and expected to increase. However, when the price of oil is lower and stable, and industry activity is lower, all investment must be welcomed. This was the situation at the time the Mulroney government assumed the reins of power in 1984. Faith in the market as a price-setting mechanism, in the private sector as the engine of growth, and in welcoming foreign investment were all consistent with the Progressive Conservative government's general approach to the economy. However, it is argued here that international circumstances not only made these principles easier to sell, but perhaps imperative to adopt.

Other circumstances were also propitious in 1985, compared to the current situation. Oil prices were not falling rapidly, as they were to do early in 1986, nor was the petroleum industry in great financial difficulty, as it now is. Central Canadian interests were willing, as well, to see the Canadian price rise somewhat to world levels.

The 1985 energy agreements between the federal government and the three producing provinces ended a quarter-century of regulated pricing for oil and gas in Canada. The governments have opted to let the Canadian price ride the international roller-coaster. The impact of this change on Canadian federalism, and on the interrelationship among the various regions of the country, could be enormous.

The Current Crisis

There is vast surplus capacity in the world oil market. Low cost reserves of oil remain large, and are being depleted very slowly. Oil use was about the same in 1983 as it was in 1970.[15] There is now an absolute shrinkage in oil consumption worldwide. Oil prices, near $30 U.S. per barrel in December of 1985, tumbled to $9.75 U.S. in early April of 1986. By autumn 1986, they hovered in the $14-$16 U.S. range,[16] and at year's end were targeted by OPEC to rise to $18. The world price collapse was the direct result of a decision by OPEC to flood the market, and through this strategy, to recover its world market share. In 1977, OPEC supplied about 65 per cent of the world oil market. By 1985, it supplied only 35 per cent.[17] Although the world consumed 18 per cent less oil in 1985 than in 1977, the non-OPEC nations were producing 33 per cent more.[18] By oversupplying the market and driving the price down, OPEC sought to convince non-OPEC countries to restrict their petroleum output, and thereby maintain a "managed" price.

For the first six months of 1986, OPEC production reached up to three million barrels per day in excess of current consumption, although the cartel agreed to a four million barrel per day cut, temporarily, for September and October.[19] The accord limiting world oil supplies was subsequently extended until the end of the year.[20]

The new oil price crisis has evoked a number of calls for government action. Carl Beigie, chief economist for Dominion Securities Pitfield, advocated in February of 1986 that the federal government set a floor price for oil, in order to ensure that Canadian production is maintained.[21] The Independent Petroleum Association of Canada (IPAC) called for an "interim survival" policy in March, involving the removal of the PGRT and provincial royalty adjustments.[22]

The Government of Alberta responded in April by announcing a $400 million aid program focussed on job maintenance and job creation in the "oil patch".[23] Nor did Alberta Premier Getty dismiss the possibility of a return to government intervention in the market.

> If it's proven to me (that) the floor price or some kind of stabilization is necessary, I couldn't care less what's (been) said in the past."[24]

Saskatchewan Premier Grant Devine went one step further, and advocated a minimum crude oil price.[25]

The Senate energy committee also entered the fray, recommending a temporary floor price of $22 (Can) per barrel for production from conventional fields, loan guarantees for oil projects in the frontier regions, and subsidies for production from conventional regions and the oil sands.[26]

The call by Alberta for a national rescue plan for the troubled petroleum industry was endorsed by the annual Premiers' Conference in August. The Premiers agreed that subsidies might be needed to protect the energy sector, and recognized the need for an income stabilization program for the industry.[27]

The federal government response to the new oil price crisis, although belated, was to eliminate the PGRT, effective 1 October 1986, at an estimated cost to the federal treasury of $1.2 billion.[28] The move, made in early September, was clearly seen as a holding action, perhaps "too little, too late" by the Canadian petroleum industry. Demands to remove the tax grew stronger in July of 1986, when the Alberta Legislature unanimously passed an emergency resolution calling on the federal government to withdraw it.[29]

Following the removal of the PGRT, the Government of Alberta announced a $1.1 billion aid package for the petroleum industry in late October. The package includes reduced royalty rates for oil and gas, royalty holidays to encourage new drilling, a royalty tax credit to help small producers, and the establishment of a Small Producers Assistance Commission. The Commission is to act as an ombudsman, and assist smaller firms renegotiate their debts.[30]

Energy Pricing and Regional Conflict

Energy can be – depending on world prices – one of the most regionally divisive sectors in Canadian public policy. Unevenly distributed throughout the nation, energy resources can have tremendous implications for a region's wealth, economic structure, and position in the federation. The country is clearly divided geographically, and along provincial boundaries, between producers and consumers, whose interests tend to be diametrically opposed.

During the period from 1961 to 1985, the federal government played the role of arbiter among competing regional demands and interests. When oil prices were low, Ontario supported the western energy industry by paying more than the world price. When prices were high, the West subsidized central Canadian manufacturing and individual consumers. With the new energy policy, this is no longer the case.

The impact of falling prices on the producing provinces is already starkly evident. One of the purposes of a "made in Canada" price for oil was to create some stability, in order to mitigate the "boom and bust" cycles of the resource economy. Since Canadian oil prices have now been deregulated, however, there is very little protection against such cycles. The Western Accord provides for government intervention only in the event of major and sudden world price shocks. Although the current decline in price has been welcomed by consumers (and by consuming provinces, such as Ontario), it is having a deleterious effect on the economy of the producing provinces, particularly Alberta. When a region suffers serious economic hardship for a prolonged period, the entire nation may have to pay the cost. This is the case whether the price of oil is so high, relative to rival producers, that it damages the international competitiveness of central Canadian manufacturing, or so low that the producing and potentially-producing regions realize no benefit from their resources.

Conclusion

What the future holds in terms of energy pricing is far from clear, and we are receiving mixed signals on the federal-provincial energy front. On the positive side, the Canada-Nova Scotia Offshore Petroleum Resources Accord was signed on 26 August 1986. The Accord, worth $225 million, replaces an earlier agreement between the province and the former federal Liberal government, and fulfills a federal Conservative election promise to give Nova Scotia a better deal.[31] On the other hand, Alberta Premier Don Getty, in responding to speculation on the price of natural gas once deregulation takes full effect on 1 November 1986, said that

Alberta will ban any "fire sale" prices for its natural gas by refusing to issue export permits.[32]

Calls for a Canadian floor price on oil, particularly strong from smaller explorers and producers in the Canadian petroleum industry, present at least the possibility of a return to government intervention in price-setting.[33] Such a possibility can be expected to provoke a spirited debate. From the perspective of the consuming provinces, one is reminded of a comment made in 1975 by the former Premier of Ontario, William Davis, with respect to the National Oil Policy of 1961.

> For over a decade we paid above the market to support the producing provinces and the oil and gas industry of this nation. [If oil on the world market were priced low again] Ontario again will be asked to serve the national interest by paying higher than world prices to support Canada's petroleum industry and oil producing provinces.[34]

From the perspective of the producing provinces, it brings to mind the West's call for a *quid pro quo* for living with a domestic price substantially lower than the world price. What has happened in recent years is that the federal government has intervened in a major way when the world price is rising (keeping domestic prices significantly below world levels), but has let the market set the price during the downswing. In these circumstances, the producing provinces are skewered both ways.

As a final note, it is interesting to compare the Clark and Mulroney governments on the issue of energy pricing, and on energy policy more generally. On a number of important issues – the Newfoundland offshore and energy pricing and revenue-sharing negotiations with Alberta – the Clark government sided with the hinterland over the heartland, and appeared to be punished because of it. Now we have the Mulroney government pursuing similar policies, and being applauded because of it. In large part, this reflects the difference in economic circumstances between 1979 and 1985. It remains to be seen if, when the economic environment and attendant political dynamics change (as they surely will), the federal government will be forced yet again to fundamentally alter national energy policy.

Notes

1. The Atlantic Accord is described in Bruce G. Pollard, "Newfoundland: Resisting Dependency" in Peter M. Leslie (ed.), *Canada: The State of the Federation 1985* (Kingston: Institute of Intergovernmental Relations, 1985), pp. 91-102.

2. Canada, Energy, Mines and Resource, *The National Energy Program* (Ottawa, October 1980).

3. Transcript of Premier Lougheed's Televised Address to the Province of Alberta, 30 October 1980, p. 4.

4. G.B. Doern and G. Toner, *The Politics of Energy: The Development and Implementation of the NEP* (Toronto: Methuen, 1985), p. 271.

5. *Op. cit.*

6. See S.M. Dunn, *The Year in Review 1981: Intergovernmental Relations in Canada* (Kingston: Institute of Intergovernmental Relations, 1982), p. 129.

7. Transcript of interview with the Honourable Pat Carney on Question Period, CTV Television Network, 29 March 1985, pp. 7-8.

8. *Ibid.* p. 6.

9. Quoted in *The Financial Post*, "High Hopes Ride on Energy Deal", 6 April 1985, p. 2.

10. Section 18 (ii).

11. Government of Canada. "Government Introduces New Frontier Energy Policy". News Release 85/160, 30 October 1985.

12. "Notes for an Address by the Honourable Pat Carney, Minister of Energy, Mines and Resources, to the House of Commons", 30 October 1985, p. 1.

13. Government of Canada, "Progress Report on Federal-Provincial Relations". Prepared for the Annual Conference of First Ministers, Halifax, Nova Scotia, November 1985, p. 16.

14. Data from Ontario Ministry of Energy, *Ontario Energy Review*, June 1979, Figure 32, p. 28; and from "What Oil Price Drop Means" in the *Financial Post*, 1 February 1986, p. 1.

15. E.A. Carmichael and C.M. Herrera (eds.), *Canada's Energy Policy, 1985 and Beyond* (C.D. Howe Institute, October 1984).

16. Data from chart on "Prices Plunge" in the *Halifax Chronicle Herald*, 17 April 1986, p. F1; "Sporadic Crude Oil Futures Prices..." in the *Edmonton Journal*, 2 April 1986, p. F1; "Canada Sees Crude Oil Prices Tumbling Again" in the *Toronto Star*, 18 September 1986, p. E1; and "An OPEC Panel Urges Price Rise to $18 a Barrel" in the *New York Times*, 15 November 1986, p. 1.

17. Data from "OPEC's Sliding Oil Share" in the Toronto *Globe and Mail*, 5 February 1986, p. B1.

18. Data from "Politics of Oil: Why World Prices Collapsed" in the *Ottawa Citizen*, 20 February 1986, p. A9.

19. See "Oil Prices Tumble Near $15 (U.S.)" in the Toronto *Globe and Mail*, 5 February 1986, p. B1 and "Oil Cartel Warns" in the *Toronto Star*, 6 August 1986, p. B1.

20. See "OPEC Members Agree on Pact to Limit Oil Supplies" in Toronto *Globe and Mail*, 22 October 1986, p. B16.
21. See "Set Oil Floor Price, Economist Urges" in the *Montreal Gazette*, 24 February 1986, p. B7.
22. See "Oil Companies Seeking Interim Survival Plan" in the *Edmonton Journal*, 26 March 1986, p. D1.
23. See "$400M Aid Programs Slated for Oil Patch" in the *Edmonton Journal*, 2 April 1986, p. F1.
24. See "Getty Studies Oil Floor Price Idea" in the *Calgary Herald*, 8 April 1986, p. A10.
25. See "Long Term Costs Flow From Cheap Oil" in the Toronto *Globe and Mail*, 9 April 1986, p. B2.
26. See "Senate Report Urges Aid for Oil Firms" in the *Ottawa Citizen*, 26 June 1986, p. D15.
27. See "Premiers Endorse Oil Plan" in the *Calgary Herald*, 12 August 1986, p. A1.
28. See "Oil, Gas Tax Removal to Cost Ottawa $1.2 Billion, Masse Says" in the *Winnipeg Free Press*, 9 September 1986, p. 1.
29. See "Drop Energy Tax, MLAs Tell Ottawa" in the *Edmonton Journal*, 15 July 1986, p. A1.
30. See "Oilpatch Gets $1 Billion Kick-start" in the *Calgary Herald*, 30 October 1986, p. A1.
31. See "Pact to Increase N.S. Revenue from Offshore Oil, Gas" in the Toronto *Globe and Mail*, 27 August 1986, p. A3.
32. See "No Gas Moves East at 'Fire Sale' Price, Getty Vows" in the *Toronto Star*, 10 July 1986, p. E1.
33. See "Some in Oil Industry Seeking Floor Price to Reduce Layoffs" in the Toronto *Globe and Mail*, 29 August 1986. The Small Producers and Explorers Association of Canada, the Canadian Association of Oilwell Drilling Contractors, and the Petroleum Services Association of Canada advocated Canadian floor price schemes.
34. "Statement by the Honourable William G. Davis, Premier of Ontario", First Ministers' Conference, Ottawa, April 1975.

8 FINANCING POST-SECONDARY EDUCATION AND RESEARCH

Ronald L. Watts

Introduction

The period since early 1985 has been marked by a myriad of reports, conferences and hearings concerning federal-provincial financing of post-secondary education and university research in Canada. Three documents have drawn particular attention: a report prepared by Dr. A.W. Johnson for the Secretary of State released on 25 March 1985, the Macdonald Commission report made public in September 1982 which in its second volume included comments and recommendations concerning post-secondary education, and the report of a Study Team on Education and Research prepared for the Task Force on Program Review which was tabled by Deputy Prime Minister Nielsen in the House of Commons on 11 March 1986.[1] The discussion which occurred during this period has demonstrated the continuing and widespread concern relating to the inadequacies of the present financial arrangements by which Ottawa and the provinces support universities and colleges and research. Despite this, governments at both levels have generally displayed little sense of urgency about rectifying the situation. Moreover, the Mulroney government in Ottawa has proceeded in the meantime with action, put into effect by its budget of 26 February 1986, and by Bill C-96 passed in June 1986, to maintain the current financing arrangements but with further measures of constraint. This solution has provoked protests from both provincial governments and from those involved in post-secondary education and research. It has, therefore, been a time of much talk on this subject, but with an outcome showing little or even negative progress.

The discussion of federal-provincial financing of post-secondary education and research has turned around five issues: (1) the need for a national federal-provincial strategy; (2) the appropriate role of the federal government; (3) the inadequacies of the current system of unconditional transfers under the Established Programs Financing (EPF); (4) university research; (5) the fostering of excellence.

The Need for a National Strategy

There has been considerable advocacy of the importance of post-secondary education and research to Canada's future economic development and international competitiveness and hence of the need for the establishment of national objectives and a national strategy which would involve both levels of government jointly. Many voices from the public sector, the corporate sector and the universities have been raised in support of the crucial national importance of post-secondary education and research.[2] They have argued that in an increasingly knowledge-based world, universities and colleges are essential for the full development of the country's most important resources, its human resources, and for the quality of Canadian intellectual life and culture. Furthermore, if Canada is to maintain its place in the even more competitive world of the future and be capable of holding its own internationally, the strengthening of post-secondary education and research is seen as crucial, especially to counteract the ravages of the constraints undergone during the past decade. Hence the call for the federal and provincial governments to end their bickering over their respective roles in financing this sector and to develop jointly a national strategy designed to meet the needs of Canada's longer-run future.

The Appropriate Role of the Federal Government

A closely related second issue has been the effort to identify the appropriate role of the federal government and the nature and level of support it should give to universities and colleges and to university research. Any realistic consideration of "national priorities" relating to post-secondary education and research requires a recognition of the constitutional and political realities, however. Given that education is an acknowledged area of provincial jurisdiction, extensive federal financial involvement in post-secondary education might appear anomalous. But as the Macdonald Commission noted, the great majority of intervenors appearing before on this subject believed that "there was a national role to be played in post-secondary education, and that in consequence, the federal government should be involved."[3] The Commission itself concurred with this view, referring to the variety of ways in which post-secondary education and research were of wider than provincial significance. It is also worth noting that virtually all other contemporary

168

federations have recognized post-secondary education and university research as areas requiring a major federal role.[4]

But mere national importance does not make a subject a federal responsibility, and jurisdiction over educational matters is assigned by Section 93 of the *Constitution Act, 1867*, to the provinces. Does this preclude a legitimate federal role? The answer is that provincial legislative authority in relation to education is not incompatible with a federal role relating to higher education.[5] Many areas which under the Constitution Acts or by convention clearly fall within the federal domain or shared federal-provincial responsibility, such as those relating to the development of the economy and the encouragement of research, are closely related to the basic activities of contemporary universities. Moreover, the federal exercise of its spending power by way of grants or institutional contributions is not prohibited by the Constitution Acts. Thus, there has already developed a long history of a shared interest on the part of the federal and provincial governments in the support of universities and colleges and of research. This shared interest makes effective coordination particularly important between the two levels of government if the universities and colleges are not to be caught repeatedly in the crossfire between governments, as has occurred frequently in recent years in Canada.[6]

But if the federal government has a legitimate shared interest in post-secondary education and research, there remains the question of the appropriate nature and level of its support. At the current time the federal government supports an extensive range of educational and research activities. The Nielsen Task Force Study Team identified some 60 programs totalling $6.6 billion in annual federal expenditures involving in some degree or other virtually every federal department or agency. Of the federal expenditures, the combined tax point and cash transfers under the EPF arrangements totalling $4.5 billion annually represent the major portion, while a further $631 million is devoted to university research and $278 million to student aid.

Although the federal expenditures are extensive, there has been less clarity about the objectives of federal involvement. From time to time, various statements of federal objectives have been made. For instance, in 1975 in response to an OECD review of educational policy in Canada the federal government prepared a document listing federal objectives, and in 1983 the Secretary of State in a document entitled *Support to Education by the Government of Canada* listed ten federal objectives for post-secondary education.[7] These ten objectives were: (1) general support; (2) educational opportunity; (3) mobility; (4) employability; (5) research; (6) official languages in education; (7) Canadian understanding, citizenship and cultural identity; (8) international relations; (9) federal direct schooling; (10) needs of the federal government as an employer. Yet by the admission of the present Secretary of State himself when appearing before the Standing Senate Committee on National Finance in May 1986, "Still we lack consensus on where we should be going and how we should get there ... and I am myself continuing to review the options."[8] Some of this lack of a clear rationale for the role of the federal government in financing post-secondary education and research may be attributed to the fact that in the past the federal-provincial financial arrangements were worked out on behalf of the federal government almost exclusively by representatives of the Ministry of Finance. It has only been within the last half dozen years that other departments, and particularly that of the Secretary of State, have had any involvement in these deliberations, although even now it is the Ministry of Finance which ultimately predominates.

The Inadequacies of the Established Programs Financing (EPF)

A third issue has been the inadequacies of the current EPF arrangements for block transfers of federal funds to the provinces in support of their post-secondary education systems. These shortcomings have led to the consideration of a variety of alternatives. Among the alternatives advanced have been the continuation of the EPF transfers with modifications to their level and allocation, the attaching of specific conditions to the transfers, the replacement of these transfers to the provinces by direct-to-student funding as a way of flowing resources to the institutions, and the phased partial or complete withdrawal of federal financial support for post-secondary education.

Federal support for post-secondary education has gone through a number of distinct stages. Prior to 1951 the federal government had provided direct support for the education of veterans. From 1951 to 1967, Ottawa provided universities with a flat subsidy per student, although because Quebec objected to this direct support, in 1960 some tax room was conceded to Quebec with the proviso that Quebec make additional contributions to its universities at the prevailing rate. In 1967 these direct grants were replaced by transfers to the provinces under the *Federal-Provincial Fiscal Arrangements Act, 1967* by which the federal government met indirectly 50 per cent of the eligible operating costs or alternatively $15 per capita escalated at the rate of growth of the eligible operating costs.[9] In 1977, with the passage of the *Federal-Provincial Fiscal Arrangements and Established Programs Financing Act* yet another major change occurred when the nature of the transfers was radically transformed from the "shared cost" principle to one of unconditional block funding. The block funding was allocated according to provincial populations and made up of a combination of cash and tax-point transfers, the combined entitlement being related to increases in population and Gross National Product rather than to post-secondary education operating costs.

From their inception in 1977 the current EPF arrangements have been a bone of contention. The Johnson, Macdonald Commission and Nielson Task Force Study Team reports all concluded that the EPF arrangements were seriously "flawed."[10] The ongoing conflict between the objectives of increasing provincial fiscal flexibility and maintaining national minimum standards has led to constant bickering between the two levels of government over their respective commitments.[11] The arrangements have not only permitted, but have encouraged, each order of government to blame the other for any apparent deficiency in the level of post-secondary funding. Furthermore, the lack of "visibility" for the federal role and the lack of assurance that increases in federal transfers would find their "unattenuated" way into universities and colleges has made these transfers a recurring target of criticism within Ottawa and seriously weakened the commitment of the federal government to them. The result has been what Johnson has called a serious "malaise" in federal-provincial relations and a failure to establish any coherent and co-ordinated federal-provincial national priorities for higher education.

Despite the widespread agreement on the serious problems inherent in the current EPF arrangements there has been less consensus about appropriate alternatives. The Johnson report proposed a modification of the current scheme which would achieve a greater degree of accountability in the disbursement of federal funds by relating the increases of the transfers to the provinces to the increases in grants made by the provinces to institutions. The federal government would offer to continue to use the present escalator for its post-secondary education transfers (the national growth of GNP, adjusted for population changes in a province), but within this upper limit Ottawa "would respect provincial priorities" by escalating the transfers to each province only by the proportion by which that province increases its grants to universities and colleges. This would, of course, create an "incentive" for provinces to move towards the maximum transfer level.[12] This proposal, predictably, was widely endorsed by members of the academic community including the Association of Universities and Colleges of Canada (AUCC) and the Canadian Association of University Teachers (CAUT), but rejected by the provincial governments as interfering with the setting of provincial priorities and therefore unacceptable.

The Macdonald Commission proposed a more radical change. Its primary objective was to develop a more competitive, dynamic and diversified post-secondary education system in Canada. In order to minimize direct federal intervention in this area of provincial jurisdiction while enabling the achievement of national objectives, it proposed that the cash portion of the EPF transfers to the provinces be replaced by direct-to-student transfers.[13] Coupled with this was a recommendation for the deregulation of fees, the resulting higher fees being met largely by the federal grants to students. Thus, federal funds would in effect flow to the institutions via the students rather than the provincial governments. The proposal aroused immediate strong opposition from students concerned about higher fees, post-secondary institutions anxious about less secure sources of revenue, and provincial governments resentful about the loss of transfers and the resulting diminished scope of provincial financial control over the post-secondary institutions. Moreover, the Johnson report had already drawn attention to the potential political difficulties likely to arise from the differential impact such a change might have upon individual provinces.[14] Despite this widespread lack of enthusiasm for the Macdonald Commission proposals, it is worth noting that in the United States direct-to-student assistance rather than intergovernmental transfers has been a preferred mode of major support by the federal government for post-secondary education.

The Nielsen Task Force Study Team presented four options without stating a clearly preferred choice. The options it outlined were: (1) to continue the present EPF arrangement, possibly with some modifications to the formula; (2) to continue financial support to the provinces for post-secondary education but establish a totally new basis for it by offering conditional transfers tied to specific standards; (3) to provide funds which flow to the institutions by way of the students, such as through a voucher system; (4) to concede that the federal government has no role in post-secondary education and to withdraw in a phased way from financial support for it.[15] The Study Team noted particularly that such a withdrawal could be justified on the grounds that the constitution does not explicitly allocate any responsibility for post-secondary education to the federal government, that the expansive circumstances requiring federal support in the 1950s and 1960s no longer exist, and that that the federal involvement has created tension all along. The fourth option and the rationale given for it aroused the ire of both the universities and the provincial governments who foresaw a major problem in funding post-secondary education adequately if federal funding were to be totally withdrawn.

Support of University Research

The fourth issue on which debate has focussed has been the quality, quantity and direction of research in Canadian universities and the need to accentuate sharply the priority given to such research. Concern about the adequacy of Canada's research effort and the support given to university research has been expressed by a wide range of sources. These have included the Johnson report, the Nielsen Task Force Study Team, the Bovey Commission, a report by the IDEA Corporation, and the business community, and this issue has been a recurring theme in the hearings of the Standing Senate Committee on National Finance during 1985-86.[16] Canada's Gross Expenditure on Research and Development (GERD) in 1984-85 was 1.3 per cent of GNP, well below that of other OECD countries such as the U.S. (2.52), West Germany (2.49), Japan (2.38), Sweden (2.33), France (1.97), and the Netherlands (1.88), and well below the target of 2.5 per cent to which the Progressive Conservatives committed themselves during the 1984 federal election campaign.[17] Moreover, as the Nielsen Task Force Study Team noted, Canada spends less on higher education research than many other countries and is in fact losing ground, as indicated by recent real growth rates (1969 to 1981) in higher education research and development: Sweden 10.3 per cent, Japan 6.8 per cent, West Germany 4.2 per cent, U.S.A. 1.2 per cent, Canada 0.6 per cent.[18] Consequently, there is an apparent urgent need for a shift in governmental priorities towards support of substantially increased university research.

An aspect of this issue which has received particular emphasis has been the need for grants from the federal granting councils in support of university research to cover not only direct costs, as they do at present, but the full indirect costs.[19] At the present time research-intensive universities find the acceptance of research grants which do not include indirect costs an additional burden which serves therefore as a brake on the expansion of university research efforts. The Bovey Commission, Johnson and Macdonald Commission Reports, among others, have drawn particular attention to this acute problem.

Fostering Excellence

A fifth issue to which much discussion has been devoted is that of fostering excellence within Canadian post-secondary education and research through encouraging greater differentiation and competitiveness among institutions and particularly through the development in research of "world class" centres of excellence. Historically, Canadian governments have tended to concentrate upon ensuring that access to post-secondary educational institutions is available to a wide spectrum of Canadians. Funding formulae based largely on enrolments coupled with governmentally restricted fee structures have contributed to a relatively uniform set of universities in Canada by contrast with the highly diversified and differentiated university scene found in the United States. The result in Canada has been a set of institutions of broadly good quality. But in the eyes of many critics there has been a failure to develop a select number of institutions and centres of research and scholarship that would be of the first rank internationally.[20] Consequently, both the Bovey Commission and the Macdonald Commission advocated policy changes (although different ones) that would induce greater competitiveness and differentiation among post-secondary institutions.[21] The Johnson report gave particular attention to the need to foster and develop "world class" centres of excellence in scholarship and research. While this objective has been endorsed by many, some doubts have been expressed about Johnson's specific proposal that the identification of such centres be made by a "blue ribbon" committee named by the federal government and composed of representatives of the public, private and academic sectors.[22] Given the poor track record of efforts to pick winners from the top down, others have argued for the provision of a healthy base for a competitive system complemented by the incentive of generous rewards for those specific centres achieving international excellence in particular fields.

The Talk

The eighteen months from January 1985 to June 1986 have been remarkable for the extensive talk about these issues. There has been an unprecedented number of reports, conferences and hearings about federal and provincial support for post-secondary education and research.

The period began in January 1985 with the release of the report of the Commission on the Future Development of the Universities of Ontario (Chairman, Edmund Bovey), *Options and Futures*. While its primary mandate related to Ontario policies, in a chapter on "Federal-Provincial Co-operation" it pointed to the national importance of the province's universities and urged upon the Ontario government the development of effective federal-provincial co-operation.[23] In a thrust complementary to that of the subsequent Johnson report, the Bovey Commission recommended that Ontario seek an agreement with the federal government whereby the two orders of government would maintain an agreed ratio between the federal transfers and provincial expenditures in support of core funding for university education and research. The Bovey

Commission also emphasized the importance of resource-intensive research and specifically drew attention to the need to provide universities with support for the indirect costs of research, and it favoured a system of incentives for the establishment and support of centres of excellence. Its report also proposed a national income-based contingency loan plan to assist students, federal government assistance for international students, and the establishment of a federal-provincial Standing Council on University Education and Research in Canada. Soon afterwards, in March, the Johnson report prepared for the Secretary of State of Canada was released.[24] It advocated a continued major role for the federal government in support of post-secondary education and research. However, it found fault with the "empty purpose" character of the existing EPF arrangements which had permitted a reduction in the "purely provincial share" of financial support to universities. This trend, it argued, had provided an incentive for federal politicians to restrict EPF/PSE transfers since their expenditure did not appear to be linked in any visible way to the purposes for which the funds were transferred. The alternatives of complete federal withdrawal of the cash transfers or the redirection of an equivalent amount to universal student grants or to research grants were each examined but rejected as not viable. Johnson proposed instead retaining the EPF transfers, but changing the rules to relate them more clearly to their ostensible purpose. Up to the current maxima, transfers would be increased at the rate of increase the provinces themselves chose for increasing grants to universities and colleges, thus providing an incentive for provinces to move their own grants to the level that would bring them the maximum transfer. At the same time, to increase the priority for sponsored university research, Johnson suggested a moderate redirection of funds from the EPF transfers (drawn from reductions in the EPF shares of those provinces where the purely provincial share of post-secondary education support had shrunk particularly sharply) to enable the indirect costs of university research sponsored by the federal granting councils to be met. He also recommended that future appropriations to the granting councils be increased each year by a rate equal to 1.5 times the rate of growth of the GNP. In addition, he advocated the establishment by the federal government of a "blue-ribbon" committee to develop proposals for funding a select number of "world class" centres of excellence. The report received quite a favourable press, especially from the university community. However, it was flatly rejected by the provincial governments. They challenged the figures presented in the report as misrepresenting the facts and were critical of the proposals which would impose constraints upon the provinces.

The spring of 1985 also saw two major conferences on these issues held in Ottawa. In March, at the annual meeting of the AUCC (the collectivity of university presidents, principals and rectors) there was an appeal for a national strategy for post-secondary education and research and for the harmonization of federal and provincial policies relating to universities.[25] Later in the spring, a *Financial Post* – Air Canada conference on financing higher education and university research attended by more than 200 university administrators, faculty members, government officials and business executives focussed its attention upon the issues of accessibility and quality.[26]

May saw three particularly significant developments. On 23 May 1985, the Minister of Finance in presenting the federal budget, announced for the first time the plans of the Mulroney government to introduce reductions in the rate of increase of EPF transfers. Intended as part of the general governmental constraint directed at reducing the serious federal deficit, the moderated rate of increase in EPF transfers starting in 1986-87 was expected to result by 1990 91 in substantial savings to the federal government in the combined transfers for health and post-secondary education. This did not help the climate when on the following day, 24 May, the Secretary of State met with the Council of Ministers of Education. At that meeting the Johnson report came in for heavy criticism and was unanimously rejected by the provincial ministers present as being unacceptable.

A week later on 30 May, the Standing Senate Committee on National Finance issued its *Fifth Report*. The report noted that it had chosen to focus its deliberations on one aspect of the Estimates for 1985-86, specifically the transfer payments to other levels of government and particularly those in support of post-secondary education. The Senate committee identified four issues which had constantly reappeared at its hearings: (1) the nature and level of federal funding; (2) national objectives; (3) the quality, quantity and direction of research; (4) the resulting staffing problems of universities. Because the committee had been able to identify issues but not their solution, it sought and received an order of reference from the Senate to examine further the support of the federal government for post-secondary education and vocational training. As a result, throughout the subsequent year, 1985-86, the committee continued to hold a series of hearings on these subjects.[27]

In September 1985, the long-awaited Macdonald Commission Report appeared. Included in the wide range of subjects considered was a review of governmental policies relating to post-secondary education.[28] The report supported a federal involvement in financing post-secondary education. However, noting the high level of dissatisfaction with the current arrangements expressed at its hearings, the commission argued that Canadian governments at both levels needed to reconsider thoroughly the financing and structure of post-secondary institutions and programs. After a review of options typical of such reports, the commission concluded in favour of the redirection of federal funding towards direct-to-student financing coupled with provincial deregulation of fees. It also advocated the reallocation of a portion of the current EPF transfers to the federal granting councils to enable them to begin to cover the overhead costs of the university research which they sponsor. While the report did refer to some form of cost-matching revision of the EPF transfers as a second-best solution, it argued strongly for its preferred solution as deserving the most serious consideration "in order to create a more competitive, dynamic and diversified system."[29] Nevertheless, these recommendations aroused little enthusiasm among students, university administrators and provincial governments. Some critics even described the proposals as unworkable, despite the working example of such arrangements south of the border where they have been the predominant pattern of federal support for well over a decade. A more telling criticism was that the report gave insufficient emphasis to the importance of university research and development as the key to Canada's future, and that in this respect the commissioners had accurately reflected the ambivalence of the country itself about the importance of this issue.[30]

19-27 October saw not only the celebration of National Universities Week, during which the contribution of the universities to Canadian society was publicly emphasized, but also a call by the university presidents, through the AUCC, for the federal government to ensure the long-term stability and development of university research and to support the proposed five-year plans of the federal granting councils.[31] The same month saw the release of yet another report, this time from the Corporate-Higher Education Forum dealing with the issue of co-operation between the universities and the corporate sector in research and development.[32]

Also in October was a conference convened by the Ontario Economic Council specifically to consider the Johnson report, although the timing of the conference enabled participants to make reference as well to the recently released Macdonald Commission report. At this conference there appeared to be agreement among most of the participants that there were serious problems in Canadian post-secondary education. Canada was in danger of seriously damaging its ability to compete in the new dynamic world environment and to develop its own cultural heritage if it did not improve the nature of its post-secondary education. The prevailing conviction was that a significant share of the blame could be attributed to three factors: the financial arrangements by which the federal government transferred funds intended for this purpose unconditionally to the provinces, the funding formulae the provinces used to support this sector, and the nature and level of support for university research and development.[33] While there was a clear consensus on the need for a major federal government role, there was less universal support for Johnson's preferred solution of modified EPF transfers, little enthusiasm for the Macdonald Commission proposals, and the discussion of a return to a scheme of transfers like those existing before 1977 proved inconclusive. There was more agreement in support of Johnson's proposals regarding research and development, although some reservations were expressed about the effectiveness of the proposed "blue ribbon" advisory committee to identify centres of excellence. Nonetheless, there was overall unanimity that a return to the federal-provincial discussion table on these issues was essential and urgent.

Despite this call, Prime Minister Mulroney at the First Ministers' Conference in Halifax defended the commitment of his government, announced in the May Budget Speech, to begin reducing substantially the rate of increase of transfers to the provinces. He insisted upon the federal government's right to do so unilaterally, and the provinces were simply left protesting. The strength of this protest was to some extent muted, however, by the provincial preoccupation with their role in the prospective free trade negotiations with the United States, and the apparent concessions to the provinces on that issue made at the conference by the Prime Minister.

At the end of 1985 the long-awaited report of the Nova Scotia Royal Commission on Post-Secondary Education made its appearance. While the report was quite naturally concerned primarily with the provincial policies, on federal-provincial co-ordination it strongly supported the Johnson report and urged the Government of Nova Scotia in its negotiations concerning EPF to adopt a position that would result in harmonization of federal and provincial increases in post-secondary education financing.[34] In this respect it took a position very similar to the earlier Bovey Commission in Ontario. At the same time the Nova Scotia Royal Commission raised the spectre of differential fees or quotas for out-of-province students.[35] Noting that Nova Scotia universities enrol disproportionately large numbers of out-of-province students, the report contained recommendations for charges for out-of-province students or out-of-province enrolment quotas. If introduced, these would represent restrictions upon inter-provincial mobility of students which have not hitherto existed on the Canadian scene.

In January 1986, the Council of Ministers of Education of Canada (CMEC) issued a document declaring that federal-provincial discussions should look beyond the unproductive issue of transfer payments which were distracting both levels of government from other areas of common concern relating to post-secondary education. This statement made it clear that the provinces would not budge from their insistence upon the unconditional nature of the EPF transfers.[36]

This was followed in February by the tabling by the Secretary of State of his first annual report to Parliament on the status and extent of federal-provincial support of post-secondary education in Canada, a report required under an amendment to the EPF Act in 1984.[37] The report gave a comprehensive review of federal-provincial spending on post-secondary education and research totalling $9.03 billion and representing 2.1 per cent of GNP. But the report failed to impress the provinces, which claimed that it understated the provincial contributions by some $1.8 billion.

Provincial concerns intensified in February when, in fulfilment of his statement in the May 1985 federal budget, Finance Minister Michael Wilson introduced Bill C-96 to moderate the growth of transfer payments to the provinces under EPF beginning in 1986-87. Soon afterwards, in the budget brought down on 26 February, it was also announced that the base budgets of the federal research granting councils would be held more or less at the 1986-87 levels up to 1990-91. This means that when expected inflation is taken into account there will be a reduction in the funding levels in constant dollars over the five-year period for the core activities of the councils, although up to $315.9 million would be added to the budgets (but not the base budgets) of the three granting councils over the five years to match any private sector contributions to the councils on a one-to-one basis up to a maximum of six per cent of each council's annual budget.[38] The university community has been critical of the announcement not only for the vagueness of the scheme for matching private sector contributions but even more for the reduction in real terms of the base budget of the councils. This will provide support for university research far short of that required to meet the country's research needs or to fulfil the Conservative promises during the 1984 election campaign to take the means necessary to double Canada's research and development spending to 2.5 per cent of GNP.

In March the 300-page Study Team Report on Education and Research for the Nielsen Task Force on Program Review was tabled in the House of Commons.[39] The eleven-member study team was led by Benson Wilson, chairman of the Ontario Manpower Commission and formerly Assistant Deputy Minister of Universities and Colleges of Ontario. The study team reviewed some 60 programs of the federal government costing an estimated total $6.6 billion in 1984-85 aimed directly or indirectly at supporting elementary and secondary school education and education and research in universities and colleges. The report presents a broad range of policy options in relation to federal support for post-secondary education through EPF, for the role of the granting councils in support of university research and for the federal contribution towards student aid. But the report lacks a sense of perspective, perhaps because the study team's original report underwent some subsequent editing by the Task Force itself. Certainly, as published the report never really addresses the issue of national priorities and fails to present any coherent set of specific recommendations on the appropriate future federal role.

The report did note that the $4.5 billion in annual cash and tax transfers to the provinces under the EPF program had been a major source of controversy. The study team reviewed the options of continuing the present EPF arrangement, converting the transfers to conditional form, substituting the flowing of funds to the institutions by way of the students rather than the provinces, and withdrawing federal support for post-secondary education. While it did not come down firmly in support of any one option, the study team did emphasize the flaws in the current EPF arrangements which have encouraged governments at each level to blame the other for failing to meet their commitments. Moreover, by the possible justification it provided for a federal phased withdrawal, and by its statement that "In spite of the heartfelt concern of the academic community, there are no objective measures to prove that the system has been significantly damaged by recent stringency in funding", the study team appeared to provide implicit support for the federal government's announced plans to scale down increases in the EPF transfers.[40] Similarly, with regard to federal support of university research, despite explicitly drawing attention to Canada's dismal showing internationally, the study team inexplicably saw no urgency in the situation and recommended against the level of funding proposed by the granting councils in their five-year plans. The negative character of the report in relation to the role of the federal government was clearest in its discussion of student aid. Here a preferred option was identified. This was to phase out the present joint federal-provincial plan and leave student aid entirely to the provinces, while providing a federal grant to the provinces to assist them. Such a proposal would appear simply to reproduce in this area the defects the study team had previously identified with the general EPF arrangements.

Not surprisingly, the failure of the study team's report to address the urgent issue of national priorities and its generally negative tone to the involvement of the federal government came in for considerable criticism, particularly from the academic community.[41] With the establishment of two new House of Commons committees, the Standing

Committee on the Department of the Secretary of State and the Standing Committee on Research, Science and Technology, both beginning hearings in May on subjects relating to post-secondary education and research including the report of the study team for the Nielsen Task Force, and with the continuing deliberations of the Standing Senate Committee on National Finance, it appeared in mid-1986 that the intense national attention to these issues would go on.

The Action

But while the talk goes on, it appears that in fact the die has already been cast. Two specific actions of the federal government during the first half of 1986, Bill C-96 introduced on 14 February and given final reading late in June after two weeks of debate and a government motion to limit debate, and the federal budget of 26 February, establish basic policies which will shape and constrain the development of post-secondary education and research during the period 1986-87 to 1990-91 and will set the pattern for federal-provincial relations relating to this sector.

Bill C-96 in effect maintains the much criticized EPF transfer arrangements. But it does so with a unilateral federal reduction in the escalator, and this will introduce a strong measure of constraint in the funds available to the provinces to improve support for post-secondary education. Clearly, the Mulroney government has seen the reduction of the national debt as more urgent than the investment of resources in Canada's intellectual capital crucial to national development and international competitiveness.[42] Under Bill C-96, the EPF transfers will continue to be linked to the growth of GNP and to population increases but the escalator has been modified so that beginning in the 1986-87 fiscal year the per capita growth rate will be two percentage points less than under the original 1977 formula. This would reduce the projected annual increase in transfers from 7 per cent to 5 per cent. To ensure, however, that the growth in transfers does not fall below the rate of inflation, there is provision for special additional payments should the inflation rate outstrip the growth in entitlements. As a result of this moderation in the growth of EPF transfers for health care and post-secondary education, the federal government expects to save $2 billion annually by 1990-91 and $6 billion cumulatively over the five year period, of which, taking the specified federal attribution, one-third would relate to post-secondary education. This, indeed, introduces a major new constraint upon the provinces for the next quinquennium. It is true, that, as emphasized by the federal government in its explanation of the bill, even after slowing down the rate of increase, the transfers are still expected to outpace the national inflation rate. But provincial officials have replied with some justification that cost increases in the sectors supported by EPF normally run well ahead of increases in the consumer price index. Moreover, constraint at this time appears to run counter to the many analyses which have pointed to the urgent need for an investment in the improvement of post-secondary education and research if Canada is to be internationally competitive in the future.

The second major action was the announcement in the February 1986 Federal Budget of the pattern of funding for the federal research granting councils for the period 1986-87 to 1990-91. By turning its back upon the five-year plans of these councils and by planning instead to reduce progressively the base budgets of the councils in constant dollar terms (assuming an annual inflation rate of 4 per cent) by a probable 18 per cent over five years, the Mulroney government has imposed a very serious constraint upon them just at a time when this area requires a massive investment to meet the nation's long-run needs. Even with the maximum additional federal and private sector contributions provided for by the new scheme for matching grants, the total federal funding for the three granting councils in constant dollar terms (again assuming an annual inflation rate of 4 per cent) would by 1990-91 have increased by only about 30 per cent from the 1986-87 levels. This hardly provides the massive governmental boost to the nation's research effort which many have argued is required, and it falls far short of the effort needed to double research and development spending as a percentage of GNP from 1.3 per cent to the 2.5 per cent which was pledged during the 1984 election. It is not surprising that the Canadian university community has expressed grave disappointment, as have both the author of the Johnson report and the retiring president of the National Science and Engineering Research Council (NSERC), Dr. Gordon McNabb.[43]

Conclusions: Lament for the Future of the Nation

Despite the widespread and intense discussions occasioned by the variety of reports, conferences and hearings during 1985-86 and the prospect of a continuing review by two House of Commons standing committees and the Standing Senate Committee on National Finance, the continuation of the current arrangements in their basic form but with an added measure of constraint appears to be the pattern set by the Mulroney government for the coming quinquennium. This outcome has major implications concerning the five issues upon which so much of the discussion during the past year and a half has centred.

First, despite all the calls for federal-provincial agreement upon a national strategy for the development of post-secondary education and university research, the two levels of government remain far apart on this issue and no concerted strategy has been developed. It would appear that both levels of government have been more concerned about deficit reduction and protecting their petty prerogatives and short-run interests rather than with the longer-run implications for Canada's intellectual and economic development. Ironically, this has occurred at a time when the ability to compete effectively will be all the more important if freer trade arrangements with the United States come to fruition. By contrast, in the U.S. there has recently been much greater federal and state government appreciation of the importance of post-secondary education and research to national development. During the period 1983-84 to 1985-86 twenty of the U.S. states with a combined population of 99 million have each increased their operating grants to universities by over 20 per cent (six of those states by over 30 per cent) compared with 13.3 per cent for the highest province in Canada.[44] Furthermore, despite severe budgetary cuts the British universities still receive significantly higher grants per student. Changes in the attitude of governments toward post-secondary education and recognition of its crucial national importance seem to be coming much slower in Canada than in many other developed countries and there appears to be little sense of the urgency of the issue. In the process of concentrating upon shorter-run considerations and failing to invest in post-secondary education and research in an energetic and coherent way, Canada may well be mortgaging its future.

With regard to the appropriate role of the federal government in supporting post-secondary education and research, the federal government by its own admission has failed to develop any clear or firm consensus.[45] Indeed, in the light of Bill C-96 and the 1986 Budget, A.W. Johnson has charged that "The government is in the course of vacating its role in the core financing of universities."[46] This is all the more regrettable at a time when some of the provinces have just begun to recognize the need to set up special funds for university excellence and renewal. Examples are Saskatchewan's $125 million University Renewal and Development Fund and the new Ontario government's implementation of some of the Bovey Commission's most important thrusts with the establishment of a $50 million University Excellence Fund supplemented by an additional $74 million for a multi-year faculty renewal program.[47] At a time when the provinces have begun, although only barely, to face up to the urgent needs of post-secondary education and research, the federal government has not only declined a more significant role but has instead imposed further constraints upon the provinces.

It now appears that the EPF arrangements of unconditional block transfers, although much criticized, will continue at least for five more years although on a scale involving further reductions in the escalator from the formula originally established in 1977. Despite the range of alternatives canvassed during the past year and a half, the federal government has chosen not to make any radical or fundamental alteration in the form of these transfers and only to constrain their level. To some extent the provincial governments have brought this further constraint upon themselves by their intransigent opposition to any alternative to the current unconditional block transfers. Given the loss of federal visibility and of federal ability to ensure accountability inherent in this form of transfer, the decline in Ottawa's enthusiasm for these arrangements was to be expected. The easy way out which the Mulroney government has taken has been to maintain the current form of EPF transfers insisted upon by the provinces, but to meet its own critics within Ottawa by constraining the rate at which these transfers will increase. The urgent need to make up Canada's international backwardness in the level of its support for university research has aroused torrents of rhetoric, but there has been little effective response on the part of the federal government. Most of the federal government's efforts have been devoted to focussing what support it gives and to encouraging greater private sector support of university research. In terms of the aggregate level of governmental support for university research, however, Canada's growth rate appears to be doomed to remain well below that of such countries as Sweden, Japan, West Germany and the United States.

With regard to fostering excellence, as the Macdonald Commission found at its hearings, there has been an increasing public recognition and concern about the importance not only of accessibility but of quality in post-secondary education and research. A number of provincial governments, urged on by reports such as that of the Bovey Commission, have begun to establish special funds to foster such a thrust. Nevertheless, there has as yet been no coherent federal-provincial action for the development of centres of national excellence in scholarship and research with support on the scale required to be competitive with the very best internationally.

Thus, for all the talk during 1985-86 about the federal-provincial financing of post-secondary education and university research, it has been a period of negative delivery. What appears to have been lacking in governments at both levels has been any appreciation of the real urgency of these issues for Canada's intellectual and economic future. Indeed, a decade or two hence this period may well come to be looked back upon as a turning point at which Canadian governments at both levels advocated increased internal and international competition but failed to take adequate action to ensure Canada's own ability to compete effectively on the world scene.

Notes

1. A.W. Johnson, *Giving Greater Point and Purpose to the Federal Financing of Post-Secondary Education and Research in Canada* (Johnson Report) (Ottawa: Secretary of State Canada, 1985); *Report of the Royal Commission on the Economic Union and Development Prospects for Canada* (The Macdonald Commission Report) (Ottawa: Minister of Supply and Services Canada, 1985), Vol. II, pp. 741-756, 765-6, 820-822; *Service to the Public: Education and Research* (A Study Team Report to the Task Force on Program Review) (Ottawa: Minister of Supply and Services Canada, 1986).

2. See for instance, The Standing Senate Committee on National Finance Hearings on Federal Support for Post-Secondary Education, *Introductory Remarks for an Appearance by the Secretary of State of Canada* (15/5/86), pp. 3-6; David Vice, President, Northern Telecom Limited, *Post-Secondary Education in Canada: A Capital Investment* (Brief to the Senate Committee on National Finance, Ottawa, 30 January 1986); Gordon McNabb in Senate of Canada, *Proceedings of the Standing Senate Committee on National Finance*, Issue No. 26, Thursday, 21 Nov. 1985, pp. 26: 13-14 and 26A: 2-3; *Service to the Public: Education and Research*, pp. 14-15; R.L. Watts, *Intellectual Development – The Universities' Role in the Nation's Future: A View from Within Canada*, reproduced in Senate of Canada, *Proceedings of the Standing Committee on National Finance* Issue No. 22, October 24, 1985, Appendix "NF-22A".

3. *Report of the Royal Commission on the Economic Union and Development Prospects for Canada*, Vol. II, pp. 741-2. See also the Commission on the Future Development of the Universities of Ontario, *Options and Futures* (Toronto: Ministry of Colleges and Universities of Ontario, 1984), p. 34; Conference of Rectors and Principals of Quebec Universities, *Brief to the Standing Senate Committee on National Finance* (22 May 1986), p. 8; Peter Leslie, "Fiscal transfers for post-secondary education: some comments on the Johnson Report", in Ardeshir Noordeh, (ed.), *Reforming the Financing Arrangements for Post-Secondary Education in Canada* (Toronto: Ontario Economic Council, 1985), pp. 5-7.

4. Watts, *Intellectual Development*, pp. NF22A:12-13.

5. Leslie, *op. cit.*, pp. 8-10; Watts, *op. cit.*, pp. NF22A:10-12.

6. *Report of the Royal Commission on the Economic Union and Development Prospects for Canada*, Vol. II, p. 754. See also A.W. Johnson, *op. cit.*, pp. 3-5; *Service to the Public Education and Research*, p. 15; *Proceedings of the Senate Committee on National Finance*, Issue No. 14, 25 April 1985, p. 14:12; Issue No. 26, 21

November 1985, (McNabb) pp. 26:13-14; Issue No. 42, 17 April 1985 (Anderson) pp. 42:6-7.

7. Peter Leslie, *Canadian Universities: 1980 and Beyond* (Ottawa: Association of Universities and Colleges of Canada, 1980), p. 374; Senate of Canada, Standing Senate Committee on National Finance, *Fifth Report* (Ottawa: 30 May 1985) p. 4.

8. *Introductory Remarks for an Appearance by the Secretary of State of Canada*, p. 11.

9. Newfoundland, P.E.I., and New Brunswick accepted the latter option.

10. Johnson, *Giving Greater Point and Purpose to Federal Financing*, pp. 3-6, 17-19, 22-23; *Report of the Royal Commission on the Economic Union and Development Prospects for Canada*, Vol. II, pp. 742-3, 754; *Service to the Public: Education and Research*, pp. 26-27.

11. These have included disputes over the calculation and attribution of the relative support of the federal and provincial governments. See for instance, in Ardeshir Noordeh, (ed.), *Reforming the Financing Arrangements for Post-Secondary Education in Canada*, the comments of Ardeshir Noordeh, pp. 153-158 and the response of A.W. Johnson, p. 146. For fuller development of a provincial view see Ron McGinley, *The Johnson Report: Some Provincial Government Concerns* (unpublished paper, Ontario Ministry of Treasury and Economics, 1985).

12. Johnson, *Giving Greater Point and Purpose to Federal Financing*, pp. 25-37.

13. *Report of the Royal Commission on the Economic Union and Development Prospects for Canada*, Vol. II, pp. 765-767, 820-822. For comments on this proposal and a suggested variant see Edwin G. West, "The universal student grant option in the federal financing of post-secondary education" in Ardeshir Noordeh, (ed.), *Reforming the Financing Arrangements of Post-Secondary Education in Canada*, pp. 65-81.

14. Johnson, *Giving Greater Point and Purpose to Federal Financing*, pp. 39-44.

15. *Service to the Public: Education and Research*, pp. 17-20, 27-31.

16. Johnson, *Giving Greater Point and Purpose to Federal Financing*, pp. 15-16, 19-20, 28-32, 34-5; *Service to the Public: Education and Research*, pp. 3536; Commission on the Future Development of the Universities of Ontario, *Options and Futures*, pp. 6-8; *University Affairs*, June-July 1985, p. 5; David Vice, *Post-Secondary Education in Canada: A Capital Investment*, Part One, pp. 4-13; Standing Senate Committee on National Finance, *Fifth Report*, pp. 5-6, and *Proceedings*, Issue No. 26, 21 November 1985, Issue No. 36, 13

February 1986. Of particular note is the presentation by Gordon McNabb, *Proceedings*, Issue No. 26, 21 November 1985, Appendix "NF26-A", pp. 26A:13.

17. *Service to the Public: Education and Research*, pp. 35-36.

18. *Ibid.*, p. 36.

19. CFDUO, *Options and Futures*, pp. 26-27, 34; Johnson, *Giving Greater Point and Purpose to the Federal Financing*, pp. viii-ix; *Report of the Royal Commission on the Economic Union and Development Prospects for Canada*, Vol. II, p. 754; *Proceedings of the Standing Senate Committee on National Finance*, Issue No. 26, 21 November 1985, p. 26A:4-5, Issue No. 36, 13 February 1986, p. 36:28; David Vice, *Post-Secondary Education in Canada: A Capital Investment*, Part Two, pp. 16-19.

20. See, for instance, the contributions of George Pedersen, John Evans, and Fraser Mustard in Ardeshir Noordeh, (ed.), *Reforming the Financing Arrangements for Post-Secondary Education*, pp. 29-39; 40-46; 49-61; 134-9.

21. CFDUO, *Options and Futures*, pp. 14-15; *Report of the Royal Commission on the Economic Union and Development Prospects for Canada*, Vol. II, pp. 748, 820.

22. Johnson, *Giving Greater Point and Purpose to the Federal Financing*, pp. 35-37; Ardeshir Noordeh, (ed.), *Reforming the Financing Arrangements for Post-Secondary Education*, pp. 43, 55-60, 136-139; *Proceedings of the Standing Senate Committee on National Finance*, Issue No. 26, 21 November 1985, pp. 26:22-26.

23. CFDUO, *Options and Futures*, pp. 34-35, 43-44.

24. Johnson, *Giving Greater Point and Purpose to the Federal Financing of Post-Secondary Education and Research in Canada*.

25. *University Affairs*, April 1985, pp. 2-3.

26. *University Affairs*, June-July 1985, p. 11.

27. Standing Senate Committee on National Finance, *Fifth Report*, 30 May 1985; *Proceedings of the Standing Senate Committee on National Finance*, Issue No. 22, 24 October 1985, pp. 22:3, 22:5.

28. *Report of the Royal Commission on the Economic Union and Development Prospects for Canada*, Vol. II, pp. 741-756, 765-6, 820-822.

29. *Ibid.*, p. 820.

30. *Proceedings of the Standing Senate Committee on National Finance*, Issue No. 36, 13 February 1986 (J.F. Mustard), p. 36:33.

31. *University Affairs*, November 1985.

32. *Partnership for Growth* (Montreal: Corporate-Higher Education Forum, 1985).

33. Ardeshir Noordeh, (ed.), *Reforming the Financing Arrangements for Post-Secondary Education in Canada*, p. 16. See also pp. 139-141.

34. *Report of the Nova Scotia Royal Commission on Post-Secondary Education* (Halifax: Nova Scotia Government Bookstore, 1985), p. 3-31.

35. *Ibid.*, p. 3-62.

36. *Principles for Interaction: Federal Provincial Relations and Post-Secondary Education in Canada* (Toronto: Council of Ministers of Education, Canada, 1986).

37. *Federal and Provincial Support to Post-Secondary Education in Canada: A Report to Parliament 1984-85* (Ottawa: Secretary of State Canada, 1986). See also *University Affairs*, April 1986, p. 5.

38. *University Affairs*, April 1986, p. 40.

39. *Service to the Public: Education and Research.*

40. *Ibid.*, p. 40.

41. *University Affairs*, May 1986, pp. 2-3.

42. *Introductory Remarks on Bill C-96 by the Minister of State (Finance) before the Standing Senate Committee on National Finance* (Ottawa: Ministry of Finance, 21 May 1986), p. 3.

43. *University Affairs*, April 1986, p. 40; *CAUT Bulletin*, Vol. 33, No. 6, June 1986, p. 5.

44. Canadian Association of University Teachers, *Brief to the Standing Senate Committee on National Finance* (Ottawa: CAUT, April 1986), pp. 13-18. See also *Proceedings of the Standing Senate Committee on National Finance*, Issue No. 26, 21 November 1985 (McNabb), p. 26:13.

45. *Introductory Remarks for an Appearance by the Secretary of State*, p. 11.

46. *CAUT Bulletin*, Vol. 33, No. 6, June 1986, p. 5.

47. *University Affairs*, June-July 1986, p. 7.

9 FEDERALISM AND FREE TRADE

Richard Simeon

Canada-United States trade, former Alberta Premier Peter Lougheed has said, is as important for Canadian federalism as energy or the constitution. Few issues engage historic and continuing regional economic interests more directly. In no other area is there such an obvious tension between the requirements of domestic politics, shaped by the division of powers and the processes of intergovernmental relations, and the imperative of effective Canadian performance in an international arena ever more critical to our economic well-being. The issues raised by free trade go to the heart of the economic constitution of Canadian federalism.

Canadian and American representatives have now launched negotiations with a view to developing a comprehensive Canada-U.S. free trade agreement. Whether or not they will succeed – and if so what the arrangement might look like – remains uncertain. Yet it is clear that federal-provincial relations will have a major effect on the outcome. The key questions concern the role of the provinces in the negotiation, ratification, implementation and enforcement of any bilateral agreement and the interaction of all these with the bilateral negotiations. In the longer run, it seems equally clear that a Canada-U.S. trade agreement could have fundamental implications for the future development of the federal system – just as it does for so many other areas of Canadian public policy. This chapter explores both the shorter and longer run questions in the context of the current negotiations.

Background: Federalism and International Trade

At first glance it might be thought that federalism should hardly be an issue in the conduct of international trade negotiations. After all, the constitution gives the federal government jurisdiction over international and interprovincial trade, including control over tariffs, and the sole authority to negotiate international treaties. More generally, it might be thought, few Canadians would challenge the overall responsibility of the government of Canada for the conduct of Canadian international relationships, or its general responsibility for management of the economy.[1] With few exceptions – such as the Quebec-Ottawa battles over Canadian representation with France and the francophone world – domestic disagreements are expected to stop at the border. Canada, it is argued, must speak with one voice abroad.

Such a traditional image of responsibility for international relations does not apply in the present case, for a wide variety of reasons. The first reason is constitutional. The dominant view is that only the federal government can speak authoritatively for Canada abroad, and only it represents Canada as an international personality in the eyes of international law.[2] Only Ottawa has the authority to negotiate and ratify treaties. But this authority is heavily qualified. The critical legal case is the Labour Conventions case of 1936.[3] The federal government's power to make treaties, the Judicial Committee of the Privy Council held, did not extend to the power to implement them. Treaties must be implemented through the passage of ordinary legislation; they do not automatically become the law of the land. And in the implementation process, the domestic division of powers embodied in sections 91 and 92 of the Constitution Act are operative: the federal government cannot enforce treaties whose provisions are within provincial jurisdiction. As Lord Atkin put it: "[Even though] the ship of state now sails on larger ventures and into foreign waters, she still retains the watertight compartments."[4]

This is in sharp contrast to some other federations. In the United States, treaties are largely self-executing: once ratified by the Senate they become the law of the land, binding equally on both federal and state governments. Moreover, even where an international trade agreement is made by executive arrangement, rather than treaty, it seems clear that the ambit of the U.S. federal trade and commerce power permits it to overrule any state activity likely to violate it. In Australia, the federal power over external affairs extends to implementing legislation, even if it trenches on state power.

Thus the authority of the federal government in Canada is sharply constrained. It can implement a treaty only in areas of its present jurisdiction. In most areas of international affairs – such as international security – this makes little difference. Nor is it of major significance when international trading rules are built around the tariff, since that too is solidly within federal jurisdiction. The difficulty arises when, as has happened recently, attention turns to "non-tariff barriers". Now the whole panoply of subsidies, purchasing policies, regulation, product standards and the like become issues in international negotiations. Many of these kinds of activities, at least potentially, fall within provincial jurisdiction.

Since existing Canada-U.S. tariffs are already low, the Canada-U.S. discussions will focus primarily on non-tariff barriers. American negotiators have made it very clear that they wish the negotiations to address provincial as well as federal barriers to trade, and that an agreement limited only to matters in federal jurisdiction would be insufficient. The more effective the agreement is in doing so, the less able the federal government is to implement it. To the extent any Canada-U.S. agreement contains provisions binding on the provinces, in their own areas of jurisdiction, it will depend on provincial consent, and provincial legislation to give it effect. Thus, the provinces have a strong constitutional hand with respect to any treaty which imposes obligations on them. It is true that other international trade agreements have explicitly contained "federal state" clauses which note that it will not be binding on the sub-national units within member states, and which pledge the central government to use its best efforts to secure compliance. On at least one occasion, a province has signed a letter of intent to abide by one of the terms of an agreement, but such arrangements do not appear to be legally enforceable.[5] Thus for any Canada-U.S. agreement to be effective, some way must be found to secure provincial compliance with its provisions. This is the sense in which there is indeed a "provincial veto".

There is, however, one great uncertainty: How far do provincial economic powers extend?[6] Or, put the other way, how much power does the federal government have to police or constrain such activities under its trade and commerce power, or even under the general power of Peace, Order and Good Government? How much potential is there to extend the boundaries of federal authority in order to outlaw provincial policies inconsistent with a Canada-U.S. trade agreement? Many of the provincial practices likely to be addressed by an agreement – such as purchasing policies and subsidies – have never been tested in the courts, even though they can be interpreted as interferences with the larger economic market. The federal trade and commerce power – unlike in the U.S. – has been interpreted narrowly, largely in the name of federalist values. In order to prevent an uncontrolled extension of federal authority, with no logical stopping place, the courts have made a sharp distinction between interprovincial trade and that taking place within a province. The latter has been preserved from federal interference.

It could be argued that in terms of economic theory this distinction between inter and intra-provincial trade has long been outdated: we continue to use it mainly for the non-economic "federalist" reason. But such interpretations, as numerous cases have shown, are not carved in stone. They can and do respond both to changing circumstances and to changing conceptions of the role of government in the economy. For example, both federalism and the constitution were able to adapt to the Keynesian economic model adopted in Canada and most other western countries after World War II. The possibility which arises now, therefore, is that the new circumstances of a possible free trade agreement – and more generally of the critical importance of international trade matters for Canadian economic performance – could allow the federal government successfully to claim a broad power to implement a trade agreement, even where it affected policies and practices now engaged in by provinces. Such an agreement would make clear the international effects and ramifications of these provincial activities, and this could invite the Supreme Court to interpret "the regulation of trade and commerce" more broadly than it has in the past. Peter Hogg notes that since the Labour Conventions case, several *dicta* have hinted that the court may be willing to reconsider the constitutional position, and that the 1932 Radio Reference case provides a precedent in which the Peace, Order and Good Government clause was used to justify an extension of federal power resulting from an international agreement.[7]

On its past record, the court is likely to look for mediating principles which retain a significant role for provincial economic powers, and will try to limit what could become limitless extensions of federal power. Nevertheless, it is possible that the line between federal and provincial authority, when redrawn, might be somewhat differently placed from where it is now. The point here is not to argue that there exists a heretofore undiscovered federal power, or that provinces have all these years been exercising authority they do not actually have. The point, rather, is to emphasize the constitutional uncertainties as Canada approaches the possibility of a comprehensive trade agreement with the U.S.. These uncertainties will complicate the bilateral discussions and could, if not clarified, leave crucial sections of the agreement in limbo. We must avoid the prospect of a draft agreement being rejected in the U.S. on the grounds that Canada is incapable of guaranteeing its applicability, or, even worse, the prospect of an agreement being followed by years of wrangling in the courts about which parts of it can be implemented by Ottawa alone. Moreover, an agreement whose provisions were applicable in some provinces but not others would be unworkable.

Beyond the constitutional uncertainties, other factors also engage federalism directly in the free trade debate. From the National Policy to the present, it has always been true that Canada's most important industrial policy has been its trade policy. But perhaps never before have domestic industrial policy and international trade concerns been so deeply intertwined. Moreover, with the relative decline of reliance on Keynesian macro-economic policy tools in economic policy, there has between a growing emphasis on the tools of micro-economic policy. Both these factors greatly increase the importance of the provinces. The first means that not only will provincial practices have potentially important international ramifications, but also that provinces, in promoting their own economic growth, will seek to influence international trade matters. We have seen both the strong provincial claim to a role in shaping Canada's national trade policies, and an increase in provincial international trade activities – the opening of offices abroad, the hiring of Washington consultants, links between groups of Canadian provinces and contiguous U.S. states in all regions, extensive trade promotion junkets and the like.[8] Thus, the assertion of provincial responsibility for regional economic development, a phenomenon of growing importance since the 1960s, has had an important international dimension. Provinces are not likely to be willing to allow federally-negotiated agreements to negate or supplant their own activities.

Conversely, the increasing reliance on micro-economic policy tools generally means that national economic performance is more dependent on policies for which the provinces are largely responsible. Thus the federal government cannot be indifferent to provincial activity. The need for federal-provincial coordination across the whole range of economic matters – including international trade policy – will be even more important in the future as federal and provincial governments must adjust their policies in light of new rules; and as ways must be found to increase the competitiveness of Canadian industry.

The complexity of the interactions between federalism and international economic relations has recently been dramatically illustrated by the softwood lumber issue.   Here was protectionist action initiated by U.S. government agencies at the behest of U.S. lumber producers.   But it involved a resource which is largely owned and under the jurisdiction of the Canadian provinces; and it called into question policies and practices undertaken at the provincial level – activities which themselves varied from province to province.   Planning a Canadian response therefore required full coordination among the federal government and the producing provinces. The Canadian industry, which had been deeply involved at the earlier stages seemed to be pushed aside as the need for intergovernmental agreement became more pressing. Canadian responses to the U.S. initiatives were slowed by the need for agreement among the Canadian parties; and on occasion, the Canadian governments appeared to be sending conflicting messages to the United States. The initial outcome was a federal export tax on provincial resources (a kind of measure which provinces had traditionally deeply opposed as a form of federal taxation of provincial resources), but the proceeds of this federal tax were to be shared among the provinces. The agreement with the U.S., however, sharply constrained the uses to which the provinces could put these revenues, barring them from use to provide direct or indirect subsidy to the industry. In the longer run, the agreement envisaged changes to provincial policy and taxation regime respecting lumber, and these too would have to be established within the same complex three-way negotiation. Federal, provincial and international dimensions of the question were inextricably intertwined – no simple formula that Ottawa is solely responsible for international trade relations, or that the provinces are solely responsible for the disposition of natural resources under their control, could possibly encompass the situation. Yet softwood lumber was only one of a potentially large class of issues which have been and are likely to be posed by the changing world and North American political economy.

The Federal-Provincial Debate

The preceding analysis suggests that there remain many unresolved crucial questions about the roles of federal and provincial governments in the free trade negotiations, and in international trade negotiations generally. Indeed, the constitutional limitations on the federal treaty power – and the lack of any agreed procedures for seeking provincial consent – is a major weakness in our institutional structure. Regional differences in interest, combined with this constitutional gap, could seriously hamper Canada's effectiveness in international trade negotiations generally, not only in those with the U.S.. We have to find some way to reconcile the internal division of powers with international needs. We need to ensure that any treaty, once written, is binding and enforceable on the provinces; and that requires that the provinces have a central role in negotiation, ratification and implementation. Such a role must go a great deal further than the successful and extensive – but informal – intergovernmental consultations which have occurred in previous rounds of international negotiation such as the GATT.

Before looking at the process in detail, let us examine some of the provincial views on the prospect of free trade with the United States. They have lined up in a way remarkably parallel to that in the constitutional and energy debates, with the western and eastern provinces – especially Alberta, B.C. and Saskatchewan – taking the lead in pushing for comprehensive free trade discussions; and the central Canadian provinces, especially Ontario, expressing the greatest caution. Now, however, Ottawa is more in tune with the governments outside Central Canada. The reasons lie partly in history, and partly in the current makeup of provincial economies. Free trade versus protection has been one of the dominant themes in Canadian regional conflict. High tariffs were used largely to create and sustain a manufacturing base in central Canada. They were resented by the West and the East on the grounds that their consumers were forced to pay artificially high prices for protected manufactured goods from Central Canada, while they were required to sell their natural resources in volatile, unprotected world markets. The tariff, it was argued, supported the centre at the expense of the hinterland. Hence, to argue for free trade now was, as the Macdonald Commission argued, to remove one of the principal sources of regional grievance in Canada.

In the present, some of the main products of the resource-producing provinces are threatened by rising protectionism in the United States, whether it is fish in Atlantic Canada, or timber products in B.C.. Thus, free trade is not only ideologically supported by governments such as B.C., or Alberta, but also is justified as a way to ensure that American protectionism can be controlled. Six months before Prime Minister Mulroney officially informed the United States of the Canadian government's desire to pursue trade talks, the Western Premiers, in May 1985, called for complete Canada-U.S. free trade, to be phased in over a five to 10 year period. In August 1985, at the Premiers' Conference in St. John's, nine of the 10 provinces called for free trade. Alberta Premier Lougheed warned of reopening old Ontario-Western divisions if Ontario continued to drag its feet on the matter.

Ontario has been the most reluctant province, though it has not tried to block the trade talks. Instead Premier Peterson has concentrated on posing hard questions about the impact of free trade on Ontario industry, especially in manufacturing. Studies commissioned by the province have suggested that the jobs of a large proportion of the Ontario workforce could be affected by free trade. Of particular concern is the Canada-U.S. Autopact, which provides important safeguards for Canadian production which Ontario fears might be lost in a general free trade agreement. Ontario's caution reflects the genuine uncertainty about the effects of free trade on it. It is more dependent on the U.S. market than any other province: it has both the most to gain and the most to lose in any free trade arrangement.

Quebec's change of government has also led to a change in the official Quebec position. Reflecting the PQ's traditional support of integration with the U.S. as a counterweight to the economic dependence on the rest of Canada, Premier Johnson supported free trade. With a greater commitment to federalism, Premier Bourassa has joined forces with Ontario Premier Peterson. Echoing the arguments he made during the Quebec referendum campaign of 1980, Bourassa also has argued that free trade would be the start of a "slippery slope" leading to ever closer harmonization and integration with the United States.

The provincial coalitions for and against free trade, however, may not be as strong as they might have been in the past. All provinces have expressed various kinds of reservations about the content of any treaty. The Atlantic provinces, for example, are especially concerned that regional development and interregional transfer programs not be threatened. Manitoba's relative caution mirrors the importance of its manufacturing sector. All the provinces seek various exemptions for agricultural interests. All have spoken of the need for a generous transition period, and for preservation of major Canadian social programs.

More generally, provincial interests appear to be less homogeneous than they may once have been. Historically, the coalition behind the National Policy was the triumvirate of central Canadian manufacturing, financial and transportation industries, all with a vested interest in creating and maintaining an East-West economy. But all three have changed considerably. While it is true that many smaller Ontario manufacturers serving the domestic market are nervous about free trade, it is significant that both the Business Council on National Issues and the Canadian Manufacturers' Association have been strong proponents of free trade. Many Canadian firms have already become less dependent on Canadian markets and are more integrated into international markets; they no longer seek protection. Similarly, banking and financial institutions have become far more international in focus. As other provinces have become more diversified they too are likely to be less united on trade matters. In Saskatchewan, Alberta and B.C., for example, there is far less agreement between Conservatives (or Social Credit) and New Democrats on trade than there was on energy in the 1970s.

Despite these caveats, provincial support on the general objective of freer trade is an important asset for the Mulroney government in the negotiations with the U.S. and with the equally important battle for public opinion within Canada.

The Process

But Provincial support for free trade does not, however, translate into provincial willingness to delegate to the federal government responsibility

196

for bringing it about. All provinces have asserted that there must be full provincial participation in the trade talks. In the first few months of the trade talks, working out a domestic procedure has consumed almost as much energy as preparing for sessions with the U.S. negotiators. By the summer of 1986, after two First Ministers' Conferences and innumerable ministerial and official meetings, a procedure was in place. A federal-provincial committee of officials would track the talks; there was to be a committee of Ministers Responsible for Trade whose role seemed undefined, and the First Ministers were to meet every 90 days to review progress. While the federal negotiating team, led by Ambassador Simon Reisman, would sit at the table with the Americans, it seemed clear that, more than any previous round of trade talks, this would be an exercise in federal-provincial collaboration.

"Full provincial participation" has proved to be a slippery concept even at the preliminary stages. It will become much more difficult as negotiators make the complex trade-offs involved in getting agreement. And as yet, there appears to have been very little discussion of the even more critical phases of enforcement and implementation.

Underlying the debate at the November 1985 First Ministers' meeting in Halifax, and in the subsequent discussions, were variations on the fundamental questions about federalism with which the country wrestled during the constitutional negotiations, and in other forums during the 1970s. Who speaks for Canada? What are the relative roles of the federal and provincial governments in economic development? What forms of consent are necessary for fundamental change?

Then, as now, two polar views are in contention. The first suggests that the federal government must be responsible for the trade negotiations. This view is reminiscent of that during the thirties. Then, the argument was that federalism was obsolete, because it was incompatible with the newly emerging social and economic roles that the state was required to play. In order to undertake these successfully, it was argued, we needed a much higher degree of centralization.

The contemporary version of this view is that federalism may be incompatible with the implications of the growth of international interdependence. That, Pierre Trudeau argued in a speech, before his resignation, has many ramifications: it means that it is more important than ever that Canadian industry be rationalized and competitive; hence the degree of fragmentation of industry within Canada – itself accentuated by interprovincial domestic barriers to trade – limits our ability to develop internationally competitive firms. International trade negotiations will become more and more important determinants of our economic welfare, and we will not be able to deal with them effectively if we speak with many voices, and if we are unable to deliver on commitments. All this then leads some to argue, as in the thirties that decentralized federalism may be a luxury we can no longer afford.

This centralist model asserts that the federal government is the primary government; that in particular it has responsibility both for the overall management of Canada's international affairs, and for overall economic management. This model – adopted in part in the Macdonald Report – suggests that this gives the federal government a legitimate role in extending its influence into areas of provincial jurisdiction, whenever that is necessary to define and carry out a broad national purpose – as with the postwar establishment of the Keynesian welfare state. Today, then, the model would imply that the new circumstances justify a strengthening of Ottawa's control over the domestic economy in order to meet international needs.

Moreover, it would argue that only the federal government has the capacity to represent the whole country, and ensure the appropriate regional trade-offs, which a Canada-U.S. agreement would require.

It follows from this model that responsibility for the conduct of negotiations lies with the federal government. It defines the mandate of the chief negotiators, and they report to it. Only the federal government is present at the negotiating table.

It would also follow that not only does the federal government have the power to ratify the treaty, but also that it should have the power to implement it, ensuring that provincial practices were consistent with the terms of the treaty, even if that meant limitations on current provincial powers. The federal government would provide the Canadian representation on any new bilateral agency to enforce the bilateral agreement.

Whatever the nostalgia of some federal officials for this model, it has not been asserted by the Mulroney government. While seeking to maintain as much control as possible over the negotiations, it has recognized the need for provincial involvement, and conceded the authority of the provinces to block any parts of an agreement which infringe on provincial jurisdiction. This is in part a reflection of the government's goal of enhanced intergovernmental cooperation and in part a recognition of the constitutional realities. It is possible that Ottawa could take a strong unilateralist stand, asserting an expanded view of its trade and commerce power, or justifying action under the "Peace, order" clause. But that would be an extraordinary act of political will, with uncertain chances of success. The federal government would have other levers too, if it chose to force the issue, for example, the threat of reducing transfers to the provinces. Such a "conditionalizing" of transfers, this time for economic, rather than social goals, has been suggested by Stefan Dupré, and others.

Despite these rather unlikely possibilities, the federal government has every incentive to encourage participation at the early stages, if only to maximize the chances that provinces will consent to any agreement. In the longer run, enhanced federal power to implement treaties would require a constitutional amendment, which, under the present amendment formula, would be extraordinarily difficult to achieve. Even provinces which strongly support free trade would be unwilling to concede to Ottawa their broad powers over economic development.

All the provinces – even those most ardently supporting the federal initiative – have espoused a collaborative model: the view that national policy and policy-making are functions of the operations of two orders of government, that neither has any logical primacy, and that crucial matters of public policy therefore must be developed in a collaborative federal-provincial forum. To the question, Who speaks for Canada? this model argues, 11 governments collectively do.

Applied to the free trade negotiations, this model would imply that both federal and provincial governments should be equally involved at all stages. Not only are matters within provincial jurisdiction directly at stake, but so are crucial regional interests, which only the provincial governments can fully represent. Thus both Ontario and Alberta have argued that the formulation of Canada's goals and negotiating position should be the joint responsibility of the 11 governments; that the First Ministers' Conference, not the federal cabinet, is the body which should determine the mandate for the negotiating team. Specifically, this meant that Simon Reisman would be responsible to the FMC.

In the negotiating stage, provinces argued that provincial representatives should be at the table or at least, so to speak, in the next room, and that there should be frequent reporting back by the negotiators again not only to the federal government, but also to the provinces. Each order of government would then have equal responsibility for implementating those parts of the treaty within their own jurisdiction. Finally, at the stage of enforcement, any bilateral adjudicatory or dispute-settling body should either contain provincial representatives, or its members should be appointed jointly by some federal-provincial body.

There are both philosophical and practical objections to such a model. Philosophically, again, many would see this as a provincialism incompatible with their conception of the country. Practically, there would be the danger that Canada's position could only be a lowest common denominator of rival provincial interests, that a fragmented Canadian position would allow American negotiators great opportunity to "divide and rule", and that the development of Canadian positions would take so long that effective negotiation was impossible. Provincial responsibility for implementation could mean either that crucial sections of a treaty could be rendered void – or that there could be a checkerboard with some provinces included and others not.

The American reactions to this would also be important. Indeed, there is an interesting contrast between Canada and the U.S. here. In both countries, the federal executive is going to be heavily constrained by domestic political pressures including regionalist forces. But these will take rather different forms in the two countries. In Canada, it is federalism and the power of the provinces that will constrain the federal executive. Americans with a more centralized federation will find this difficult to understand and will be impatient with it. On the other hand, the U.S. executive will be constrained by Congress. Canadians with their tradition of executive dominance will in turn find this difficult to understand and deal with. There is a lot of room for mutual frustration here, and for very complicated negotiations.

By the fall of 1986 negotiating procedures acceptable to both Ottawa and the provinces seemed to have been reached. The federal government remained responsible for the conduct of the negotiations and there appeared to be a high degree of communication among the governments. But it was unclear whether this harmony would extend into the period when an agreement was dropping into place. And little attention had yet been given to the critical stages of implementation. The yawning constitutional gap remained.

It is crucial to address it. How and when to do so remains questionable. Federal negotiators worry, with reason, that to try to come to agreement on such crucial procedures now could divert attention from the primary focus on the U.S. talks. Gil Winham has maintained that to argue about formal ratification and implementation now, without a concrete set of results to focus the discussion is dangerous. It is to run the risk of a replay of the "constitutional model" of intergovernmental relations, in which abstract questions of rights and status predominate over substance. Far better, he argues, to ensure that a broadly appealing deal emerges and to expect that political pressures of both sides of the border will induce compliance.[9] A further reason for this strategy is that it would avoid the question of the constitutional rules concerning trade becoming embroiled in other constitutional issues, notably those respecting Quebec's status. These are persuasive arguments; it is nevertheless useful to survey the possibilities for the longer-term.

The Macdonald Commission considered a number of alternatives which might clarify the issue.[10] One was a constitutional amendment which would give the federal government the power to implement international trade treaties. Given the provincial stakes, and our current amendment formula, that would be impossible to achieve. Such an

200

amendment would have the potential for virtually open-ended extension of federal powers over the economy into provincial spheres; it could mean that changes in the division of powers were brought in through the "back door" of international agreements, rather than through the "front door" of deliberations within Canada.

Or, the Commission suggested that there might be more support for such a federal power if treaties were ratified by an elected Senate with strong regional representation – in effect the American model.   Again, this is a distant possibility.

The Commission felt that in order to achieve its central and immediate goal of U.S. free trade, no institutional innovations could be made: the Commission called simply for extensive consultation and provincial involvement, and would leave it to political pressures on the provinces to implement the treaty as necessary.

That of course raised the interesting question of what if some provinces were to comply and others did not. It would be a kind of opting-in process, opening up another dimension of a "checkerboard Canada".   Presumably, for a province to gain whatever benefits the treaty offered, it would have to be part of the deal.   But it is very hard to see how such an arrangement would be workable given the free movement of goods within Canada, or whether it would be acceptable to the Americans.

For the longer term, the Commission did propose a constitutional amendment to deal with ratification and implementation.   It would create a more democratic ratification process than we have at the moment.   Any treaty would have to be ratified by Parliament.   And where a treaty imposed obligations within provinces' constitutional authority, then the relevant sections would also have to be ratified by them, using the same formula as for constitutional amendment – seven provinces with at least 50 per cent of the population.   Once ratified in this way, then the terms of the treaty would become the law of the land, binding on both orders of government.   Such a procedure would close the constitutional gap, and would reflect both the Parliamentary and federal character of Canada.   Given the importance of international trading agreements for domestic economic policy in the future, some such amendment to the constitution is a desirable development for the future.   But it is not likely to be attained within the tight deadlines within which the current Canada-U.S. negotiations are being conducted. Moreover some important questions would remain. Would the opting-out procedure of the present amendment formula be retained?   And how would it be determined which sections of the treaty were subject to provincial ratification?   Some would argue that a provincial role in ratification would be too much of a concession to a provincialist view of the country.

Clearly no constitutional amendment – whether to give the federal government the future power to implement treaties touching on provincial jurisdiction, or to build in a direct provincial role – is attainable within the context of the current Canada-U.S. negotiations. Yet the problem remains a pressing one. If a draft Canada-U.S. agreement is achieved, how can we, or the Americans, know it will be implemented? One other device does exist. That is the possibility of an intergovernmental Accord which would define a federal-provincial agreement on the terms of the treaty and commit each government to abide by them as they affected their own spheres of jurisdiction.

Intergovernmental Accords are a relatively new instrument in Canadian federalism. Recent examples are the 1985 Canada-Newfoundland Atlantic Accord with respect to management of off-shore resources, and a series of bilateral agreements between Ottawa and the western provinces, concerning oil pricing and revenues. The Atlantic Accord is the most far reaching. It sets out a detailed regime for management of the off-shore; it commits the federal and Newfoundland legislatures and governments to specific courses of action; and it creates joint management bodies. Such Accords have grown with the need for more precision in intergovernmental arrangements both for the governments themselves, and for private actors. They have no constitutional status; and have never been tested in the courts. To the extent that they commit and constrain future governments, their legal standing is uncertain. The Macdonald Commission, recognizing the utility of an agreement, which was less rigid than a constitutional amendment, suggested that such Accords be given a more formal, enforceable status. Even without that step, an Accord might be an appropriate instrument to record federal and provincial assent to the provisions of a draft Canada-U.S. treaty, and to commit each to its implementation. It would ease federal concerns that it could not deliver on commitments made to the U.S., while relieving provincial fears that Ottawa would use the agreement to assert a much wider range of trade and commerce powers. An Accord would also probably satisfy U.S. demands for assurance of provincial compliance.

Even such an Accord might be hard to reach. Certainly it presumes a highly successful outcome to the negotiations, and a strong national and intergovernmental consensus on the result. There is still no guarantee of provincial unanimity – but for practical purposes the exclusion of one or two smaller provinces would not likely be fatal to the treaty.

Treaty Enforcement

Any Canada-U.S. trade agreement would need to include some form of dispute-settling mechanism, some forum for discussion of trade irritants and a policeman for the specific provisions. A strong enforcement agency would be particularly important for Canada, since its main goal in the negotiations is security of access to the U.S. market, which means that the ability of U.S. agencies to take arbitrary actions against Canadian exports must be reduced. The powers of a bilateral agency could vary from informal – advice, research, education and publicity – to formal – with specific powers to order compliance with its rulings. Canada would probably want to opt for the more formal end of the continuum, and to ensure that both countries would be weighted equally.

To the exent that the agreement encompasses provincial policies and actions, they will come before the tribunal. So it becomes important to know what role the provinces will play in its powers and membership. If all Canadian members were appointed by the federal government, expertise on provincial policies and interests might be lacking. Purely federal representation could increase any tendency of the agreement to extend federal powers. On the other hand, direct provincial representation would make for a large and cumbersome body. The Americans would no doubt argue for state representation as well. Perhaps the most satisfactory compromise would be to have the Canadian representatives nominated by the federal government, followed by some form of provincial ratification. Such a device has frequently been proposed for appointment of Supreme Court justices and members of federal regulatory bodies with important provincial and regional roles.

Once a free trade agreement is in place, it will pose numerous challenges to Canadian governments, in order to assure that Canadian industry gains the maximum advantages. Three kinds of policies will be especially important. First, those designed to cushion and ease the inevitable transition. process, from those industries and firms whose competitive position will be weakened to those which will be strengthened. It is likely that the transition process will be a lengthy and complex one. Even such a staunch advocate as the Macdonald Commission called for a massive Transitional Adjustment Assistance Program. Second is the need for policies to assist Canadian industries in developing access to the new markets which presumably are to be opened up. Small businesses, especially, often have little expertise, and few resources, to penetrate foreign markets. Export promotion and capital assistance to help Canadian firms acquire effective distribution systems in the U.S. will be vital. Third, there must be policies which more generally are aimed at improving the competitiveness of Canadian industries; structural and micro-economic issues such as efficient labour markets, training of skilled manpower, etc. will be critical.

All these policy challenges are complex enough. But an additional characteristic of free trade is that it will constrain the instruments which governments can bring to bear on them. Direct assistance programs to industry, together with any policies designed to protect the domestic market, are likely to be just the sort of non-tariff barriers the treaty will be designed to catch, especially given the U.S. emphasis on the "level playing field".

More important for the purposes of this analysis, responsibility for meeting these challenges will fall to both levels of government simultaneously. Neither the provinces nor the federal government will have a monopoly on the authority or policy instruments to be employed.

The economic impact of a free trade arrangement, for good or ill, will depend heavily on how the adjustment process will be managed. Adjustment issues will extend into many current areas of federal-provincial arrangements: Economic and Regional Development Agreements, manpower training, fiscal arrangements and the like. It is clear that the challenges to the institutions of Canadian federalism only begin with the signing of the agreement.

***

So far we have explored how federalism is likely to affect the negotiation and implementation of a Canada-U.S. trade agreement. As the early months of the negotiations have shown, managing the domestic environment has occupied almost as much attention as have discussions with U.S. negotiators. As we move towards a possible agreement these issues are likely to become even more complex, despite the apparent satisfaction of all sides with the arrangements in place in the summer of 1986. Yet another set of questions is of even more fundamental importance. What will be the consequences of any free trade arrangement for the future of Canadian federalism? Here we must be even more speculative, since answers depend so much on the kind of agreement that might be achieved. At one extreme, there could be a very limited treaty – which eliminated tariff barriers, left a great many industrial sectors exempted, and merely set up consultative mechanisms on non-tariff barriers.

At the other extreme would be full free trade, with abolition of both tariff and non-tariff barriers, together with rules about many domestic economic and social policies which indirectly affect the competitive position of Canadian and American industry. These are what the U.S. means when it talks of a "level playing field".

Politics may well mean that if we end up with anything it will be at the first pole, more symbolic than real. That might satisfy the political goals of both President Reagan and Prime Minister Mulroney, though it would make little actual difference to Canadian-American trading patterns.

But the logic of free trade pushes towards a much more comprehensive agreement. That is because the single primary argument for free trade is to give us "security of access" – in other words certainty that the U.S. market is open to us, and that we will not suddenly be hit by rules or quotas which close it down. That requires that we ask of the Americans sharply to constrain *their own* political process – that the treaty place clearly defined limits on Congressional and state action. And if we were to achieve this, the price would likely be concessions from our side on the "level playing field" question. If that is so, a huge range of Canadian policies come into the net, whatever the initial protestations that we can in fact insulate most Canadian domestic economic, political and social policies.

Free Trade and National Unity

The first question to ask is what might be the effect of free trade on regional conflict within the federal system. One of the strongest arguments made by the Macdonald Commission is that it would promote national unity by removing one of the prime historic sources of regional grievance and conflict. It finally buries the national policy by which central Canadian manufacturing, transportation and financial interests were protected at the expense of the West and the East. Western grievances in particular stemmed in large part from the fact that they were required to buy their manufactured goods from central Canada at higher than world prices, while they had to sell their own goods on volatile world markets at world prices – or, as in the case of energy in the 1970s , were forced to sell their oil and gas to central Canadians at less than world price. Free trade would indeed remove this source of grievance: no longer would Westerners feel discriminated against in this way.

More importantly, free trade would sanction and promote something which is already far advanced. The National Policy was based on the assumption that nation-building depended on the creation of a national economy, one built on East-West lines, and aimed at strengthening economic linkages within the country. The country which trades together stays together. Free trade makes another set of assumptions. Political unity and economic unity are quite separable. There is no particular virtue in Canadians trading with one another. Indeed, if this internal trade is artificial, not dictated by market forces, then it is bad economics because it reduces efficiency in the allocation of resources, and thus reduces aggregate incomes, and it is politically inefficient because it increases conflict as some regions are coerced into it. If there is no natural fit, then far better to allow each region to develop the most advantageous linkages with anywhere in the world.

This is quite persuasive. But there is another side. First, we must ask what goes along with trade. If trade is also a carrier of cultural values, interpersonal ties and the like, then we give up – have already done so – a lot by reducing trade within the country. We run the risk of reducing the capacity to build national support, across regions for common national purposes. The Royal Commission addresses this but not very persuasively. It argues that we can make a sharp distinction between economy, culture and polity; economic efficiency can be pursued without spilling over to harm our capacity to pursue cultural, social and political goals. It also argues for an enhancement of what it calls the national state's "symbolic" and social management roles to counteract any erosion of sovereignty or other values. Yet the observation that the reduction in the relative importance of economic linkages within Canada attendant on free trade would make the eventual separation of Quebec, for example, more feasible is persuasive.

Another implication of these changing trade patterns which would again be exacerbated, but not created, by free trade, is what they might do for our commitment to sharing – to interregional equalization and regional development. There are two aspects here.

First what do they do to our normative commitment to sharing? In an integrated economy, redistribution has a circular, reinforcing quality. For example, a dollar which goes from Ontario to New Brunswick in equalization is likely eventually to find its way back to Ontario in the purchase of its manufactured goods – it is, so to speak, an integrative dollar. Or in energy, a dollar which goes to Alberta in higher prices, but then gets spent in buying Ontario drill pipe is also an integrative dollar. But a dollar which goes from Ontario to Fredericton to Boston, or from Ontario to Edmonton to Houston can have quite different implications.

Second, what about the future of regional development policy? There are both direct and indirect possibilities here. Regional policies might, of course, be fully protected in a free trade agreement. GATT for example explicitly allows its member countries to engage in regional development programs. But it is not at all clear that they could easily survive once raised in free trade negotiations. We have already seen major U.S. challenges to elements of regional development policy in Canada – for example, to provisions of unemployment insurance and other measures to protect the Canadian fishing industry.

Many of the instruments of regional development policy, especially subsidies, loans and grants are just the sort of non-tariff barriers a free trade agreement would be designed to catch. At a minimum, free trade would alter the form and the instruments employed in regional policy – leading to more emphasis on infrastructure and less on direct assistance to industry.

But even if explicit regional development policy survives, the logic of free trade could undermine it. The big claim for free trade is that it will promote efficiency through forcing Canadian industry to become more competitive by responding to market signals. There are strong pressures in this direction anyway – and they lead to more and more calls such as those from Tom Courchene that Canadian economic policy generally, must look more to efficiency and aggregate growth and less to redistributive policies.[11] Free trade would massively strengthen that argument. Mobility – moving people to jobs – would become more important; the traditional Canadian commitment to preservation of less economically vigourous regions would be harder to sustain.

Third, what about the effect of free trade on provincial industrial policies? The growth of such policies in the last two decades has been one of the most striking features of Canadian federalism, though as Young, Faucher and Blais have recently shown, their extent can be exaggerated and there is some indication that the thrust behind them has worn off, as their effectiveness has been challenged, and as provincial revenues have become increasingly constrained.[12] But again the instruments used in province-building – subsidies, loan guarantees, tax provisions, etc. – are very often just the sort that free trade would be designed to curb. Hence, at a minimum, free trade is likely to constrain provincial activism, and to shift provincial industrial policies to more indirect forms, such as education, manpower training and the like.

There is much uncertainty about this. It could be replied that even the degree of economic integration achieved within the European Common Market has not stopped France and Germany, for example, from having very different industrial strategies. So why not for Canada, and its provinces, in a free trade arrangement with the United States? More work is needed on these questions. But it seems reasonable to expect that when Canada-U.S. free trade is combined with the already high degree of integration in other spheres, the pressures for harmonization will be greater than they are in the European community, as Quebec Premier Robert Bourassa has argued.

It is also possible that free trade could actually enhance provincial industrial development activities rather than diminish them. One reason for the growth in these policies was an increasing sense of the ineffectiveness of federal policies. And one reason for that ineffectiveness, it could be argued, is the existence of major international constraints on the kinds of policy instruments most used by the federal government. From this perspective, it is not the provinces which stop Canada having an effective fiscal policy, or an autonomous monetary policy – it is open world capital markets, our dependence on foreign trade and investment, and the like. If a free trade agreement were to reduce federal economic powers even further, then the incentives for provinces to explore what they can do will be all the greater. There are considerable indications that a similar phenomenon has happened in the United States: reduced economic development activity by the Reagan government has helped stimulate a rapid increase in such activities by states and cities.

In addition, a possible effect of free trade is that it would do a better job at catching and controlling the big, visible, federal policies – constraining Ottawa even more – than it would succeed in catching the much more varied and diverse provincial policies. It will be harder to police the activities of 10 provinces – or 50 states – than it will two national governments. One recent survey of state industrial activities demonstrates an extraordinary variety and inventiveness in state and local industrial policies; they will not be easy to control.[13] It is also interesting to note that recently the U.S. state governors passed a resolution calling on the federal government not to limit their own international trade promotion activities.

Thus it is conceivable that under free trade we will end up with a weaker and more constrained federal government, without equal constraints on provinces.

Related to industrial policy is the way in which the internal Canadian debate about the economic union interacts with the free trade debate. In a sense the issues are perfectly parallel: enhancing the Canadian economic union tries to stop provinces doing to each other what free trade would try to stop Canada and the U.S. doing to each other.

All indications are that the political will to tackle the economic union question within Canada has been weak, and action is likely to be very slow. But it could be speeded up dramatically by free trade. It is very hard to imagine that we could continue to accept barriers within Canada which were not acceptable between Canada and the U.S., either practically or politically. Canada-U.S. free trade, therefore, could bring about, via an international agreement, something which cannot be achieved by domestic political processes alone. (Indeed, one important rationale for some advocates of free trade is precisely that: to create a set of rules which tie the hands of Canadian governments, barring them from policies seen to be inefficient and distorting).

208

The economists also make another argument about the link between free trade in Canada and that between Canada and the U.S.. That is, if we got free trade with the U.S. – with all the rationalizing, competition-enhancing features this implies – then the economic union within Canada simply would not matter any more, at least in economic terms. The assumption here is that free trade within Canada is a "second-best" to free trade with the United States.

Finally, is free trade likely to be centralizing or decentralizing for domestic Canadian politics and the structure of Canadian federalism? The most common view is that it would likely be profoundly centralizing. Indeed, those who see the Macdonald Report as largely a centralist document have pointed precisely to free trade as one of those elements. Free trade, this view suggests, dictates and requires unity and singleness of purpose within each one of the partners.

Such a view is based on the assumption that Canada-U.S. free trade is an arrangement between two cohesive entities. Canada and the U.S. are each in a sense single actors, whose interests are to be negotiated. Politically, this means we must get our act together, speak with a single voice and nationalize our domestic economy in order to strengthen Canada's ability to do well in the continental competition. There is also the assumption that whatever their domestic disagreements, Canadians rally together – and look to the federal government – once issues transcend Canadian borders. Finally, there is the assumption that to do all this requires, or tends towards, strengthening federal powers, especially in international and economic matters.

But the more I think about it, the less plausible this model seems. In fact the model it is derived from is really a mercantilist model, which sees trade as an affair between distinct sovereign entities managed by authoritative governments.

But the inspiration of free trade is not mercantilist at all – it is overwhelmingly based on a market model. Governments will indeed play a major role in writing the rules, but once written, those rules will constrain and limit governments. Free trade weakens rather than strengthens political authorities; it shifts power from them to private economic actors. It means that economic linkages, whether within Canada or between it and the United States, are no longer to be defined, regulated and mediated by and through governments, but are to be left to these private interests. It becomes much more difficult to think coherently about an economic entity called Canada, much less one whose destiny could be guided by a central government. Ottawa would simply become less important, both for the provinces (all of which would no doubt soon open Washington offices to influence policy where it really counts) and for the private sector.

This, combined with the real possibility that the trade agreement itself may constrain Ottawa less than provinces, means that a possible effect of free trade would be increased decentralization, a weaker rather than a stronger federal government. Free trade, along with other international integrative forces, undermines the historically most important federal economic powers, such as the tariff, and places much greater weight on the kinds of powers – education, training, industrial relations and the like – which are largely provincial. The federal government might claim it now needs more control over such policies, but it is by no means clear that it could mobilize the support to get them.

Central authority has always been greatest in Canada when the federal government has been able to mobilize broad support for a "National Policy" which could only be achieved through federal action, whether that be the National Policy of the Nineteenth Century, or the building of the Keynesian welfare state in the 1940s and 1950s. Free trade is a national strategy all right, but it is one which denies the very idea of a national policy, and denies the federal government the power to mount one, even if it could be defined. Hence free trade may shift initiative, if not power, not only from the public to the private sector, but also from the federal to the provincial spheres.

This analysis is very speculative. Whether or not it is the centralizing or the decentralizing potential in a trade agreement that prevails depends greatly on the terms of the agreement, and on the degree to which the provinces are able to ensure a powerful voice, not only in the negotiations, but also in the subsequent ratification, implementation and enforcement stages. In the autumn of 1986, many readers might also conclude that the analysis is moot, since the prospects for a comprehensive Canada-U.S. agreement are so limited. On both sides of the border, powerful forces are arrayed against it.

Nevertheless some of the lessons apply whether or not the current initiatives succeed. Many of the consequences which many fear (and others welcome) from a free trade agreement are already apparent, and will not diminish without an agreement. External challenges to various aspects of federal and provincial resource management policies, or to aspects of regional development policy involving unfair subsidies exist in any case. The link between domestic economic policies and external trade policies can only increase. The subjects of international trading discussions will increasingly focus on the activities of provincial governments. Greater global economic integration is likely to promote even further regional differentiation within national economies, and to reduce the significance of internal trading relationships. Adjustment policies will need to be ever more responsive to international developments. Hence, the working out of effective federal-provincial arrangements as they relate to the international arena will remain a crucial issue for federalism in the next few years. More generally, much more attention needs to be paid to how we adapt our domestic policy-making structures to the exigencies of a world more integrated in both global and North American terms. The realization that these pressures dramatically constrain our autonomy and freedom of action must be accompanied by a search for those levers which we can still pull effectively and for the areas within which we can still make real choices. That will all require rethinking of our democratic processes, both as represented in federalism and in parliamentary government.

We have only just begun to explore the possibilities with respect to such questions as the role of provinces in international negotiations, the integration of provincial trade development policies with those of the federal government, the sharing of responsibilities in trade negotiations, the role of provinces in treaty negotiation and implementation, and the division of economic responsibilities in light of these international economic pressures and of the need to define and implement a role for Canada, and for each of its regions, in the global economy.

Notes

1. Richard Johnston. *Public Opinion and Public Policy in Canada* (Toronto: University of Toronto Press, 1985). pp. 204-205.
2. See, for example, J.J. Quinn. "The International Legal Environment: An Overview," in John. J. Quinn, ed. *The International Legal Environment* (Toronto: University of Toronto Press, 1985). pp. 90-94.
3. Reference Re Labour Conventions, [1936] S.C.R. 461
4. Quoted in Peter Russell, ed. *Legal Constitutional Decisions* Revised edition. (Toronto: McClelland and Stewart, 1973). p. 161.
5. Quinn, *op. cit.* p. 89
6. These issues are explored in John Whyte, "A New Look for Federal Powers over the Economy?" Paper presented to the Sixth Annual Workshop on Commercial and Consumer Law. University of Toronto, October, 1986. Mimeo.
7. Peter Hogg. *Constitutional Law of Canada* Second ed. (Toronto: Carswell, 1985). pp. 373, 450-2.
8. For a thorough review, see George Szablowski, "Treaty-Making Power in the Context of Canadian Politics," in C. F. Beckton and A. W. MacKay, eds., *Recurring Issues in Canadian Federalism* (Toronto: University of Toronto Press, 1985). pp. 142-83. See also Tom Keating and Don Munton, eds., *The Provinces and Canadian*

Foreign Policy Proceedings of a Conference, Edmonton, March, 1985. (Toronto: Canadian Institute of International Affairs, 1985.)

9. Gil Winham, Paper presented at Carleton University Conference on Canada-U.S. Free Trade, October 1986.

10. Royal Commission on the Economic Union and Development Prospects for Canada. Report. Vol. One, pp. 368-73; Vol. Three, pp. 151-156.

11. T. J. Courchene, "The Fiscal Arrangements: Focus on 1987," in Courchene, David Conklin and Gail Cook, eds., *Ottawa and the Provinces: The Distribution of Money and Power*. (Toronto: Ontario Economic Council, 1985). pp. 6-11.

12. R. A. Young, Philippe Faucher, and Andre Blais, "The Concept of Province-Building: A Critique," Canadian Journal of Political Science. 17: 4 (December, 1884), pp.783-818.

13. Earl Fry, "The Role of State and Provincial Governments in Canada-U.S. Sectoral Integration", in *Canada-United States Law Journal*, Vol. 10, 1985. pp. 169-188.

IV

CHRONOLOGY

CHRONOLOGY OF EVENTS 1985

Stephanie Thorson and
Avigail Eisenberg

A list of recurring entries begins page 257

January 13

*Northwest
Territories
- Political
Jurisdiction
Division*

An agreement on the boundary to divide the Northwest Territories into two independent political jurisdictions is reached. The eastern territory will be populated mainly by Inuit who live in the eastern Arctic. Living in the west are Dene Indians, Metis and Inuvialuit with a slight white majority. The Beaufort Sea is allocated to the western territory but the agreement allows the eastern territory to share oil and gas revenues. Revenues from resource deposits in either territory will be pooled and divided among the federal, Nunavut and western governments. Indian and Northern Affairs Minister David Crombie endorses the move in early February, setting out a tentative timetable for the division and citing 1987 as the earliest date.

January 15

*Education -
Ontario
Universities*

The Commission on the Future Development of the Universities of Ontario releases its report. The report recommends a 50 per cent increase in tuition fees over the next few years, a six per cent cut in enrolment, and provincial-wide entrance exams. The purpose of these measures is to place Ontario universities on financially stable ground without sacrificing excellence in instruction and research. The Commission also recommends new arrangements for provincial government financing of universities which include tying government grants to graduate student fellowships and academic research grants.

January 23

*Regional
Development
- Quebec*

Regional Industrial Expansion Minister Sinclair Stevens and Quebec Industry Minister Rodrigue Biron sign a $350 million, five-year industrial development agreement, pursuant to the 10-year, $1.8 billion Economic and Regional Development Agreement (ERDA) between the federal and Quebec governments signed in December, 1984. The new agreement ensures only one level of government will handle negotiations on individual investment projects in Quebec, depending on what jurisdiction the project is under. Grants or subsidies for industrial projects will be offered, each government providing half the financing.

January 24

*Constitution
- Quebec*

Quebec MP Raymond Garneau affirms the need for the Quebec and federal governments to discuss a resolution passed in the Quebec National Assembly in November, 1981, before further constitutional negotiations take place. The resolution calls for a Quebec society with the attributes of a distinct nation, to include its own language, culture and institutions. Garneau says the Quebec government should modify the resolution so that negotiations can proceed, and calls on the Prime Minister to outline what changes should be made.

January 31

*Constitution
- Charter of
Rights*

Minister of Justice John Crosbie presents to Parliament the government's first proposal for bringing federal statutes in line with the Canadian Charter of Rights and Freedoms. Over 50 statutes are to be amended, some of which contain discrimination on the basis of age and gender. Ottawa announces plans to set up a special committee of the House of Commons to hold public hearings on Charter related questions.

February 1

*Communications
- Quebec
Regional
Development*

The federal and Quebec governments sign a $40 million agreement to stimulate research and development in the Quebec communications industry. The agreement which is part of the umbrella Economic and Regional Development Agreement (ERDA) signed between the governments in December 1984, is the first agreement in the communications sector to be signed between the Quebec and federal governments.

February 4

Housing

A report entitled *A Consultation Paper on Housing* is released by William McNight, Minister responsible for the Canada Mortgage and Housing Corporation. The report suggests the government should: define the roles that various levels of government should play in the housing industry; clearly identify the priorities for housing expenditures; and create programs that are effective in meeting intended objectives.

February 7

Fiscal Federalism - Northwest Territories

Finance Minister of the Northwest Territories Tom Butters introduces a budget giving the Territories' government the ability and responsibility to identify its own priorities and allocate its own resources, functions previously carried out largely by the federal government. The federal government will transfer money to the territories in one lump sum for a given year, replacing the current system of providing funds on an ad hoc basis.

February 11

Energy - Atlantic Accord

Prime Minister Brian Mulroney and Newfoundland Premier Brian Peckford sign an offshore energy agreement called the Atlantic Accord. The Accord gives the province substantial decision making power over offshore energy development such as the power to set and collect royalties and taxes. A $300 million grant, 75 per cent federally funded and 25 per cent provincially funded, is set up for offshore oil and gas development. The federal and provincial governments will share Crown revenues from offshore development equally. An offshore management board will be set up and consist of equal representation from both governments. The Accord will not affect equalization payments to the province. (For a full account, see B. Pollard: "Newfoundland: Resisting Dependency", in *Canada: The State of the Federation 1985*.)

February 14, 15

First Ministers' Conference

The agenda for the First Ministers' Conference on the economy, held at Regina addresses investment, training, regional economic development and international trade. The first ministers agree to meet at least once per year for the next five years. The premiers urge the federal government to pursue a free trade agreement with the United States. The federal government announces it will redirect $695 million, previously budgeted job training programs in an attempt to combine the operations of the two levels of government and private companies in the area of worker retraining. New training and job creation programs are announced: $125 million for programs aimed at women and youth; $350 for job creation for the long-term unemployed; $80 million for those whose jobs are threatened by technology; $40 million will be spent on declining communities; and $100 million for pilot studies and experimental programs. Total federal spending on job creation for the 1985-86 fiscal year will be the same as the previous year, $2.2 billion. The principles of a national strategy for export development are supported by all the ministers. The premiers' request for an upper limit on interest rates is not met.

February 17

Aboriginals
- Charter of
Rights

A leaked federal cabinet document reports that there are sections of the Indian Act which violate the equality section of the Canadian Charter of Rights and Freedoms. The document predicts it will cost the federal government $420 million to restore the rights and benefits of 26,700 Indians who are affected by the Act.

February 22

Regional
Development -
Quebec
(Domtar)

The federal Department of Regional and Industrial Expansion withdraws a $100 million grant, promised by the previous government, to modernize a Domtar Inc. fine-paper mill in Windsor, Quebec. The Quebec government says it will donate $83 million to the project if the federal government reinstates the grant. On April 5, a federal-provincial package, including a $150 million interest-free loan, is accepted by Domtar Inc.. The loan will be provided by a Quebec government agency and interest charges will be split evenly between the two governments. A $21 million grant will be contributed by Quebec's energy and resource department.

February 23

The agreement to divide the Northwest Territories into two political jurisdictions is set back because

Northwest Territories - Political Jurisdiction Division	the Nunavut Constitutional Forum (NCF) rescinds its support. The NCF, which represents Inuit interests and is based in the Eastern Arctic objects to the present agreement because it places Inuvialuit communities of the Beaufort Sea in the western territory and allows four central Arctic Inuit communities a choice as to which side they will join. The NCF state that their aim in the division is to create an Inuit homeland.
February 28 *Aboriginals*	Indian Affairs Minister David Crombie introduces Bill C-31, legislation which enables Indian women who have married non-natives to regain their Indian status and rights. Many Indian groups oppose the legislation and see it as yet another example of federal intervention into matters over which native groups ought to have autonomous power. The legislation is passed June 20 and is given Royal Assent June 28.
March 1 *Employment Labour Code*	Amendments to the Canada Labour Code come into effect. These include provision for an extra 24 weeks of unpaid paternal leave (to be added to the 17 weeks already provided) for parents employed in industries under federal jurisdiction, without loss of their previous positions at work. In addition, employers are being encouraged to further protect employees from sexual harassment. Finally, amendments require that disabled employees under federal jurisdiction be paid at least federal minimum wage.
March 1 *Economic and Regional Development Agreements*	To date, 52 sub-agreements under the umbrella of the Economic and Regional development Agreement (ERDA) have been signed between the federal and provincial governments. The new agreements allow for an increase of the amount of federal money to be spent on regional development in the next five years. Spending presently stands at 12 per cent of total federal spending per year or $12.96 billion. The sub agreements place an emphasis on technology and research and development.
March 6	Fisheries Products International Limited in Newfoundland receives $25 million in government

subsidies: $15.5 million from the federal government; $6.5 million from the Newfoundland government; and $3 million from the Bank of Nova Scotia, to be used on strengthening trawlers for ice navigation and resumption of operations. The federal government owns 62.5 per cent of the shares and the Newfoundland government owns 25 per cent of FPI; both declare that privatization is the ultimate goal for the company.

March 6

*Constitution
- Quebec
- Senate Reform
- Charter of
Rights*

Quebec Justice Minister Pierre Marc Johnson announces Quebec will sign the Constitution only if it recognizes that Quebec is a distinct society, which needs special powers to protect its unique character. Specifically, Quebec wants control over the "linguistic situation" in the province, referring to the need for modifications to Article 23 of the Charter of Rights, which guarantees French and English minorities education in their language across Canada. Quebec will not agree to any constitutional amendments desired by the rest of the country until its own constitutional demands have been met. For example, Quebec will not assent to a proposed constitutional amendment limiting the length of time the Senate can debate a money bill.

March 12

Pension Reform

Federal Health and Welfare Minister Jake Epp releases a report by the Canada Pension Plan Advisory Committee. The recommendations of the report include (1) a modified "pay-as-you-go" funding for the CPP, to begin in 1994 and designed to maintain enough funds on hand to cover two years of benefits and administrative expenses; (2) adjusting contribution rates to pay for changes in benefits; (3) commencement of federal-provincial talks in order that decisions can be made well before 1994.

March 15

*Energy -
Atlantic Accord
- Environment*

Minister of Energy Pat Carney and Newfoundland Energy Minister Bill Marshall announce the schedule for the submission of the Environmental Impact Statement (EIS) for the Hibernia Development Project and the establishment of a federal-provincial panel to review the EIS. Hibernia operator Mobil Oil Canada Ltd. releases its EIS May 15, announcing the number of jobs created at Hibernia will peak at 2,085 in 1989. The Newfoundland government had predicted 15,000 to 20,000 jobs would be created. A safety program, to be included in all stages of the development, is included in the EIS. It also states that the probability of an oil spill is low. Mobil Oil announces July 31 it will use a concrete production system instead of a floating system to develop the Hibernia oil field. The cost is an estimated $5 billion, with a maximum capacity of 150,000 barrels a day, and operation will begin by the early 1990s.

March 26

Official Languages - Manitoba

Official Languages Commissioner, D'Iberville Fortier, releases a report entitled *Fifteen Years Later: Renewal or Reversal, The Minority Challenge*. The report warns that French in Manitoba will become extinct without a concerted effort by the federal and provincial governments to expand the provision of French services in that province. On March 27 the Manitoba government indicated that it would not hasten the pace by which the present program is expanding the provision of French language services.

March 27

Education - Ontario

Ontario Liberal leader David Peterson says the Ontario government is passing on to Ontario colleges and universities an increase of only five per cent rather than the 7.5 per cent increase in transfer payments from the federal government that the province received for post-secondary education for the 1985-86 fiscal year. The 2.5 per cent difference amounts to almost $29 million.

March 28

Energy - Western Accord

An energy agreement between the federal government and the Alberta, British Columbia and Saskatchewan governments is announced. The agreement will cost the federal government $500 million a year. The Petroleum Compensation Charge, an oil import subsidy, will be eliminated. Energy Minister Pat Carney estimates 300,000 jobs will be created. As a result of the deal, a three to five cent per litre tax on oil will be included in the next federal budget. She says the deregulation will give the oil industry an estimated $800 million a year. The provinces involved agree not to impose additional royalties as a result of the higher oil prices. A task force is to be set up to create a gas pricing deal to make gas prices more sensitive to market forces. On June 1, the Canadian oil market is deregulated. On November 1, 1986, natural gas prices are to be deregulated, subject to federal-provincial agreement.

March 29

Regional Development - Newfoundland

The federal and Newfoundland governments announce a six-year, $180 million highways construction agreement pursuant to the Economic and Regional Development Agreement (ERDA) signed between the two governments in December, 1984. The money is to be used on both upgrading and construction of the Trans-Labrador and Trans-Canada Highways. The agreement is signed June 24.

March 30

Quebec Nationalism

The Rassemblement Démocratique pour l'Indépendance (RDI), an offshoot of the Parti Québécois, holds its founding convention. The RDI is a movement dedicated to the independence of Quebec. The movement's temporary leader Camille Laurin says the RDI will decide in the autumn whether to turn the movement into a political party.

March 31

Crown Corporations - Canagrex

The Crown corporation Canagrex, the central agency for exporting farm goods, will be dismantled by the federal government. It has authority to extend credit to foreign buyers, to set up joint ventures with Canadian farmers and to buy and sell agricultural products. Canagrex has been in operation since January 1, 1984. Operations will end in September, 1985. The federal government says dismantling the corporation will save $6.6 million.

April 1

Fiscal Federalism - Equalization

The federal government increases equalization payments by $285 million to the six least wealthy provinces: New Brunswick, Newfoundland, Nova Scotia, Manitoba, Prince Edward Island and Quebec. According to an announcement made on February 27 by Finance Minister Michael Wilson, the provinces were to receive a decrease in transfer payments of $397 million with Quebec receiving a cut of $263 million, Manitoba $72 million, Nova Scotia $52 million and Prince Edward Island $3 million. Newfoundland and New Brunswick were not affected by these cuts. Under the new arrangement, cuts for Quebec are reduced by $110 million, for Manitoba by $50 million, for Nova Scotia and New Brunswick by $20 million each, for Newfoundland by $15 million and for Prince Edward Island by $5 million. The new figures were determined by guaranteeing 95 per cent of the previous year's payments in the case of Manitoba, Quebec and Nova Scotia and providing a per capita average, based on the payments for those three provinces, for the three poorer have-not provinces. The transfer payments are dictated by the federal Fiscal Arrangements Act, which took effect in 1982 and ends in 1987.

April 1

Law - Young Offenders Act

A section of the Young Offenders Act setting 17 as the maximum age for young offenders, comes into effect. Under the old Juvenile Deliquents Act, each province had the power to determine which age groups would be sent to adult and juvenile court. (British Columbia, New Brunswick, Nova Scotia, Ontario and Saskatchewan pressured the federal government to postpone the implementation of the section of the Act which sets the maximum age.) On March 20, the Saskatchewan government announces a $13 million program to fulfill the province's responsibilities under the Young Offenders Act which include the provision of facilities for people aged 12 to 17 who commit crimes under the Criminal Code. On April 2, the Alberta government announces the introduction of the Alternative Measures Program which provides an alternative to formal court proceedings allowed for in the Act. Under the Act a young offender may be required to attend counselling sessions, to compensate the victim financially or to provide service to either the victim or the community. In mid-May, the Ontario Supreme Court rules that offenders charged before April 1 should still have their trial conducted before a youth court. In Nova Scotia, youths aged 16 and 17 charged before April 1 will continue to be tried before adult court. At the September 19 meeting of six provincial attorneys general, consensus is reached that changes in the Act are needed, but agreement is not reached on what should be changed or how drastic the changes should be.

April 2,3

First Ministers' Conference - Aboriginal Self-Government

Agreement is not reached on the federal government's proposed amendment regarding aboriginal self-government at the First Ministers' Conference on Aboriginal Constitutional Matters. The federal proposal sought to "recognize and affirm the rights of the aboriginal peoples of Canada to self-government", to have these rights given effect through negotiated agreements, and to commit governments to such negotiations. About one-half of the provincial governments were reluctant to make a constitutional commitment to negotiate, while several aboriginal peoples' organizations were concerned that the amendment would diminish their rights.

April 3

Tax Reform

The House of Commons committee studying social programs for families recommends that the existing $710 tax exemption on each dependent under 18 years be reduced. The revenue from the cuts which will go to both federal and provincial governments should be redirected by both levels of government to other social programs. The committee also recommends that the current family allowance system should be retained, that a surtax to tax back those benefits from the wealthy not be entertained and that tax discounters be banned.

April 7

Aboriginals - Self-Government

Alberta Premier Peter Lougheed suggests the federal government change its focus on entrenching native self-government in the Constitution by only negotiating with status Indians who fall within federal jurisdiction, and leaving the provinces to negotiate with the Metis.

April 15

Minister of State for Finance Barbara McDougall's discussion paper on financial institutions entitled

Regulation of Canadian Financial Institutions: Proposals for Discussion, is released. The paper proposes that federally-incorporated financial holding companies (FHCs) be allowed to operate banking businesses. The government requirement to set up an FHC would apply to all investors who hold more than 10 per cent of two or more regulated financial institutions, at least one of which is federally incorporated: the two institutions must fall under different pieces of legislation. A new class of banks, Schedule C banks, could also be owned outright by an FHC. Schedule C banks would be subject to most of the rules governing Schedule A and B banks, and their owners would be permitted majority control. A proposed Financial Conflicts of Interest Office is to be modelled on the operation of the United States Securities and Exchange Commission. This report and the Wyman Report are forwarded to the House of Commons Committee on Finance, Trade and Economic Affairs. The Senate Banking Committee report, studying changes to the Canada Deposit Insurance Corporation is released the week of December 9.

April 17

*Constitution
- Charter of
Rights*

The equality clause, section 15, of the Canadian Charter of Rights and Freedoms comes into effect. It guarantees equality before and under the law and equal protection and benefit of law. Subsection one provides for affirmative action programs. Although the Constitution Act came into effect on April 17, 1982, governments were given three years to amend their statutes before section 15 became law. Nova Scotia, Saskatchewan and Manitoba governments introduce legislation to make provincial laws conform to the Charter. On April 18, Prince Edward Island passes similar legislation. British Columbia introduces legislation April 16. Ontario Premier Frank Miller announces plans for equal pay for work of equal value legislation for the civil service, but will not immediately force private industry to do the same. Due to the election call, introduction of legislation is delayed until June 11. The Alberta government announces legislation will be introduced in early May. On April 18, the Newfoundland government announces legislation will be introduced April 25. The New Brunswick government does not set a date to introduce legislation. Section 33 of the Charter allows provincial governments to override the equality section.

April 18

Aboriginals

A report is leaked by cabinet proposing $169 million would be cut from the Department of Indian Affairs and Northern Development's (DIAND) budget, and 3,500 of DIAND's 5,000 employees would be redirected. (On May 7, New Democratic Party leader Ed Broadbent reveals a secret cabinet document recommending $311 million be cut from DIAND's budget.) New Brunswick Premier Richard Hatfield and Manitoba Premier Howard Pawley announce their opposition to any transfer of constitutional responsibilities regarding Indian affairs from the federal government to the provinces.

April 23

Law
- Prostitution
- Pornography

A federal report on prostitution and pornography recommends prostitutes be allowed to work in their homes. The report recommends that the Criminal Code be modified so that the licensing of brothels and the sanctioning of red-light districts by provincial and municipal authorities is possible. Other recommendations include halting criminal sanctions against many forms of explicit adult pornography that do not involve violence or human degradation while tightening restrictions on child pornography. Justice Minister John Crosbie announces that amendments to the Criminal Code will be introduced in early May to get prostitutes off the streets. The Saskatchewan and Nova Scotia governments announce they will not introduce legislation to legalize prostitution. Amendments to the Criminal Code, Bill C-49, are introduced May 2, are passed November 20 and receive Royal Assent December 20. The legislation provided for a review of the section of the Criminal Code dealing with prostitution, to be undertaken by a House of Commons committee.

| April 24 | The Supreme Court of Canada strikes down the federal Lord's Day Act as violating religious freedoms and hence the Canadian Charter of Rights and Freedoms. Alberta, British Columbia, Manitoba, Ontario and Saskatchewan have their own municipal or retail business holiday laws that govern Sunday store closings; the impact of the Supreme Court's decision on these provincial laws is unclear. |

*Constitution
- Charter of
Rights*

| April 25 | The Quebec government proposes that contributions to the Quebec Pension Plan almost double over seven years, beginning in 1987. The contribution rate would rise from its present level of 3.6 per cent of gross salary, with the employee and the employer each paying half, to 4.0 per cent in 1987, reaching 6.4 per cent in 1993. Regarding private plans, the government proposes to make them portable for people changing jobs. In addition, employers would be required to offer plans to employees after two years of employment. |

*Pension Reform
- Quebec*

| April 25 | Fisheries Minister John Fraser announces commercial salmon fishing will be banned in the Maritime provinces in 1985 and part-time Newfoundland fishermen will have to give up their licenses. The move is aimed at allowing stocks of Atlantic salmon to recover. |

*Natural
Resources -
Maritimes
- Fisheries*

| April 30 | The federal and Quebec governments sign a $300 million, five-year forestry development agreement as part of a $1.6 billion Economic and Regional Development Agreement (ERDA). The money will be spent primarily on reforestation projects. The governments hope 16,000 person-years of jobs in reforestation will be created. |

*Natural
Resources -
Quebec
- Forestry*

| April 30 | A report prepared by the Hall committee, a group appointed by former Liberal transport minister Lloyd Axworthy, unanimously recommends that all of the Crow benefits be paid to grain producers instead of the railways, which currently receive the payments. The $658.6 million grain stabilization payments would be made to grain producers on the basis of delivery of eligible grains. The funds |

*Agriculture
- Crops*

would be administered under the grain stabilization act and would be called the Grains Transporation Refund. The report stated that this refund system would result in additional growth in the West, increasing the incomes of farmers in Alberta, Saskatchewan and Manitoba.

April 30

Senate Reform

Prime Minister Brian Mulroney agrees to a full-scale constitutional conference on Senate reform by 1987. Eight of the 10 provinces previously agreed to support a constitutional resolution which will place a 30-day limit on the time the Senate can hold up money bills and a slightly longer limit for other legislation passed by the House of Commons. Quebec, which did not sign the Constitution, and Manitoba, which is in favor of abolishing the Senate, do not support the resolution. On February 26, Mulroney threatens to give Senate reform higher priority in light of the Senate's refusal to pass a finance borrowing bill before the government's 1985-86 spending estimates were tabled. As a result of the delay, an estimated cost of $10 million in additional borrowing charges was incurred. On March 6, the Alberta, British Columbia and Ontario governments announce they are not in favor of abolishing the Senate. The Quebec government announces Quebec will not endorse any constitutional change concerning the Senate as long as Quebec has not signed the Constitution. On March 23, a committee of the Alberta Legislature recommends an elected Senate with six Senators for every province. On May 1, Mulroney says he wants to hold the conference before the end of his mandate. On May 14, Crosbie says he will push ahead with reforms even though Ontario Premier Frank Miller will not support the reforms unless his minority government receives backing from one of the two opposition parties. If Ontario does not approve the amendment, the resolution will lack the necessary population requirements to amend the Constitution. A Gallup poll released December 2 reveals 41 per cent of Canadians would prefer an elected Senate, 26 per cent would abolish it and 15 per cent would retain the Senate in its present form.

May 14,15

Western Premiers'
Conference -
Tax System
- Free Trade
- Farmers'
Programs

At the Western Premiers' Conference, the premiers call for the implementation of the proposed Canada Equity Plan, a system of tax credits providing incentives for investment. The plan is similar to the Quebec Stock Savings Plan, already in effect. The premiers agree to the principle of free trade with the United States. A series of communiques call for stabilization programs for farmers.

May 15

Francophone
Summit

External Affairs Minister Joe Clark announces he will wait to invite Quebec to the Francophone Summit until the Canadian and French governments settle the dispute surrounding Quebec's role at the summit. The summit is to be held in January in Paris. On May 24, Prime Minister Brian Mulroney approves Quebec's participation in the Summit, without specifying what Quebec's role will be. On December 10, Quebec Premier Pierre-Marc Johnson accuses Mulroney of betraying Quebec by giving New Brunswick the same status as Quebec in the Francophone Summit.

May 17

Constitution
- Quebec

Quebec Premier René Lévesque releases The Draft Agreement on the Constitution. On May 25, Quebec Intergovernmental Affairs Minister Pierre-Marc Johnson says reaching an agreement on the Constitution does not mean acceptance of the federal policy of bilingualism. Liberal leader John Turner supports initiatives to have Quebec sign the Constitution, but not if the initiatives are to the detriment of the Charter of Rights.

May 21

Communication
- Quebec

A report prepared by the federal and Quebec governments outlines an agreement on the future of Quebec television, recognizing that both French and English television systems, with separate rules governing each, are required in Canada. Changes being contemplated include: maintaining Radio-Canada as a general interest service if the mandate of the English equivalent is redefined as a cultural channel; creating French content requirements for those stations outside Quebec which have over 500 francophones in the community; and requiring Quebec television stations to spend profits above a certain level on French productions.

May 23

*Education -
Established
Programs
Financing*

In presenting the federal budget, Minister of Finance, Michael Wilson, announces reductions in the rate at which EPT transfers will increase. EPF transfers are federal funds which go to the provinces in order to fund health care and post-secondary education. The cuts will affect EPF funds in starting in 1986-87.

May 23

*Constitution
- Charter of
Rights*

The Supreme Court of Canada will consider whether employers in every province should be legally accountable for discrimination practised by their employees. Depending on the Court's ruling, victims of discrimination by store clerks or office workers could sue employers for damages. Such legal rights presently exist only in British Columbia and Ontario.

May 23

*Federal Budget
- Fiscal Transfers
- Income Tax
De-indexation
- Cape Breton
- Agriculture
- Tourism
- Pensions
De-indexation
(Withdrawn)*

Finance Minister Michael Wilson presents his first budget. Features relevant to federal provincial relations are as follows: 1) The rate of growth in federal transfer payments to provincial governments will be limited, yielding savings to the federal treasury of $2 billion annually by 1990-91; the minister will meet with his provincial counterparts in the fall to discuss "how quickly and how best we can move to secure the savings the government intends to achieve." 2) The indexation of personal income tax exemptions and tax brackets will be reduced, reflecting only the annual increase in the consumer price index greater than three per cent, yielding increased tax incomes for Ottawa. Because all provinces except Quebec levy their taxes as a percentage of the federal tax (about 50%), their revenues too will increase (at about half the rate of the increase in federal revenues). 3) Atomic Energy of Canada Ltd. will close its two heavy water plants on Cape Breton Island, Nova Scotia. The plants, which employ 800 workers, have cost the government over $100 million annually for five years.

However, a major adjustment program for Cape Breton Island will be put in place. 4) Ottawa will re-negotiate agreements on crop insurance and agricultural stabilization programs to obtain a more "equitable balance of financial obligations" among federal and provincial governments and producers. 5) Provision of tourism facilities will be left solely to the private sector and the provinces, ending partial funding under existing Economic and Regional Development Agreements (ERDAs).

In addition to the above, the minister announces that the indexation of old age pensions will be limited to increases in the consumer price index beyond three per cent. (This measure, if it had been implemented, would have reduced the purchasing power of pensions by three per cent annually.) This announcement provokes a storm of protest, causing withdrawal of the proposed partial de-indexation.

On June 11, the Maritime premiers express concern over the federal budget, the partial de-indexing of old age pensions in particular, but do not take a joint stand against the decision, at the 61st session of the Council of Maritime Premiers. In June, both Prince Edward Island Premier Jim Lee and Newfoundland Premier Brian Peckford criticize the federal government for not taking measures in the budget to correct regional disparities. On May 27, a finance department document, released by Liberal MP Raymond Garneau, reveals taxpayers will pay $2.2 billion more in the form of added revenues for provincial governments, $2 billion of which the federal government wants to extract from the provinces. $6.4 billion a year will be gained through the de-indexation of old age pensions and income tax exemptions.

May 25 The federal and British Columbia governments announce a $300 million reforestation agreement,

Natural Resources - British Columbia	as part of a $525 million, five-year Economic and Regional Development Agreement, signed on May 15. The reforestation will be on private, Crown and Indian lands. The governments will split the costs evenly.
May 27 *Energy - Western Accord*	Energy Minister Pat Carney announces over $15 billion worth of energy projects will be implemented as a result of the Western Accord between the federal government and the western producing provinces.
May 28 *Aboriginals - Self-Government*	Inuit leaders reject Prime Minister Brian Mulroney's proposed constitutional amendment on aboriginal self-government. The leaders say that federal and provincial governments should be required to negotiate the details of self-government with native groups.
May 28 *Political Alliance - Ontario*	The Ontario Liberal and New Democratic parties sign a pact to defeat the Progressive Conservative government in the Ontario legislature through a non-confidence vote. The accord makes it impossible for the Liberal administration to be defeated for two years on a matter of non-confidence. In the first legislative session, the government plans to: implement separate school financing; ban extra-billing by medical doctors; increase youth employment and training; reform the tenant protection laws; and proclaim the section of the Environmental Protection Act dealing with toxic chemical spills. In the long term, the government promises to: promote affirmative action; finance a housing plan for non-profit units; create new pollution controls; reform services for the elderly and job security laws; and increase aid for farmers. In the area of legislative reform, the government plans to change the powers of House committees and individual members, reform the freedom of information and privacy acts, and alter election financing.
May 29 *Crown Corporations*	The Conference Board of Canada releases its study on the role of the board of directors in the accountability of Crown corporations. It calls for an overhaul of the legal and administrative

(Management)	structures within which the boards must operate. The study recommends that the government, as a shareholder, must make its goals known to board members, and directors should be allowed to participate in key decision making and corporate policy formulation. Also, government must not respond to political pressures by making a Crown corporation concurrently responsible to a series of different groups. The board should also be responsible for developing a corporate strategy, fixing capital and operating budgets and choosing a chairperson, company president and new directors.
June 5 *Aboriginals* *- Alberta*	The Alberta government proposes that Alberta legislation for the province's Metis be entrenched in the Constitution. The legislation is an amendment to the Alberta Act, granting title of existing Metis settlement lands to Metis corporations and protecting the title in the Constitution. The Metis Association of Alberta criticizes the policy because it fails to affect Metis not living in designated Metis settlements in Alberta.
June 12 *Constitution* *- Charter of* *Rights* *- Saskatchewan*	The Saskatchewan Court of Queen's Bench rules that an accused has the right to have his trial conducted in French. The decision is based on section 15, the equality section of the Canadian Charter of Rights and Freedoms. On June 24, Saskatchewan Justice Minister Gary Lane announces that the government will appeal the decision.
June 13 *Constitution* *- Charter of* *Rights* *- Manitoba*	The Supreme Court of Canada declares virtually all of Manitoba's statutes and most of its subordinate legislation invalid because they are in English only and not in French. The judgment renders Manitoba laws temporarily valid from the date of the judgment to "the expiry of the minimum period necessary for translation, re-enactment, printing and publishing." The case was first brought before the courts on May 29, 1980 by Roger Bilodeau. The judgment conforms to the provisions of the Canadian Manitoba Act of 1870. On June 14, Manitoba Premier Howard Pawley says Manitoba needs time and financial aid

from the federal government in translating its laws into French.

June 14

Regional Development - Nova Scotia

Regional Industrial Expansion Minister Sinclair Stevens announces that federal efforts to bring industries to Cape Breton Island are underway. Three Ontario companies are interested in building plants on the island.

June 17

Financial Institutions

A private sector committee, appointed by Minister of State for Finance Barbara McDougall in January, releases its report on deposit insurance, the *Wyman Report* which recommends co-insurance be adopted by the Canada Deposit Insurance Corporation. Insured depositors would carry some of the loss in the case of a financial institution's failure. The committee recommends co-insurance be phased in over a three-year period. In the first year, coverage would remain at its present level of up to $60,000. Beginning in the second year, the total insured amount would increase yet, the depositor would risk 10 per cent of his or her money.

June 17,18

Premiers' Conference - Acid Raid - Energy

At the thirteenth annual Conference of Eastern Premiers and New England governments, Quebec and Atlantic province leaders adopt a short-term acid rain reduction plan, committing themselves to 34 per cent sulphur dioxide emissions reduction. The New England states agree to cut their output by 24.7 per cent. The leaders endorse development of east coast natural gas off Nova Scotia and oil off Newfoundland. The issues of free trade and Canadian fish exports, which the United States complains are protected by federal government subsidies, are not resolved.

June 20

Science - Quebec ERDA

The federal and Quebec governments sign a five-year, $100 million agreement to finance research and development in Quebec as part of the Economic and Regional Development Agreement signed by the two governments in December. The overall costs are to be shared equally between the two governments. The largest beneficiary of the agreement is The Institute of Optics which will receive $34 million over the next five years.

June 24

*Regional
Development -
Saskatchewan*

An extension of a five-year Economic and Regional Development Agreement (ERDA) between the federal and Saskatchewan governments is announced. $45 million will be used for irrigation and transportation development in Saskatchewan.

June 25

*Education -
Quebec*

The Quebec Superior Court strikes down Bill 3, which attempts to reorganize the Quebec school system according to language rather than religion, as unconstitutional. Bill 3 calls for the abolition of most denominational school boards in favor of French or English-language school commissions. The Court rules that school boards that existed before 1867 are protected as denominational schools under section 93 of the Constitution Act of 1867, as are dissident boards set after that time. On June 26, the Quebec government announces its intention to appeal the decision.

June 27

Pension Reform

The federal government announces a reversal of the May 23 budget proposal of partially de-indexing old age security payments. To pay for the move, Finance Minister Michael Wilson announces a one cent per litre increase in gasoline taxes starting in 1987 and the extension of a special surtax on large corporations.

June 28

Employment

The federal government announces a $2-billion annual employment program called the Canadian Job Strategy, which is to be in full operation by September. The program emphasizes training rather than job creation and is made up of six programs designed to aid people unemployed for over 35 weeks, youth, women, those in social assistance and those whose jobs are threatened by technological change. Studying alternative industries and development for single industry communities is also included in the program. It is estimated to benefit 400,000 people. On August 24, the ten premiers issue a communique demanding that the federal government postpone the September 5 deadline set for the commencement of the training iniatives, saying the provinces were not consulted sufficiently in designing the training programs. On September 10, Employment Minister Flora MacDonald says four provinces (Alberta, Manitoba, Newfoundland and Saskatchewan) have signed individual agreements with the federal government on training programs and three others (New Brunswick, Nova Scotia and Prince Edward Island) are close to giving their final approval. On September 3, a preliminary agreement with Quebec is accepted.

July 1

Aboriginals - Charter of Rights

The federal Indian Act is amended to comply with the equality section of Canadian Charter of Rights and Freedoms. It restores Indian status and band membership to native women (and most children) who lost those rights by marrying non-status Indians.

July 4

Housing Ministers' Conference

The federal, provincial and territorial housing ministers agree to the transfer of certain social housing programs from federal to provincial control. Each province or territory is to negotiate its own housing agreement with the federal agency, Canada Mortgage and Housing Corporation. The ministers announce their unanimous support for a mortgage-backed securities proposal as a way of providing homeowners with stable long-term fixed rate mortgages. The move will require changes to the federal Interest Act. The ministers agree to a set of principles to govern future federal/provincial/territorial activity in the area of social housing aimed at improving the ability of the governments to target housing programs to those most in need, reduce duplication, improve the efficiency of program delivery and reduce the cost of these programs.

July 4

Aboriginals - Federal Policy

Indian Affairs Minister David Crombie appoints a five-member task force to review the federal comprehensive land claims policy in light of recent constitutional developments and court cases related to aboriginal land claims.

July 4

Ontario Education Minister Sean Conway introduces Bill 30 which will extend public financing of Catholic high schools. The move is made by Cabinet decree; the government does not wait for approval from the Legislature. The Ontario government formerly funded all grades up to grade 11. The government is seeking to extend funding to grade 12 starting September, 1986 and grade 13, in September, 1987. On July 11, the bill gets second reading. On July 16, the Legislature's Social Development Committee begins hearings which conclude on November 19. Consideration of the bill is deferred until the Ontario Court of Appeal rules on its constitutionality. Until the judgment is made, the government provides funding on an interim basis. Under the bill, separate schools are obligated to accept non-Catholic students only if space is available. The Progressive Conservative members support the legislation in principle, but call it discriminatory because full access for non-Catholics is not granted.

July 8

*Regional
Development -
Quebec*

The federal and Quebec governments sign a $170 million subsidiary agreement on the development of transportation in Quebec as part of the Economic and Regional Development Agreements of 1984. Each government will pay $85 million, to be spent on research and development, air, marine, highway and urban transportation.

July 9

*Regional
Development -
Nova Scotia -
Communications*

A five-year technology transfer agreement between Nova Scotia and the federal government is signed as part of the Economic and Regional Development Agreement (ERDA). The agreement is intended to enhance Nova Scotia's computer centres and advance technological training. The costs will be shared 70 per cent by the federal government and 30 per cent by the Nova Scotia government.

July 15

*Health -
Extra-billing
- Manitoba
- Saskatchewan*

Extra billing by physicians for insured medical services is banned in Manitoba and Saskatchewan. In Manitoba, doctors may not charge more than the scheduled rates of the province's health plan. In Saskatchewan, physicians may opt out of the province's health plan.

July 15

Transportation -
Deregulation

Transport Minister David Mazankowski proposes deregulation of airline, railroad and trucking companies and shipping lines, in a white paper entitled *Freedom to Move*. The firms would be free to set their own prices and decide what routes they would serve and the frequency of service. Mazankowski also proposes replacing the Canadian Transport Commission with a new agency with minimal powers to review air fare increases. Current restrictions on mergers and takeovers will be eliminated, but Cabinet will have the power to disallow such transactions where the assets involved are worth $20 million or more. Crown corporations in the transportation industry will be discouraged from "engaging in non-businesslike pricing and in loss-making activities." On February 28, provincial-territorial and federal transport ministers agree to significantly deregulate the operation of the Canadian trucking industry. An approved timetable of implementation sets autumn of 1986 as a target of completion of the deregulation of the trucking industry.

July 16

Education
- Official
Languages
- New Brunswick

The federal and New Brunswick governments conclude negotiations for 1984-85 regarding the Official Languages in Education Agreement. The federal government will give the New Brunswick government $23 million to ensure equitable educational opportunities for the French and English including second language instruction. Under a separate agreement, the federal government will give over $3.6 million to the New Brunswick government toward two francophone school-community centres.

July 24

Constitution
- Charter of
Rights
- Alberta
- Education

An Alberta Court of Queen's Bench gives francophone Albertans "the right to a degree of exclusive control over French minority instruction for their children in Alberta." The present law governing education was labelled unconstitutional by the court for violating section 23 of the Canadian Charter of Rights and Freedoms, which deals with minority education rights.

July 30

*Natural Resources -
British Columbia
- Mining*

The federal and British Columbia governments sign a $10 million mineral development agreement, as part of the federal Economic and Regional Development Agreements (ERDA).

August 1

*Health -
Extra-billing*

The Canadian Medical Association files a statement of claim that the federal Canada Health Act is unconstitutional and sections fall out of the federal government's jurisdiction. Under the Act, passed in 1984, the federal government withholds $1 in transfer payments to provinces for every dollar patients pay directly. The money is reimbursed if the province outlaws extra-billing within three years.

August 1

*Agriculture -
British Columbia*

The federal and British Columbia governments sign a five-year $40 million agreement to expand farm production in the province pursuant to the Economic and Regional Development Agreement (ERDA) signed between the two governments in December, 1984. The money will be spent on product and technology research, market development, farmer and public education and soil and water conservation efforts. Costs will be shared equally by the two governments.

August 5

*Premiers'
Conference -
Lumber*

A task force on lumber trade between Canada and the United States is announced at the annual meeting of the National Governors Association, attended by Canadian premiers. The six governors on the task force are from lumber producing states in the Pacific northwest; the task force will be suggesting to their national governments ways to resolve lumber trade problems which include non-tariff barriers.

August 8

*Aboriginals -
Housing*

The Native Council of Canada sets up a committee to ensure suitable native housing is provided, following a federal government decision to begin transferring responsibility for a native housing program to the provinces.

August 12

Petro-Canada purchases 1,800 petroleum service stations and four petroleum refineries from Gulf

Canada Ltd. for $886 million. The service stations and refineries are located in Ontario and the western provinces. On July 16 Petro-Canada received authorization from the federal Cabinet to spend as much as $1.8 billion to buy some of Gulf Canada Ltd.'s assets.

August 15

Alberta
Environment
- Waterfowl

The Alberta government announces its support of a $1 billion agreement between the federal and provincial governments and the United States government called the North American Waterfowl Management Plan. The agreement is to be signed by the governments in April 1986.

August 15

Natural Resources
- Maritimes
- Fisheries

Fisheries and Oceans Minister John Fraser announces the establishment of the Atlantic Regional Council of Fisheries created to advise the federal minister on fisheries policy.

August 21

Premiers'
Conference -
Regional
Development
- Free Trade

A joint statement is released by the premiers expressing concern that the principles agreed upon at the February first ministers' conference are not being followed by the federal government in areas such as regional development and the federal budget. The principles call for stronger federal-provincial cooperation and more balanced regional development. Ontario Premier David Peterson casts the only dissenting vote on the issue of free trade with the United States. As a result, no communique is issued on the subject.

August 29

Social
Assistance -
CAP

The Health and Welfare Ministerial Task Force on Program Review studying the Canada Assistance Plan (CAP) publishes its results. The task force reports that nearly half of all Canadians on social assistance are employable and unable to find work. Also, the cost of the program for the federal and provincial governments was over $4 billion in 1984-85 and if the growth in the proportion of employable Canadians who receive social assistance continues, CAP payments would reach $8.5 billion a year by 1989-90. Health Minister Jake Epp recommends easing the restrictions on the amount of private earnings that social assistance recipients can receive before their welfare benefits are reduced, so that the regulations do not discourage work activity. On September 18, Epp and his provincial counterparts approve a seven-point agreement removing certain financial penalties for welfare recipients participating in job training or placement programs. Benefits such as denticare can be maintained for a 12-month transition period under the agreement. The federal government's Canadian Job Strategy training and employment programs will will be made more accessible and training allowance will supplement social assistance payments.

September 1

Education -
Ontario - Catholics

The Ontario government extends public financing of Catholic schools. On September 11, the Ontario Cabinet passes an order-in-council providing grants to Catholic school boards to finance grade 11 programs for the 1985-86 academic year. On September 23, the Ontario Court of Appeal begins hearing arguments for and against the constitutionality of Bill 30. On September 24, Ontario Attorney General Ian Scott says the province has the constitutional authority to establish separate schools and the courts cannot stop the provincial government from establishing and financing a Catholic school system.

September 10

Health -
Ontario
Drug Prices

The Ontario government announces it will oppose federal government moves to change the system of licensing generic drugs unless the changes are accompanied by firm guarantees of benefits. Under the present law, competing firms pay a royalty to companies who patent the drugs and are then able to produce inexpensive generic equivalents.

September 12

Natural Resources
- Lumber

The federal and provincial forestry ministers announce their unanimous support for efforts to block United States protectionist measures against Canadian lumber.

September 13

Energy -

A set of agreements between the federal and Prince Edward Island governments is unveiled to reduce P.E.I.'s electricity rates by as much as 25

Prince
Edward Island

per cent. The federal government will contribute 80 per cent of an $8.5 million program to reduce the rates.

September 19

Constitution
- Charter of
Rights
Manitoba

The Supreme Court of Canada strikes down a provision in the Manitoba Public Schools Act which gives school boards the authority to set the age for mandatory retirement. The court rules that the Manitoba Human Rights Act, which prohibits discrimination based on age, takes precedence over other provincial statutes.

September 25

Constitution
- Charter of
Rights

The federal government announces that under the newly expanded court challenges program $1 million in the current fiscal year and $2 million in each of the next four years will be provided to help to finance important court challenges under the Canadian Charter of Rights and Freedoms. Cases involving equality rights, sexual equality and multiculturalism are eligibe for funding through the program.

September 25

Natural Resources
- Forestry

The Canadian Council of Forest Ministers is established. The forest ministers from across the country meet for the first time as an independent group.

September 26

Agriculture -
Stabilization Act

Amendments to the Agriculture Stabilization Act are announced by Agriculture Minister John Wise. Provincial governments will be given five years to join a national farm income stabilization plan, which guarantees farmers a floor price for certain products to protect against price fluctuations. Provinces can join the program during that period and leave at any time. Provinces that join must phase out their provincial subsidies so that farmers in every province eventually receive equal treatment. The program will be financed equally by the federal and provincial governments and participating farmers. The plan will be implemented immediately for hogs and cattle, and other agricultural products will be included at a later date. On November 21, the Alberta government announces its own assistance plan for farmers. The government will provide $150 million in farm fuel subsidies and $62.9 million will be given to livestock producers. On November 25, Ontario joins the income stabilization plan; Ontario farmers will receive $42 million in compensation for low prices earlier in the year.

September 29

Agriculture - Manitoba

A federal-provincial committee recommends Manitoba use its $1 million aid package to expand insurance coverage for livestock feed instead of giving farmers individual payments to compensate for the drought in Manitoba. A long-term forage security program presently being offered in 20 municipalities could be expanded to include the whole province and forage could be added to the list of crops protected. The plan is managed by the Manitoba Crop Insurance Corporation which is funded by both the federal and Manitoba governments.

September 30

Natural Resources - Pearse Report (Water)

Currents of Change, the report of an inquiry on Federal Water Policy chaired by P.H. Pearse, releases its report. The $1.5 million inquiry recommends homeowners and industries be required to pay the full costs of the water they use, as a way of discouraging waste. The report does not rule out exporting water to the United States, and it states Canada's supply of fresh water is threatened by pollution and regional shortages. Environment Minister Thomas MacMillan announces the appointment of a task force to examine the inquiry's 56 proposals for water diversion to the U.S.. The report also calls for the federal and provincial governments to negotiate a Safe Drinking Water Act, to improve municipal sewers and sewage-treatment plants, and to spend more money on water research.

October 1

Parliamentary Representation - Electoral Boundaries Act

Proposed amendments to the Electoral Boundaries Act are introduced in the House of Commons. A House of Commons committee will study the recommendations which call for slowing the rate of growth of the House of Commons. Under the new legislation, the House of Commons would expand from the present 282 seats to 289 instead of 310 under the current redistribution system. After 1991, there would be 293 seats instead of 343 and after 2001, 296 seats would exist instead of 369.

October 2

Newfoundland - Fisheries

The federal and Newfoundland governments announce a $105 million refinancing plan for Newfoundland's Fishery Products International (FPI). The federal government provides 62.5 per cent of the grant, the Newfoundland government provides 25 per cent and the Bank of Nova Scotia provides 12.5 per cent. Also, in its five-year business plan, the company states it intends to sell or lease 15 of its inshore plants to private industry. Newfoundland Premier Brian Peckford says the 15 plants listed for privatization are not entitled to money from the $105 million refinancing plan. On October 3, Nova Scotia Fisheries Minister John Leefe says the move will jeopardize the east coast fishery because it will encourage countervail duties on Canadian fish from the United States.

October 13

Environment - Forestry

The results of a scientific survey released by Minister of State (Forestry), Gerald Merrithew, warns that unless pollutants are cut in half, forest productivity declines will be nationwide and "substantial". As a result, the minister promises to redouble efforts to have the United States reduce its airborne pollutants. The survey was conducted by Canadian Forestry Service between September 1984 and February 1985.

October 15

Constitution - Charter of Rights

Justice Minister John Crosbie announces the federal government will introduce legislation in the winter to make federal laws conform to the Canadian Charter of Rights and Freedoms. Areas to be discussed are: allowing homosexuals in the Canadian Forces, the RCMP, schools and government; removing mandatory retirement; and allowing women in combat roles in the military.

October 23

Social Assistance

Finance Minister Michael Wilson rejects an Opposition recommendation to withdraw a bill to partially de-index family allowances. The NDP referred to a report stating that the number of families living in poverty had increased in 1984 for the fourth year in a row, bringing the number over one million families or 15 per cent of all families.

October 28

Newfoundland
- Fisheries
- Emergency
Aid Fund

The federal and Newfoundland governments announce the creation of an emergency fund of up to $9.5 million to aid Newfoundland fishermen affected by the poor fishing season in 1985. Because of the poor season, fishermen and plant workers do not have a sufficiently long employment period to be eligible for employment insurance for the winter months. The fund will be used to create special employment projects which will run for two to 20 weeks.

October 30

Constitution
- Charter of
Rights

A report is released by an all-party parliamentary committee established to review federal statutes and laws to make sure they conform to the equality section of the Canadian Cahrter of Human Rights and Freedoms. The report, entitled *Equality for All*, recommends mandatory retirement be abolished in Canada. The committee also says that public civil servants should get more political rights, that spouses on military bases should be allowed to take part in community activities and lobby for increased services, that the government should begin enforcing the concept of equal pay for work of equal value in federally regulated firms and that part-time workers should get more benefits and protection.

October 31

Energy -
Western Accord

Details of the federal policy on natural gas are released. Prices charged by Canadian producers will be frozen for one year. The federal government will cancel the Canadian Ownership Special Charge (this was announced in the spring). Alberta agrees to absorb higher transportation costs. On November 1, 1986, gas prices will be totally deregulated. Canada's single export price will be dropped in favor of regional export prices, so that Canadians do not pay more for gas than Americans in nearby areas. The new export system is estimated to increase exports to the United States by $500 million to $4.5 billion this year. On December 11, a study by the Canadian Petroleum Association is released, reporting Atlantic Canada would experience out-migration and economic hardship as a result of deregulating natural gas export volumes.

November 6

*Financial
Institutions
- House of
Commons
Committee
Report*

The House of Commons Committee on Finance, Trade and Economic Affairs examining the McDougall Green Paper and the *Wyman Report* releases its report, entitled *Canadian Financial Institutions. Report on the Standing Committee on Finance, Trade and Economic Affairs.* It recommends tougher regulation of all financial institutions to protect consumers from loss of funds and to prevent improper deals by corporate insiders. Also, there should be fewer restrictions on non-bank institutions' financial activities so that diversification into related fields is possible. It recommends the December 31 merger between Canada Trust and Canada Permanent be blocked until an ownership policy for financial institutions is formulated by the federal government. The committee advocates the creation of a National Financial Administration Agency (NFAA) which would perform the functions handled by the Inspector General of Banks, Department of Insurance and Canada Deposit Insurance Corporation. The NFAA would be controlled by a board made up of federal, provincial and industry representatives. It rejects two of Minister of State (Finance) Barbara McDougall's main mechanisms to allow more competition among financial institutions: the financial holding company and Schedule C banks.

Justice Minister John Crosbie announces a maximum of three factory freezer trawler licenses for the Atlantic fisheries industry will be granted by the federal government. Newfoundland Premier Brian Peckford accuses the federal government of a breach of trust, referring to a 1983 federal-provincial fisheries restructuring agreement which prohibits the use of FFTs in harvesting northern cod. Peckford argues the licences will result in a loss of hundreds of jobs in the province's onshore fish processing plants. Crosbie says the industry will not be affected.

Ontario Attorney General Ian Scott announces Ontario's francophones will have the right to a trial in French in any of Ontario's courts. This right will take effect in most courts by July 1, 1986. Full language rights in the courts will be implemented by December 31, 1986. Previously, francophones have been able to have trials in French only in courts that were in regions in the province designated as having a significant number of French speaking people in the population.

November 13

Crown
Corporations
- Northwest
and Yukon
Territories

The Northwest Territories Energy Minister, Tagak Curley, says he will request that the federal government write off a $125 million debt owed by the Northern Canada Power Commission before it turns the Crown corporation over to the Northwest and Yukon territories in March, 1987. Erasing the debt would create $10 million in revenue for the territories, money otherwise spent on interest for the loan.

November 14

Education
- Ontario
- Catholics

The Ontario Supreme Court orders a temporary stop on the Ontario government's payments to the province's Catholic schools until the courts have ruled on the legality of the Cabinet decree authorizing financing. The courts must determine if the funding contravenes the Canadian Charter of Rights and Freedoms. On December 12, the Ontario Supreme Court reserves judgment on the constitutionality of the legislation. Since payments were to begin mid-December, Catholic school boards are forced to borrow money to pay for grade 11 programs.

November 14

Transportation -
Deregulation

Transport Minister Donald Mazankowski rejects truckers' bid for slower implementation of deregulation, saying the truckers are only clouding the issue by claiming higher costs than their U.S. competitors. In October, provincial and federal transport ministers agree to remove regulations on the trucking industry by January 1, 1987. Ontario Transport Minister Edward Fulton promises truckers he will move slowly on deregulation and will only act after he knows what effects it will have on the industry.

November 16

Education -

A government financed study on the educational needs of franco-Ontarians prepared by the Ontario Institute for Studies in Education, reports that at least 30 per cent of Ontario's francophone residents are in danger of being assimilated within the next 20 years partly because their education system is not as good as that of the anglophone residents of Ontario. The study on elementary and secondary education cites problems for francophones in almost every aspect of the school system including the training of teachers, school organization and the political control over the structure of the school board. The report states that franco-Ontarians do not need to attend bilingual schools in order to become bilingual and should not be encouraged to do so. Rather, they should be attending French-language schools.

November 19

*Energy -
Western Accord*

Ontario Energy Minister Vince Kerrio charges that most Ontario natural gas consumers will not see price cuts due to deregulation for at least a decade because, according to Consumers Gas figures, approximately 85 per cent of contracts for natural gas sold in Ontario do not expire until 1995; only a minority of consumers have access to short term contracts for natural gas.

November 19

*Parliamentary
Representation
- Electoral
Boundaries Act*

The federal cabinet approves amendments to the Electoral Boundaries Bill. Due to their growing populations, Alberta, British Columbia and Ontario will each be given more seats in the House of Commons in the next election. Each province will get two more seats than were proposed under the original bill. The House of Commons will expand to 295 seats under the new legislation. Legislation passed on September 16 gives Alberta three additional seats in the House of Commons.

November 20

*Maritime
Premiers -
Agriculture
- Natural Resources*

The Council of Maritime Premiers endorses a Feed Sufficiency Strategy which calls for a 35 per cent increase (from 25 to 60 per cent) in feed freight rate assistance from the federal government and outlines a job creation program. The council supports a proposal submitted to the federal government for mapping resource information in the Maritimes.

| November 21 | The Supreme Court of Canada rules that according to section 35 of the Canadian Charter of Rights and Freedoms a 233-year old treaty guaranteeing native Indians hunting and fishing rights takes precedence over Nova Scotia's 1967 Lands and Forests Act. Section 35 guarantees existing aboriginal and treaty rights which include pre-Confederation treaties. |

November 21

*Aboriginal
Rights -
Land Claims -
Nova Scotia*

The Supreme Court of Canada rules that according to section 35 of the Canadian Charter of Rights and Freedoms a 233-year old treaty guaranteeing native Indians hunting and fishing rights takes precedence over Nova Scotia's 1967 Lands and Forests Act. Section 35 guarantees existing aboriginal and treaty rights which include pre-Confederation treaties.

November 21

*Regional
Development -
Quebec*

The federal and Quebec governments sign an agreement to help Hyundai Motor Company of South Korea finance a $300 million auto plant in Bromont, Quebec. The federal government will help Quebec pay interest for five years on a $200 million loan. The federal and Quebec governments will each pay half of up to $110 million in interest payments over five years.

November 25

*Crown
Corporations
- Canada
Development
Corporation*

The House of Commons gives final approval of a bill permitting the federal government to sell its 47 per cent share in the Canada Development Corporation. Under the legislation, no foreign investor or allied group of foreign investors may own more than 10 per cent of the company. No Canadian company or allied group of companies may own more than 25 per cent.

November 28, 29

*First
Ministers'
Conference
- Free Trade
- Agriculture
- Fiscal
Federalism
- Fisheries*

Prime Minister Brian Mulroney does not give in to premiers' demands to drop his budget proposal of cutting transfer payments to the province by $2 billion. An agreement on an approach to free trade negotiations with the United States is reached. Under the agreement, full provincial participation in the negotiations is agreed upon, although the term "full participation" is left undefined. A 90-day deadline is set for the two levels of government to work out common goals for a free trade agreement. The Ontario government proposes that the provinces be made almost equal to the federal government in the conduct of free trade negotiations. The proposal suggests the chief free trade negotiator Simon Reisman receive instructions from a special committee of federal and provincial ministers. The negotiator's strategies could also be reported back to each of the premiers. Reisman's final proposal would be examined by the committee for approval or rejection. Prime Minister Brian Mulroney agrees to work towards establishing a long term national agricultural policy. Federal and provincial agriculture ministers will spend the next months negotiating the policy. A priority will be working out details of a new permanent disaster relief program. Mulroney does not agree to the premiers' request for low interest rates loans to farmers on a large scale. Comprehensive crop insurance and increased agricultural research spending are also tabled for negotiation. Nova Scotia Premier John Buchanan says the federal government is discriminating against Nova Scotia in its feed freight costs subsidies. He says the federal government has not increased feed grain assistance in 10 years and since Nova Scotia imports two-thirds of its feed grain, it pays the highest grain costs in Canada. Newfoundland Premier Brian Peckford calls for more provincial say in fishery management, and New Brunswick Premier Richard Hatfield requests new approaches to federal-provincial co-ordination in fishery development.

December 2

Elections - Quebec

The Quebec election results give 99 seats to the Liberal Party (58 per cent of the popular vote) and 23 seats to the Parti Québécois (PQ) (37 per cent of the popular vote). The Liberal campaign consists of: job creation and increasing manpower retraining; reducing the deficit by $800 million, raising revenue through privatization and creating a favorable investment environment; a four-year deadline for signing the Constitution; increasing school financing; improving social and health services; a one per cent reduction in income taxes effective January 1, 1986; increasing welfare payments to those under 30 years of age; the elimination of a surtax on automobile, health, personal disability and accident insurance; guaranteeing English language health and social institutions; improving health and social services; investigating the feasibility of including homemakers in the Quebec Pension Plan;

providing interest-free loans to farmers; creating a closer relationship between management and labour; encouraging more competitive business and decreasing government intervention. The PQ campaign includes: increasing job creation and job protection; the mandatory participation of Quebec in any free trade discussions that would affect the province; increasing environmental protection, recycling and pollution prevention; improving social and health services, particularly emergency ward care; the entrenchment of the right of anglophones to receive social and health services in English; increasing agricultural assistance; creating a closer relationship between management and labour; encouraging more competitive business and decreasing government intervention; and improving the lot of women. The PQ leaves open the possibility of making Quebec politically sovereign at some future time.

December 2

Crown
Corporations
- De Havilland

Crown corporation de Havilland Aircraft of Canada is sold to Boeing Co for $155 million. The federal government's expenditure on the corporation was $834 million over 11 years. The federal government has promised Boeing an estimated $58 million to help finance the costs of expansion and modernization projects which have been proposed.

December 5

British Columbia
- Forestry

The federal cabinet authorizes, a five-year renewal of a project to promote overseas exports of British Columbia lumber. The federal and provincial governments and the Council of Forest Industries will each shoulder one third of the $35,372,200 cost.

December 5

Free Trade -
Quebec - Ontario

Quebec Premier Robert Bourassa and Ontario Premier David Peterson agree the provinces need a veto in free trade negotiations with the United States.

December 9

The Senate banking committee report is released proposing major changes to the Canada Deposit Insurance Corporation. The committee proposes

Financial
Institutions
- Senate
Banking
Committee
Report

full insurance be provided on the first $25,000 of deposits and 80 per cent insurance be provided on the next $50,000. It recommends that more powers be given to the corporation to prevent self-dealing among member institutions that do not have adequate regulations themselves. In addition, the corporation should have more power to deal with financial institutions that get into trouble yet it should not be able to close down institutions. The report recommended that the federal cabinet appoint a new board of directors.

December 9

Health -
Federal
Guidelines

Federal Health Minister Jake Epp announces the establishment of guidelines limiting the amount of ethyl carbamate in alcoholic beverages. The federal guidelines take precedence over provincial standards.

December 10

Social
Assistance

Secretary of State Benoit Bouchard announces the federal government will spend $16 million over five years to provide community support for disabled people. He announces a secretariat will be established to deal with concerns of disabled people, to join the provinces and various groups in providing financial and technical resources for research and education, and to convene a federal-provincial-territorial conference to discuss the needs of disabled people.

December 10

Aboriginals
- Alberta

The Alberta and federal governments agree to set up 62 square kilometres as a reserve for the Lubicon Lake Indian Band. The federal government will give the band $1.8 million in benefits.

December 12

Social Policy
- Housing

The federal government releases a report on changes to federal housing programs, entitled, *A National Direction for Housing Solutions*. The program emphasizes aiding the needy. The provinces will be allowed some say in the programs used in their jurisdictions. The Canada Mortgage and Housing Corporation's (CMHC) budget will not be cut. In the non-profit housing programs, tenants will not pay more than 25 per cent of their income for rent. Starting in early 1986, a system of mortgage-backed securities will be guaranteed by the federal government. Wider distribution of grants under the Residential Rehabilitation Assistance Program to bring older homes up to building code standards is included. The cooperative housing program will link financing to the cost of living, replacing the old system which provided subsidies. The Rural and Native Housing Demonstration Program will involve 500 units over a five-year period with the government supplying the funds and the communities supplying the labour.

December 12

Energy -
Western Accord

A study prepared by the Canadian Petroleum Association estimates that deregulation of natural gas exports would cut the federal deficit by $110 billion over the next 25 years through increased economic activity, gas exports and new explorations, but would cost the Atlantic provinces $23 billion in decreased disposable income and retail sales.

December 12

Education
- Official
Languages
- Ontario

Legislation is proposed in the Ontario Legislature which would guarantee representation for francophones on every school board in the province that operates a French-language school or class. The legislation calls for the creation of the province's first independent French-language school board, to be established in Ottawa-Carleton by 1988. The bill would provide for the election of French-speaking representatives to 28 public school boards and 30 separate school boards in Ontario.

December 12

Constitution
- Quebec

Quebec Premier Robert Bourassa says he wants to negotiate a constitutional agreement within two years. On December 13, Prime Minister Brian Mulroney agrees to begin negotiations soon. On December 18, Quebec Intergovernmental Affairs Minister Gil Rémillard says the Quebec stance on constitutional negotiations will be based on the new Liberal government's convictions rather than those of the Parti Québécois. Rémillard refuses to outline the stance in front of the National Assembly before the negotiations with Ottawa begin. Mulroney says he cannot promise Quebec a veto because that decision belongs to the other provinces.

December 13

*Social
Assistance -
Pensions*

The federal and provincial governments convene to augment contributions to the Canada Pension Plan, as of January 1, 1987. The CPP rate increase will be 0.2 per cent per year for five years. The current rate is 3.6 per cent of salary. The maximum CPP contribution increase in 1987 will be $24.10.

December 13

*Economy -
Transfer
Payments*

Federal Finance Minister Michael Wilson announced a new Established Programs Financing formula, which determines federal funding for health care and post-secondary education. Under the new formula funding will increase five per cent each year instead of the seven per cent which the previous arrangement provided. The Finance Minister stated that this will save the federal government $6 billion by the end of the 1990-91 fiscal year. Provincial opposition to the new arrangements is based upon the federal government's unilateral imposition of the new formula without consulting the provinces and the worry that the tax burden will have to be shifted to other people in order to maintain the present quality of health care and post-secondary education services.

December 17

*Social
Assistance -
Aboriginals*

Two accords to negotiate future child and family services agreements are signed by the First Nations Confederacy and the provincial and federal governments. The accords provide for the negotiation of an extension of existing Indian child and family services for another year and for the discussion of new arrangements for operation and funding for the future.

December 18

*Transportation -
Deregulation*

The House of Commons Transport Committee calls for changes to government proposals on transportation deregulation and a reduction in recently increased airline passenger taxes. The committee recommends specific regulations to protect low-density air routes and northern air travel from the full impact of a completely deregulated environment. The committee also advises giving priority to the full or partial privatization of Air Canada. New Brunswick Premier Richard Hatfield and Newfoundland Transport Minister Ron Dawe told the committee further study and consultation is required to adequately address the topic of deregulation and how it will affect the Atlantic provinces. Hatfield said transportation must be recognized as a key to regional economic development in a new National Transportation Act.

December 19

Environment -
Acid Rain

Environment Minister Thomas McMillan says the federal government will not grant Ontario its request of $85 million to control industrial acid emissions until the other provinces have submitted their requests for financial assistance. The federal government has a $150 million budget for reducing acid emissions of the country's major polluters.

December 19

Health - Extra-
billing - Ontario

A bill is introduced in the Ontario Legislature by the Ontario government to ban extra-billing by physicians for insured medical services.

December 19

Financial
Institutions
- Bank Failures

The Senate banking committee reports that the high risk corporate strategies and poor management practices followed by the Canadian Commercial and Northland banks are the primary reasons for the banks' failure. The Canadian Commercial Bank failed September 1 and the Northland Bank failed September 30. A judicial probe was launched October 2, headed by Mr. Justice Willard Estey. The Senate report says the banks made themselves vulnerable in the recession by having the overriding objective of increasing their assets in good and bad years. The Senate committee also criticizes the directors and external auditors of both banks, the inspector general of banks and the Bank of Canada. The report says auditors did not provide an independent check on the statements for shareholders, the inspector general of banks did not act quickly enough on reports that problems existed at the banks, and the Bank of Canada has no way of assessing the value of collatoral banks put up.

December 20

Aboriginal -
Self-government
- Ontario

Federal Indian Affairs Minister David Crombie, Ontario Attorney General Ian Scott and five native leaders sign an agreement providing for aboriginal self-government negotiations among the three groups of representatives.

CHRONOLOGY:
LIST OF RECURRING ENTRIES

Aboriginals, February 17, 28, April 2, 3, 7, 18, May 28, June 5, July 1, 4, August 8, November 21, December 10, 17, 20.

Agriculture, April 30, May 14, 15, 23, August 1, September 26, 29, November 20, 28, 29.

Alberta, June 5, July 4, August 15, December 10.

British Columbia, May 25, July 30, August 1, December 5.

Communications, February 1, May 21, July 9.

Constitution, January 24, 31, February 17, March 6, April 17, 24, May 17, 23, June 12, 13, July 1, 24, September 19, 25, October 15, 30, December 12.

Crown Corporations, March 31, May 29, August 12, November 13, 25, December 2.

Education, January 15, March 27, May 23, June 25, July 4, 16, 24, September 1, November 14, 16, December 12.

Employment, February 14, 15, March 1, June 28.

Energy, February 11, March 15, 28, May 27, June 17, 18, September 13, October 31, November 19, December 12.

Environment, March 15, June 17, 18, August 15, October 13, December 19.

Financial Institutions, April 15, June 17, November 6, December 9, 19.

First Ministers' Conference, February 14, 15, April 2, 3, November 28, 29.

Fiscal Federalism, February 7, April 1, November 28, 29.

Fisheries, March 6, April 25, August 15, October 2, 28, November 8, 28, 29.

Forestry, April 30, September 25, October 13, December 5.

Free Trade, February 14, 15, May 14, 15, August 21, November 28, 29, December 5.

Health, July 15, August 1, September 10, December 9, 19.

Housing, February 4, July 4, August 8, December 12.

Law, April 1, 23.

Manitoba, March 26, June 13, July 15, September 29.

Mining, July 30, September 19.

Natural Resources, March 6, April 25, 30, May 25, July 30, August 15, September 12, 25, 30, November 20.

Newfoundland, March 6, 29, October 2, 28.

Northwest Territories, January 13, February 7, 23, November 13.

Nova Scotia, June 14, July 9, November 21.

Official Languages, March 26, July 16, November 9, December 12.

Ontario, January 15, March 27, May 28, July 4, September 1, 10, November 9, 14, December 5, 12, 19, 20.

Parliamentary Representation, October 1, November 19.

Pension Reform, March 12, April 25, May 23, June 27.

Premiers' Conference, May 14, 15, June 17, 18, August 5, 21.

Quebec, January 23, 24, February 1, 22, March 6, 30, April 25, 30, May 17, 21, June 20, 25, July 8, November 21, December 2, 5, 12.

Regional Development, January 23, February 1, 22, March 1, 29, June 14, 20, 24, July 8, 9, August 21, November 21.

Saskatchewan, June 12, 24, July 15.

Senate Reform, March 6, April 30.

Social Assistance, August 29, October 23, December 10, 12, 13, 17.

Tax Reform, April 3, May 14, 15.

Transportation, July 15, November 14, December 18.

List of Titles in Print

Bruce G. Pollard, *Managing the Interface: Intergovernmental Affairs Agencies in Canada*, 1986. ($12)

Peter M. Leslie, editor, *Canada: The State of the Federation 1985*, 1985. ($14)

Peter M. Leslie, *Politics, Policy, and Federalism: Defining the Role of the Institute of Intergovernmental Relations*, 1984. ($7)

Catherine A. Murray, *Managing Diversity: Federal-Provincial Collaboration and the Committee on Extension of Services to Northern and Remote Communities*, 1984. ($19)

Peter Russell *et al*, *The Court and the Constitution: Comments on the Supreme Court Reference on Constitutional Amendment*, 1982. (Paper $7, Cloth $15)

The Year in Review

Bruce G. Pollard, *The Year in Review 1983: Intergovernmental Relations in Canada*. ($16)

Revue de l'année 1983: les relations intergouvernementales au Canada. ($16)

S.M. Dunn, *The Year in Review 1982: Intergovernmental Relations in Canada*. ($12)

Revue de l'année 1982: les relations intergouvernementales au Canada. ($12)

S.M. Dunn, *The Year in Review 1981: Intergovernmental Relations in Canada*. ($10)

R.J. Zukowsky, *Intergovernmental Relations in Canada: The Year in Review 1980, Volume I: Policy and Politics*. ($8) (*Volume II not available*)

D. Brown, *Intergovernmental Relations in Canada: The Year in Review 1979*. ($7)

Queen's Studies on the Future of the Canadian Communities

Keith Banting, *The Welfare State and Canadian Federalism*, 1982. (Published with McGill-Queen's University Press. Distributed by University of Toronto Press.)

Allan Tupper, *Public Money in the Private Sector: Industrial Assistance Policy and Canadian Federalism*, 1982. ($12)

William P. Irvine, *Does Canada Need a New Electoral System?*, 1979. ($8)

Discussion Paper Series

22. Robert L. Stanfield, *National Political Parties and Regional Diversity*, 1985. (Charge for postage only)
21. Donald Smiley, *An Elected Senate for Canada? Clues from the Australian Experience*, 1985. ($8)
20. Nicholas Sidor, *Consumer Policy in the Canadian Federal State*, 1984. ($8)
19. Thomas Hueglin, *Federalism and Fragmentation: A Comparative View of Political Accommodation in Canada*, 1984. ($8)
18. Allan Tupper, *Bill S-31 and the Federalism of State Capitalism*, 1983. ($7)
17. Reginald Whitaker, *Federalism and Democratic Theory*, 1983. ($7)
16. Roger Gibbins, *Senate Reform: Moving Towards the Slippery Slope*, 1983. ($7)
14. John Whyte, *The Constitution and Natural Resource Revenues*, 1982. ($7)
13. Jack Mintz and Richard Simeon, *Conflict of Taste and Conflict of Claim in Federal Countries*, 1982. ($7)

Bibliographies

Federalism and Intergovernmental Relations in Australia, Canada, the United States and Other Countries: A Bibliography, 1967. ($9)

A Supplementary Bibliography, 1975. ($10)

A Supplementary Bibliography, 1979. ($5)

Aboriginal Peoples and Constitutional Reform

PHASE ONE

Background Papers (second printing)

1. Noel Lyon, *Aboriginal Self-Government: Rights of Citizenship and Access to Governmental Services*, 1984. ($12)
2. David A. Boisvert, *Forms of Aboriginal Self-Government*, 1985. ($12)
3. NOT AVAILABLE
4. Bradford Morse, *Aboriginal Self-Government in Australia and Canada*, 1985. ($12)
5. Douglas E. Sanders, *Aboriginal Self-Government in the United States*, 1985. ($12)
6. Bryan P. Schwartz, *First Principles: Constitutional Reform with Respect to the Aboriginal Peoples of Canada 1982-1984*, 1985. ($20)

Discussion Paper

David C. Hawkes, *Aboriginal Self-Government: What Does It Mean?*, 1985. ($12)
Set ($75)

PHASE TWO

Background Papers

7. David C. Hawkes, *Negotiating Aboriginal Self-Government, Developments Surrounding the 1985 First Ministers' Conference*, 1985. ($5)
8. John Weinstein, *Aboriginal Self-Determination Off a Land Base*, 1986. ($7)
9. Marc Malone, *Financing Aboriginal Self-Government in Canada*, 1986. ($7)
10. Jerry Paquette, *Aboriginal Self-Government and Education in Canada*, 1986. ($10)
11. Richard H. Bartlett, *Subjugation, Self-Management and Self-Government of Aboriginal Lands and Resources in Canada*, 1986. ($10)
12. C.E.S. Franks, *Public Administration Questions Relating to Aboriginal Self-Government*, 1987. ($10)
13. Ian B. Cowie, *Future Issues of Jurisdiction and Coordination Between Aboriginal and Non-Aboriginal Governments*, 1987. ($7)

14. Delia Opekokew, *The Political and Legal Inequities Among Aboriginal Peoples in Canada*, 1987. ($7)

Discussion Paper

David C. Hawkes, *The Search for Accommodation*, 1987. ($7)

Position Papers

Martin Dunn, *Access to Survival, A Perspective on Aboriginal Self-Government for the Constituency of the Native Council of Canada*, 1986. ($7)
Inuit Committee on National Issues, *Completing Canada: Inuit Approaches to Self-Government*, 1987. ($7)

Workshop Report

David C. Hawkes and Evelyn J. Peters, *Implementing Aboriginal Self-Government: Problems and Prospects*, 1986. ($7)

Bibliography

Evelyn J. Peters, *Aboriginal Self-Government in Canada: A Bibliography 1986*, 1986. ($12)

Publications may be ordered from:
Institute of Intergovernmental Relations
Queen's University, Kingston, Ontario K7L 3N6